THE AWKWARD OZARKER

THE AWKWARD OZARKER

A CURIOUS TALE OF SELF-REINVENTION IN A SCANTILY SETTLED LAND

BLANT HURT

FAIRBOURNE PUBLISHING

Copyright © 2016 by Blant Hurt.

All rights reserved. No part of this publication may be reproduced, distributed, or transmitted in any form or by any means, including photocopying, recording, or other electronic or mechanical methods, without the prior written permission of the publisher, except in the case of brief quotations embodied in critical reviews and certain other noncommercial uses permitted by copyright law. For permission requests, write to the publisher, addressed "Attention: Permissions Coordinator," at the address below.

Illustrations copyright © 2016 by Amber Heard

Cover Design by Dane Low

Book Design by H. K. Stewart

The Awkward Ozarker is a work of non-fiction. The names and identifying characteristics of some individuals have been changed.

>Fairbourne Publishing
>2623 Commerce Drive
>Jonesboro, Arkansas 72402
>www.blanthurt.com
>www.theawkwardozarker.com

First edition

ISBN: 978-0-9973256-0-7

Printed in the United States of America
This book is printed on archival-quality paper that meets requirements of the American National Standard for Information Sciences, Permanence of Paper, Printed Library Materials, ANSI Z39.48-1984.

"I do not understand how anyone can live without some small place of enchantment to turn to."

— Marjorie Kinnan Rawlings

IZARD COUNTY

SHARP COUNTY

★ Melbourne

Sage

To the Flatlands of the Arkansas Delta →

Sidney

Lunenburg

Mt. Pleasant

Cave City →

Guion Sand Mine

Lafferty

Little Rock and the World Beyond ↓

INDEPENDENCE COUNTY

Contents

Prologue 11
First Autumn
   1. Whither Hogback Mountain....................................17
   2. Settling In 22
   3. Beargrease and Company 28
   4. Wonders under Our Noses 36

First Winter
   5. The Essential Four-Wheeler 47
   6. Fortunes Built on Sand 52
   7. Wintertime Amusements 60
   8. Power and Water, Please!..68
   9. Enter the Land of the Preppers 84

Springtime
   10. Clinging to Religion...93
   11. Hanging Out with Dennis 102
   12. The Many Uses of a Cave 111
   13. Schemes and Dreams...114
   14. Further Explorations 122
   15. Springtime Rites 132
   16. The Two Dannys...143

Summer
- 17. The Chicken Bandwagon 151
- 18. Sacrament on the White River 155
- 19. Fishing and Fishy Stories 162
- 20. Local Characters of Different Sorts...................................170
- 21. Meetup of a Mountain Clan 185
- 22. Drama at the Cave Cinema...189

Second Autumn
- 23. Among the Arts and Crafts Gentry...................................197
- 24. The World Underground..201
- 25. The Fall Churn 205
- 26. Bear Mountain Flirtation 213
- 27. Close Encounters with Fellow Dreamers..........................218
- 28. Genuine Ozark Wedding 225
- 29. The Glories of Bean Fest 233

Second Winter
- 30. Deer Season, Full On 243
- 31. Prepper Fatigue 251
- 32. A Dreaded Campout 256
- 33. Deep Wintertime...263
- 34. Chimney Sweep Triumph 268

Epilogue...272

Prologue

The path to self-reinvention is as varied as the human race, yet I daresay few people have stumbled upon the catalyst for a transformative journey at the cash register of a run-down convenience store in the Delta of eastern Arkansas. I'd stopped at this particular c-store to get gasoline—it was just after quitting time on a Friday evening. But soon I discovered the credit card reader at the gas pump wasn't working. So it was there, at the store's cash register, alongside the plastic bucket filled with multi-colored Bic lighters, where I spotted the loose brochures advertising Bear Gap, a bed-and-breakfast somewhere up in the dark heart of the Ozarks.

The notion of going to an achingly modest bed-and-breakfast about a hundred and ten miles to the west had never before crossed my mind. *Why would it?* Typically, to have some fun on weekends, my wife, Susanne, and I drove over to Memphis, some sixty-five miles the other direction, for shopping and dining and entertainment. This was our way of enjoying a modicum of sophistication; a chance for me, once a resident of Boston and New York, to get what I called my "city fix."

Still, the brochure intrigued me. Susanne and I were ready for something new to go with our new lives. We'd only been married three months, each of us closing in on age fifty, empty nesters feeling our way towards our mutual future. Plus, the truth was that unless I came up with somewhere to go fairly soon—like in the next hour or so—we faced another long, sultry July weekend at home in Jonesboro, stuck in the mosquito-infested, not-much-to-look-at flatlands. So I tucked one of the brochures into my shirt pocket and drove home.

Not surprisingly, Susanne was not so keen on a spur-of-the-moment excursion over to Bear Gap.

"We're staying here this weekend," she said with a wrinkle of her nose. "I've got a lot of chores to do, and you can help me."

"But this bed-and-breakfast has a swimming pool." I offered her the brochure and pointed out the hot tub too. She loved hot tubs. "It could be romantic," I added hopefully.

Susanne looked closer at the crude map on the back of the brochure. "Do you have any idea where this Highway Nine is?"

"No. But it can't be *that* hard to find. Can it?"

She continued to study the brochure. "I know this area," she said, noting the meandering blue line that represented the White River. "When I was a little girl, my dad used to take me and my sisters trout fishing not too far from there."

"Well, I guess we could go fishing on the river, if you want to," I said, even though I wasn't much of a fisherman.

"But anyway…" She flipped the brochure across the countertop. "We're staying home this weekend."

"Come on, let's get out of here!" I added, trying, with my stubborn enthusiasm, to carry the day. "It will be an adventure, and if the bed-and-breakfast is terrible we'll drive right back home after just a one-night stay. Let's pack up and get in the car!"

Turned out, Bear Gap was indeed hard to find—this particular stretch of Highway 9 is one of the curviest, most confounding roads in all of the Ozarks. Susanne and I wound up staying at Bear Gap the entire weekend. The trip served as our brief introduction to this little lost corner of the Ozarks and sort of our second honeymoon (alas, our real one was in Paris).

Prologue

It's odd now to think that if on that hot July evening I hadn't stopped for gas at that particular run-down convenience store—a store soon after shut down—Susanne and I would never, ever have set down roots of any sort up in the backwoods of Izard County, Arkansas. Chance and serendipity play a larger role in our lives than we often care to admit, and this is what makes things so interesting and unpredictable.

1.

Whither Hogback Mountain

The Ozarks have been called an arrested frontier, a place where civilization and savagery meet. Perhaps savagery is too strong a word; then again, maybe not. Regardless, as a devotee of the cosmopolitan life, I knew I was ill suited for the wilds of Highway 9. But I plowed ahead anyway. Like a dray horse, my course was set. On a hilltop almost a thousand feet high—let us generously call it a mountain—I stood beside Barry Helton, who, bless his heart, was suffering a fleeting case of seller's remorse. Already, his wife and two kids were back in Houston, fed up with their hard living in the Ozarks. The sale of his family's not-quite-finished cabin on twenty-seven acres of land—to Susanne and me—was just official. Near the front steps was a portable outhouse, a hillbillyish sight that caused the city boy in me to smile, though it was certainly no cause for mirth among the Heltons—who, rather incredibly, had lived on this mountain for two years without electricity or running water.

"I bought that outhouse from a furniture maker up the road," Barry said. "It's made of pure cedar."

"I guess that makes things smell better." My glance confirmed that Barry wasn't even slightly amused. "Look," I said in a more beseeching tone. "You don't really want to haul that outhouse all the way back to Texas, do you? Your moving truck is already full."

"I'll take fifty dollars for it. And that's a good deal! I bought it for a hundred bucks."

Susanne and I would definitely need an outhouse, at least until we drilled a well—and we had no idea when that would happen—so I handed over the cash.

Barry Helton claimed to be a pastor, though he had no church. He said he'd been a missionary in Costa Rica, but he didn't speak much Spanish. His former company built foundations for homes, yet the cabin he'd built for his own family—the cabin I'd just bought—was propped on cinder blocks and shimmed with shards of wood. Its crude, boxy shape was covered with four-inch strips of cedar laid vertically like pinstripes. Nearby was a barn with dirt floor and, down the hill, a makeshift lumber mill and a pig trailer: Barry ran a part-time boys' camp and, during the campers' paintball wars, the pig trailer served as their fort.

Though on this mountain practically everything touched by man was an eyesore, the land itself was blessed by nature. The hillsides were thick with post oaks and red cedars and shagbark hickory trees. Off the cabin's living room was an eastward view over a big hollow and a distant ridge of mountains impressive enough to impart a sense of scale and even a touch of grandeur. The front porch offered a close view of Izard County's third tallest mountain, Brandenburg, named after a long-gone German settler. Even though the cabin itself was pretty much regrettable, the beauty all around was of a kind that travelers to places beyond the Ozark hinterlands pay rather a lot of money to experience.

The week before, my father-in-law had unwittingly named our place when he gazed up from the roadside lookout on Highway 9 and said the profile of our mountain, which ran along the top of a humpbacked ridge, looked like a hog's back. Of course, *hogback*—a geological term that means "a long, sharply crested ridge"—can describe virtually any hill in the Ozarks. Nevertheless, the word aptly described our new property, and, besides, as long-ago graduates of the University of

Arkansas, Susanne and I had a thing for razorbacks. Already, we'd taken to calling our place Hogback Mountain—or at least I had, and I was determined to make it stick.

All this had happened rather suddenly. It was only a month ago when Susanne and I—then on our second weekend stay at Bear Gap—had casually driven along Highway 9, the nineteen-mile stretch from Melbourne down to the White River at Sylamore, a road said to have more than a hundred curves in it. (The Harley riders call it the Dragon's Tail.) On a wicked blind curve, we glimpsed a sign in big black letters: SOLAR HOUSE, 27 ACRES.

We pulled over and wandered up the driveway, a dangerous thing to do out here in the boonies. Casual travelers like us could wind up with a shotgun in our faces. We peered into the front windows of the cabin and wondered, *What if?* We returned a week later, and this time, the owners were home. It was late September; the mountain air was crisp, the leaves just turning hues of red, orange, yellow. After some back and forth, a deal ensued. *Were we really doing this?*

Now, as Barry Helton and I stood at the crest of Hogback Mountain, it was far too late to back out. He handed over the keys to the cabin, his final surrender. He was to drive his moving truck into the night, then camp out on the roadside with his ragtag crew of movers. Goodness knows he had plenty of camping gear for his trip back to Texas, including the turkey fryer his poor wife had used to heat water for her sponge baths.

Per the terms of our sale, Barry was supposed to clean up the property. But as our dealings had evolved over the last few days, I was having serious doubts that he was really going to send anyone out to clear out the spare tires, empty tin cans, piles of scrap wood, the deflated blow-up kiddie swimming pool, the useless washing machine still on the side porch. Trash and messes were everywhere.

"How about I'll clean up the property?" I said as he got into his moving truck, "and I'll just deduct it from the money I still owe you for your four-wheeler. What do you say?"

With little resistance, Barry nodded. My sense was that he just wanted to leave this mountain and never have anything more to do with it. In this, he and his wife were yet another example of the back-to-the-landers who move to the Ozarks and find out they can't hack it, or simply don't want to stick it out because it just isn't worth it. It did not escape me that perhaps Barry and his wife had figured out something Susanne and I were about to learn.

I watched Barry drive his moving truck down the gravel driveway. After a few loud motorcycles came around the blind curve, he eased out onto Highway 9. With his departure, Hogback Mountain—such as it was—was ours.

The name Izard, as in Izard County, rhymes with *lizard* and *gizzard*: it sounds hickey and backward. George Izard was the second territorial governor of Arkansas and one of its most capable administrators. He was schooled in Paris and London. His father served in Congress in America's earliest days, and the family settled in Charleston, South Carolina. Young George Izard, given his pedigree, likely figured he'd be a candidate for high office one day, perhaps even an ambassador to France or England.

But after commanding an ill-fated skirmish with the Iroquois in upstate New York, Izard's leadership abilities were severely criticized. Eventually, in 1825, President Monroe appointed him to head down to Little Rock. His wife never set foot in Arkansas, and I am fairly confident that George Izard never set foot in this particular part of Izard County—for if he did, he traveled almost a hundred miles up the White River by keelboat and then tromped for miles over some of the craggiest hillsides between the Appalachians and the Rockies.

All in all, it's easy to imagine George Izard often wondering just how in the hell he wound up in Arkansas, and in the days immediately after we purchased Hogback Mountain we had similar thoughts. *What in the world had we gotten ourselves into?* If this ratty little cabin out in the middle of nowhere was to be the road to our new lives, our re-upped selves, it wasn't immediately obvious to either of us, much less anyone else. Our friends and family back in the flatlands thought we'd lost it.

2.

Settling In

Dennis Gillihan arrived on a four-wheeler with his pistol and machete strapped to the gas tank. I of course was unarmed, and this contrast—our differentness in practically all respects—reminded me of what a greenhorn I was up here in this rugged land. We were back on what I called Hogback Road, an old logging trail behind my cabin rendered nearly impassable by downed trees and overgrowth. As Dennis dismounted, he dragged his stiff right leg (years ago, he'd almost been killed in a head-on car crash). He was a sturdy, blue-eyed, ruddy-complexioned Scots-Irishman; in his early sixties, he was ten years too young to be my father and ten years too old to be a peer, though Dennis's relationship with both age and time was complicated, to say the least.

"Hello, young man," he said, his usual greeting. He gave me another of his cool-cat soul-brother handshakes, his way to show he wasn't some provincial hillsman living in a time warp, though without question Dennis Gillihan was the purest Ozarker one could ever hope to meet.

"How are you?" I said.

"If things were any better, it'd be perfect."

I handed Dennis the money I owed him for the work he'd done to pull down a chicken-wire fence behind my barn.

"Thank ya much," he said, tucking the bills away. "You know, it's like Christmas money to me."

As we walked along the overgrown road, he hummed one of his cheerful, unrecognizable little melodies, a tic of his. We surveyed a felled tree and agreed he'd come back in a few days with his chainsaw to clear it. Then, he reached down and pulled up a thorny plant by its roots. "I had four cows that went buzzard-eating dead from eating this. It's called mint weed, and it turns their lungs into mush—they suffocate. Not many people know about it."

Certainly, I knew nothing about mint weed. But I did understand that Dennis owned a lot of cattle. Up here on the mountain ridge that overlooked the Gillihans' 220-acre ranch at the base of Dark Hollow, I often overheard the distant mooing of his cows and the call of his wife's peacocks, the latter a sound *(may-AWE, may-AWE)* so out of context that I sometimes felt as if I was living above a zoo.

Dennis tossed the mint weed over his shoulder and with a slow, descriptive sweep of his gloved hand, said, "I could bring my tractor up here and mow this whole trail for you. Just clean it up and make it nice. It won't take me very long."

I eagerly agreed. My new property was not worth owning unless I could get out and walk on it. But to clear the land, I had no tractor, not even a lawn mower. Even at this early stage of my new part-time life in the Ozarks, I knew that Dennis's ongoing assistance would be required if I was to have any chance at all of a graceful existence up here.

"I never went wrong buying land," Dennis said, no doubt sensing my trepidation. "Just enjoy your land. That's what I always say, just enjoy your land."

It was a land that, indeed, Dennis Gillihan knew well enough to thoroughly enjoy. These mountains along the southern rim of Izard County were filled with Gillihans. It all began with three brothers who migrated from Tennessee in the 1840s. Perhaps they'd chosen this area because just further west into the next county was Indian Territory; or because this particular spot reminded them of a place they loved back in the Appalachian mountains; or maybe their covered wagon broke down; or by chance a harsh winter came on. Regardless, the original Gillihan brothers were the consummate Scots-Irish hillsmen, and among their many descendants around these parts, Dennis was one of the most accomplished.

"Who owns the land back behind me?" I said, motioning towards the wilderness.

"It was bought three years ago by a fellow from central Arkansas named Dr. Jackson," Dennis replied. "He owns over twelve hundred acres. But he's not around much because his wife doesn't like it up here."

Dennis seemed to be acquainted with most everyone around this area whether they were related to him or not, so I said, "I guess you know him pretty well, huh?"

"Me and him had a steak supper over in Batesville just a few weeks ago. He's a nice fella."

"Hmm." I went on staring longingly in the direction of Dr. Jackson's property.

Dennis, as if he'd read my mind, said, "I don't want to own all the land; I just want to own all the land that touches mine."

In fact, Dennis *had* read my mind: up in the Ozarks, something about the clear air and the mountaintop vistas encourages grandiosity, in spite of any and all obstacles. Already, my head was filling up with ideas about how to improve my land and someday build a bigger, nicer cabin. It was going to be grand, eventually. (My mother always said that, from a young age, I was a planner, her kind way of saying that I was a bit of a schemer.)

To survey another downed tree, Dennis and I walked further along the overgrown road whereupon, not surprisingly, he started humming another of his happy-go-lucky ditties.

I said, "Did you know that Barry Helton left behind a monkey cage in my barn? I wonder if that monkey is back here somewhere in these woods? I figure that at some point he just turned it loose."

"There's a place called Monkey Island on the White River not too far downstream from here," Dennis replied with a top note of authority. "They say a few monkeys once lived there, but I doubt they lasted very long." He hummed a bit longer—letting what he'd just said sink in—and then, as if he'd decided I could handle more of his tale, he spoke of a local man named California who dressed up in a full-length gorilla suit, then lurked in the tree line along Highway 9 and jumped out in front of passing cars. It was a wonder California didn't get shot, Dennis noted: a good point, considering the fondness of Izardites for guns. Per Dennis, this curious fellow named California eventually settled down and married a woman who claimed he was great to her and her two kids.

His story concluded—and, for now, our mutual business done—Dennis remounted his four-wheeler, swinging his stiff right leg over the well-armed gas tank. "If you think of anything else you want me to do, just call me," he said before he cranked the engine. "I'll help you-uns any way I can."

On a cool afternoon, I was splitting logs for our wood stove—our sole source of heat—when Larry Kirby's beat-up white car came up our driveway. He and his son, Wayne, had driven to Hogback Mountain to get a check for the work they'd done so far on our cabin and barn.

As soon as he got out, young Wayne shook his red-haired head dismissively in my direction and said, "Let me show you how to do that." Slight like his father, he took my maul, spit on his hands, and widened his stance. Then, with rhythmic, compact swings, he split four logs with a speed and efficiency that I did not think possible.

"There you go," Wayne said as I slinked off to the porch to talk with his dad.

Thankfully, Larry Kirby was well along on the work required to render our cabin livable, namely weatherproofing it and making it reasonably safe to walk around in. The front porch, with its loose boards, was particularly dicey. "I'll start on your new deck next week," Larry said. "Provided all of my crew aren't out in the woods. Folks up here don't work much when deer hunting season starts." We reviewed his plans for the deck off the living room. I wanted to add an elbow-high wooden ledge with an accompanying footrest—basically creating a makeshift outdoor bar—a small, yet critical detail, which Larry grasped with only minimal explanation.

A builder of Larry Kirby's caliber wouldn't have considered a small job such as finishing out our cabin and barn if we weren't in the midst of the Great Recession. At my father-in-law's request, another builder had driven up from the flatlands, surveyed our cabin for thirty minutes, then told us to bulldoze it off the hillside and start all over. I'm quite certain this builder only stayed as long as he did as a courtesy to my father-in-law.

Before hiring Larry, Susanne and I had seen his work at Lick Fork, a development near Mountain View, over in Stone County. Few homes in this region of the Ozarks were elaborate or expensive: a $150,000 house was considered high end. An acquaintance in the area had laughingly recounted how the Mennonite craftsmen who'd built his modest, two-bedroom cabin had asked in curious awe if he and his wife were both wealthy doctors; after he told them that he was just a salesman for a chemical company and his wife a mere guidance counselor, the Mennonites seemed crestfallen.

With Larry Kirby on our job, each weekend trip up to Hogback Mountain was a revelation. Oh, the foundation looks so much better when it's fully supported! Oh, the walls upstairs are finished, so now wasps can't get inside! Oh, a door for the bathroom really makes a big difference! Oh, aren't the front steps so much safer with handrails to hold onto!

I handed Larry his check. He had blue eyes and a scraggly gray beard, and even with his paunchy belly, he looked thin to the point of undernourishment. He was another descendant of the potato-famine Irish who'd migrated to this area—or at least with his slight build and the Irish redness in his face he looked like he was.

Larry said, "You'll be back up next weekend, right?"

"Where else would I go? I'm having such fun up here trying to split wood and picking up all the trash around my property. Besides, I can't wait to see the new deck when you're finished." I pointed at the base of the outer wall on the porch—his workers had installed the wooden trim upside down.

"Dadgummit," Larry said with a wince. "I'll have to get those guys who did this trim work out of the deer woods."

I was relieved that I'd noticed this boo-boo rather than my wife, who was less than thrilled with the work Larry had done so far on the foundation of our cabin—and she was right, it still wasn't very solid. But, for crying out loud, he was doing the best he could considering what he had to work with.

I walked Larry and Wayne to their car to see them off. I waited until they were well down the driveway and out of sight before I took up my maul to split more logs, for that night promised to be the coldest so far of the fall.

3.

Beargrease and Company

"Where did that dog come from?" Emily, my college-aged stepdaughter, said as she looked out a window of our cabin. We were in our living room, watching college football on television thanks to the portable generator I'd rigged up—my first and so far only triumph of backwoods engineering.

The stray dog was black with white and gray markings—half Border collie and half blue heeler, we supposed. He was lost and scared and hungry—the gleam in his eye was delirium. We gave him water and food. He was the kind of dog one becomes attached to quickly, like in about thirty minutes.

Friedrich Gerstäcker, the intrepid German, wrote of his travels in the Ozarks in the 1840s. His dog, Beargrease, saved him in a fight with a bear, or so Gerstäcker recounted in one his many letters to his mother, which she published back in Germany, leading to her son's fame as a writer. Back then Germany was getting hunted out and overpopulated according to some, so Gerstäcker had set out for the remote Ozarks in search of adventure, which he apparently found in abundance.

"Come here, Beargrease," I said. "Here, boy."

"Beargrease?"

I told Susanne about Gerstäcker's dog.

"We can call him Bear," she said. "He sort of looks like a bear. A skinny bear anyway."

"Well, his full name is Beargrease. That's what's officially on his birth certificate."

She rolled her eyes. "His name is Bear."

Later that afternoon, we drove to the farmer's co-op in Mountain View, eleven miles west, and bought an automatic feeder, a water bowl, and a kennel; when Sunday night came, we left Bear on the front porch and told him we'd be back the next weekend. Meantime, while we were gone, he had the run of our place.

The workweek passed quickly, and on Friday night we again headed back up to Hogback Mountain. As we drove across the Black River—the winding tributary marking where the flatlands of eastern Arkansas transition to the rolling hills of the Ozarks—there was a phone call from Emily, now back at college.

"Is the dog still there?"

"We haven't gotten to our cabin yet," I said. "Give us about an hour."

Before we got to Hogback Mountain, she called again, her eagerness to learn of the dog's fate superseded only by mine. We were halfway up our driveway when Bear jumped into our car's headlights. When I got out of the car, he pounced on me.

All weekend, Bear and I had a ball hiking together all over the forest. He was a herder by instinct and when ahead of me, he turned back regularly as if to say, *Hey, man, are you coming?* With Bear around, I felt safer in the woods. He could probably tie up a bear or a wild hog long enough for me to run away, if it came to that. Not that I had seen any such beasts. All I'd encountered so far were squirrels and deer, which Bear chased with reckless abandon. But later, from somewhere on the hillside, I heard him panting, and he returned with his tongue hanging out, his black-and white snoot covered with cobwebs and cockleburs. He preferred to drink the water in my canteen.

Sunday night came too soon. Susanne and I packed up to return to the flatlands. After doing chores all weekend up at Hogback Mountain, we were in desperate need of a hot, soaking bath and an indoor toilet. But I knew that a dog like Bear needed lots of land to roam. The thought of keeping him cooped up in our town house in Jonesboro didn't seem fair, so we left him plenty of food and water on the porch of our cabin and told him we'd be back again the next weekend.

Two days later, Dennis Gillihan called. "Have you lost a dog?"

"You tell me. I'm not up at Hogback Mountain, though I wish I was."

"He showed up this morning for breakfast."

"I guess Bear heard all the noise from your cows and chickens and peacocks. You can't blame him for wanting some company. There's a lot of fun to be had down at your place."

Dennis told me his favorite dog—long dead—was also named Bear. Too, he'd had dogs named Pooter and Fussybutt. "I'll keep Bear for a few days," he added. "You-uns can pick him up when you get here this weekend."

And so began our handy arrangement of co-parenting a dog. Pretty soon, on weekends I wouldn't even have to drive down to the Gillihans' house to get Bear. I just went to the edge of our porch, rang our chuck wagon dinner bell, and called loudly down into the big hollow until he sprinted up the mountain, eager to see me.

One Sunday evening, as we again departed Hogback Mountain, I dropped Bear off at the Gillihans' house, a modest single-level home they'd built thirty years ago. I walked Bear to the front door to make sure they knew I'd returned the dog.

"Hello there, young man," Dennis said, his usual greeting. Also as usual, he shook my hand soul-brother style, but this time, before he yanked on my arm, I pulled on his as if we were mock arm-wrestling.

"There you go!" he said, his mouth half full of whatever the Gillihans were having for dinner. "I try this handshake on a lot of people, but you're the only one who gets it."

"I understand where you're coming from—I get you. Now, here's Bear. He had some dog food about an hour ago, but he might still be hungry."

"Well, I just ate his steak," Dennis said with a food-speckled grin.

I petted Bear one last time. "Seriously," I said to Dennis. "What will we ever do with this dog when y'all go out of town?"

From behind him came a mocking laugh—it was his wife, Carol. "Oh, don't worry about that," she interjected. "We haven't been anywhere in fifteen years."

Up at Hogback Mountain, James Bell sat at our kitchen table with Trouble, his little Pekingese dog, in his lap. He was tall and handsome in a decidedly weathered, grayed-out way, though apparently he still considered himself quite the sexual athlete. The front of his old red truck bore a license plate that read IZARD COUNTY STUD.

"I've brought a housewarming gift for you." James handed over a plowshare with two horses—Hee & Haw—painted on it. "It's just a little something," he said. "Nothing major."

I hung the odd-shaped chunk of painted metal near our kitchen sink. The images of Hee and Haw were reasonably well portrayed. Even now I sensed this plowshare would serve as a memento of James, whom I feared might not be our neighbor much longer given his attitude towards his ex-wife, Peggy, who owned the trailer home and eighty acres where he resided, basically rent-free.

"You can't tell Polish women anything," James said breezily. He sipped from his water bottle to bathe his cancerous throat. "I can't even pronounce her last name."

Of course I coveted Peggy-the-Polish-Lady's eighty acres of land. *I don't want to own all the land; I just want to own all the land that touches mine.* Our porch looked out onto one side of Brandenburg Mountain, which she owned. When I'd hiked up there recently, it seemed I could see all the way to Oklahoma.

So, Peggy wants to pass her land on to her children, huh? Now, where exactly do her children live? So, Peggy owns some sort of business near Memphis that involves vending machines, right? I couldn't imagine her little business to be very lucrative. Perhaps she'd entertain a fair offer for her land?

These were the subjects I wanted to discuss with James. But he had his own ideas about where our conversation should go. And so it went, as he spoke on in his raspy Mississippi drawl. Of this, Dennis Gillihan, knower of all around these parts, had forewarned me: James typically sat at home by himself for weeks on end and made his birdhouses and repaired a few small engines. Finally, lonely and stricken with cabin fever, he'd load Trouble into his old red truck and drive down to Dennis's place, where he'd talk nonstop for an hour or so until, finally petered out, he'd load up Trouble and return to his trailer home at the foot of Brandenburg Mountain.

Eventually, I lured James out to our porch to enjoy the crisp late-fall weather and to admire the northward view of Brandenburg Mountain, which was a foot shy of a whopping 1,100 feet tall. Despite James's tendency to ramble on, his powers of description were sometimes keen. Speaking of Bear, who napped at my feet, he said, "That's a fine-looking specimen of a dog you've got there."

"I know. I'm so blessed he showed up. No telling where he came from."

James sipped his water, his eyes on the dog. "I like it how his paws and chest are that buckshotty color," he said, drawing out his last few words to a syrupy effect.

A poet laureate could not have described the color of Bear's mottled gray-white markings any better.

On Hogback Mountain, we still lacked electricity and running water—a predicament with no immediate end in sight. Our outhouse was well used. Cooking presented its challenges too since all we had was a cooktop grill that Susanne and I had received as a wedding gift, plus our wood stove. On most Saturdays, to escape our isolation, I ventured into Mountain View for lunch at the Rainbow Cafe. The restaurant served above-average home-style food, but what I really loved about this joint was its tidy, one-seater bathroom with its clean commode, hot water, and plentiful toilet paper. What a godsend!

My business finished, I washed my face and hands several times, luxuriating in it all, reluctant to leave the bathroom. Above the paper-towel dispenser was a plaque:

> HOLE IN 1
> JIM A. NEWMAN
> HOLE 4, PAR 3, DIVINE 9
> AUGUST 8, 1994
> TIMBER LAKE, IL.

I lingered, stuffing extra paper towels into my coat pocket. There was an insistent knock at the bathroom door—I'd taken too long. *Did this intruder have any idea what I was up against at Hogback Mountain?*

I returned to my front-window table to finish my plate of pinto beans, green beans, fried zucchini, beets, glazed carrots, and Texas toast: my usual fare.

"I was with him when he got his hole-in-one," Pat Maheny said of the plaque honoring her deceased husband. "I still haven't gotten an ace yet."

Pat had dark hair and rosy cheeks and wore a white Harley Davidson vest; black jeans and white tennis shoes completed her matronly yet somewhat racy look. With an air of easy command, she told one of her waitresses how to fix a botched order. I overheard her say that another waitress had taken off work that day to get certified as a black belt in karate. Duly noted.

The Rainbow Cafe was the only restaurant I've ever been in with advertisements on its ceiling. When eating a jalapeño burger, or soup beans and cornbread, any customer wondering where to find a local bargain can look up and see a dozen three-by-five foot panels advertising places like POOL MILITARY SURPLUS & FLEA MARKET—2 DOORS DOWN (with a rightward-pointing arrow). Or perhaps a customer needs a warm bed after dinner—STAY ACROSS THE STREET AT INN ON THE SQUARE.

Even with this unique commercial assault from overhead, the true decorative inspiration here was Elvis Presley. On a back wall was a floor-to-ceiling print of The King with his sultry eyes and curled upper lip. Other walls were festooned with Elvis photos, signs, posters, paintings, and even dolls.

"It's all from the era I grew up in," Pat said as if she expected every seventy-year-old to share her lifelong crush on Elvis.

I tipped my waitress, Allison, quite well—she'd fixed my usual iced-tea-to-go, no matter that the cold weather outside called for something hot. But I wasn't ready to go. I tapped at the front window and waved at Bear to make sure he saw me. I'd tied his leash to the newspaper stand outside the front door, where he patiently waited for the hamburger steak I always ordered for him: his reward.

I was reading a story in the *Stone County Citizen* about how the local police had busted up a ring that manufactured methamphetamine, when a lanky, long-bearded, slump-shouldered man in faded denim overalls approached my table. Matthew Arnold ate lunch here almost every day—he was here every time I came to the restaurant—and though he looked like a postcard version of an Arkansas hillbilly, appearances are often deceiving up in the Ozarks. Matthew hailed from New York State, but years ago he'd moved to Mountain View with his wife, who was now very sick. Like many folks up in these hills, he was a man of few words—he just stood there, expecting me to carry on our halting conversation.

How's your wife? What have you been up to? Tell me again now, where exactly do you live around here? Was he aware of the English poet and critic who had the same name as his? Indeed Matthew Arnold knew about his namesake, referencing the white cliffs of Dover.

Finally, bored with our one-sided chitchat, Matthew walked over and picked up his round-topped hillbilly hat from atop the old jukebox where he always placed it and went out the door.

Before I left, I circled back to the tidy, golf-themed bathroom one last time, for I knew I wouldn't see another functioning indoor commode—or have any hot running water—until Susanne and I returned the next night to our proper home back in the flatlands.

4.

Wonders under Our Noses

With the onset of cold weather, it was hiking season. Thankfully, Bear and I were surrounded by some fifteen hundred acres of land to roam with no fences or fussy neighbors to stop us from exploring. Whenever in the woods, I felt as if discoveries of all sorts awaited.

One day, I saw random pieces of white scattered across the ground, as if someone had haphazardly shredded some Styrofoam cups. These were actually little bulbs of ice, as intricate as snowflakes, that had collected at the base of long-stemmed plants; I later learned they are called frost flowers. When I tried to pick them up, the delicate bulbs disintegrated in the space between my fingers.

Down the wooded hillside from our cabin was a fifty-foot deep gorge that, as soon as I came upon it, I named Little Grand Canyon. I sat on a promontory and caught the wind and heard the rush of water below as it coursed through West Twin Creek. On the other side of the canyon was a wall of dark limestone worn smooth by eons of erosion.

It finally stopped raining. I climbed down and hiked along West Twin Creek, through a gulch of boulders as big as two-bedroom houses. Further upstream, I came upon a waterfall with a torrent of runoff spilling over its limestone ledge. The water dropped thirty feet and splashed against the creek bed that, at this particular spot, was as flat and smooth as a parking lot.

I was amazed at my discovery, for even though this thirty-foot waterfall was not on my land, I was nevertheless only a quarter-mile down the hillside from our cabin. I lingered just beyond the splash and scooped up the cold water that had been filtered through the karst topography of Brandenburg Mountain. Dennis Gillihan had once said that when it rained, these mountains, like hole-riddled sponges, filled up with water—this but another of his dead-on observations.

Bear barked, ready to move on. He didn't like for us to stop hiking for long. After aborting the most obvious route around the waterfall, I eventually scaled a ledge so steep and slippery that I had to give the dog a boost to get him up.

Just a quarter mile further along West Twin Creek, I heard the distant roar of a second waterfall. *Are you kidding me?* As I walked closer, the gravel bar along the creek transitioned to a bed of small boulders, and the low, creviced walls along the creek steepened into a fifteen-foot high bowl. This waterfall too gushed in a torrent; behind it was a recess deep enough to build a campfire and flat enough to sleep on. I sat in wonderment at the edge of the pool where, just above the water, a line of maidenhair fern grew like a green mustache. It was easy to imagine that Indians once lived here. There was shelter and plenty of wood for fuel, and it would be convenient to hunt the wildlife that came to the pool for a drink.

Giddy with joy, I hiked on up West Twin Creek for another quarter of a mile, and just past a thicket of felled trees, I came to *yet another* waterfall. This third fall was nestled into the deepest nook of the hairpin curve along Highway 9, and though only ten feet high, it was perfect in shape and proportion, as if designed by a landscape architect. The bowl-shaped setting was like a romantic grotto.

I sat at the edge of the clear little pond, six feet from the falling water. Above me, the wind whipped, but I was shielded by the rock bowl carved out over millions of years. The rock was striated and splotched with moss, and atop it—in the thin, hard-won topsoil—a thatch of cedar trees had taken root. The waterfall concentrated the flow of the water and culminated in a loud splash that pleased my eye and ear. Here, I felt a peace and calm of the kind only felt in nature, though if someone, or *some thing*, came up behind me, I'd have been scared out of my wits, for I could not have heard anything approaching.

To reach the top of this waterfall, I climbed a narrow trace. Underneath the cedar trees was a knob of rock to sit on. The swift-flowing water curved around me as it narrowed into a funnel. The sun peeked through the clouds, and the rushing water danced in the sharp light.

For months now, I'd driven the highway that encircled this hollow with its three hidden waterfalls. At first glance, this land didn't seem like much—basically just a winding valley dissected by a power line. I suspected the Ozarks were full of places of such unexpected, out-of-the-way beauty. All one had to do was to get out into the woods and look for them.

I headed back for our cabin: I couldn't wait to show Susanne the pictures I'd taken on my cell phone. This was one of my best days so far at Hogback Mountain, even though the three waterfalls I'd found were not technically on our land.

At our kitchen table, Susanne carefully examined the pictures. "Now, where were you when you took these?" she said.

"Down in the creek bed to our west. Right at the base of this mountain."

"Wow!" Then, "You sure?"

"Or course, I'm sure," I said and then predictably—given my reflexive lust for property—I added, "I wonder how we can buy these waterfalls?"

"Who owns the land?"

"I have no idea."

"Maybe we should try to find out," she said.

"Ah, good idea."

Susanne soon launched an exhaustive Internet search followed by a flurry of phone calls. Eventually, she made contact with the owner of the three waterfalls, a woman in Dayton, Ohio. Fortunately, they hit it off; as devoted Christians they shared a concern about the-end-of-the-world-as-we-know-it, also known as TEOTWAWKI.

The Dayton lady said her father had homesteaded the property; he'd basically squatted on the land, then eventually came to own it. Before him, an old German had lived there, but he'd vanished during World War II when the federal government interred him, suspecting him of spying. The old German always wore gold jewelry, we learned.

I found all of this history of the property adjacent to ours to be mildly interesting, but more to the point, would the lady from Dayton sell us her sixty acres? She hadn't seen the land since she was a little girl, she said. But she'd think about it.

Susanne hung up the phone. "She told me there's a cave somewhere on the property too. She gave me a general idea of where it was. She said that, even now, she vividly remembers it."

"*Seriously?* Not only are there three waterfalls on her property, there's also a cave!"

"She said the cave was pretty big."

We ran out and searched the western edge of Panther Ridge, just above West Twin Creek and across the highway from the property owned by an Indian woman named Wind Daughter, whom we'd yet to meet. It was quite exotic to have a neighbor named Wind Daughter. Her presence confirmed that we truly lived on the arrested frontier, surrounded by Indians—well, by at least one Indian anyway. Too, her whereabouts confirmed how diverse the Ozarks could be. This wasn't just a white man's haven up here. Izard County *really was* a big tent, even if in all my days spent up here I had not yet seen an African American. Already, it seemed that Wind Daughter, in absentia, had evolved into such a mythic presence in our minds that it wasn't even necessary to meet her. Regular references to her flowed off our tongues: "I'm going hiking over in the direction of Wind Daughter's," or "Bear went over to Wind Daughter's to see her dogs," or, as we passed by her blood-red mailbox with *West Winds* written in swooping cursive letters, we'd casually remark to our guests, "Oh, yes, our neighbor Wind Daughter lives there."

Eventually, in our excited search for the cave, Susanne and I came to an opening in the ground. This opening was not very big, but there was definitely a hole of some sort down there.

"If we had a rope I could lower you into it," I said.

Susanne, who sometimes bragged about having been a gymnast, gave me an icy stare. There was no telling what was down in that hole.

"This can't be the cave that the Dayton lady described to me over the phone," she concluded.

We pushed on for about three hundred yards until we saw a crease in the bluff line: the cave was back in the corner, situated at the base of a high crescent-shaped limestone bowl and guarded by giant boulders. The cave had a wide walk-in mouth, a deep recess, and a floor of soft brown sand. Susanne and I hugged each other as if we'd just set foot on the moon.

Yet, clearly, we were not the first earthlings to find this cave. Near the mouth were a fire pit and a set of old rusted bedsprings. Further back were waist-high potholes where some hillbilly archeologists had long ago dug for bones, pottery, arrowheads, buried treasure, whatever. These big craters effectively segmented the cave into various apartments and made the floor look like a bombed-out battlefield.

Still, it was fun to ponder what might be under the cave's dirt floor. Were Indians buried here from as recently as two hundred years ago, before they were moved just across the White River and then on to Oklahoma along the Trail of Tears? Had Ozarkers hid out here during the guerrilla-war days of the Civil War? What about ancient animals like the woolly mammoth and hell pig? The sediment on the floor of the cave could be explored in layers, as if going back in time.

The perfect tire-sized circle in the ceiling, likely the bottom of a petrified tree stump, particularly intrigued Susanne. She called this circle the All-Seeing Eye of God, or as Henry Rowe Schoolcraft, one of the first Ozark explorers, described in his journal of 1818, "The Spirit of the Cavern."

Not too far from the cave, we found the homesite of the Dayton lady's father. The fallen-down place had all the makings of a simple frontier life. The foundation stones were underneath the collapsed joists, and the house, some six hundred square feet in size, did not appear to have had any long wooden beams to support it nor much mortar to hold it together. Out on what had been the porch was a rusted screen door and the metal carcass of a couch where the occupant had probably sat and listened to the water spill over the waterfall just down the hillside.

A week or so passed, but still no word came from Dayton. So even though we didn't legally own the cave, Susanne and I began to act as if we did. We'd learned from Dennis Gillihan (who else?) that the locals called it Sandy Wallow Cave.

One cold night, we took friends down to the cave and, outside the mouth, built a campfire and huddled around it to keep warm. I sat facing Brandenburg Mountain to the north, and the cars, as they traversed the dark highway along the base of the mountain above us, seemed like comets streaking across a black sky. All of it—the firelight, our friends, the dark mystery of the cave—was magical.

I cozied up to Susanne as we toasted our feet beside the flames, so hot that the rubber soles of my hiking boots were gummy. "We've just got to own this cave," I said. "Somehow. Some way."

"I agree," she said with resolve. "Who do you know that can say they own three waterfalls and a cave?"

Thomas, our fourteen-year old nephew from Little Rock, was again our guest for the weekend. His visits to Hogback Mountain were a respite from a tough situation back at home, where his father was very sick. For weeks now, he'd helped us with chores. Susanne and I had worked him so hard that we could have been busted for child labor violations.

His latest triumph was painting our cinder-block foundation while wearing only boxer shorts and house slippers.

Yet with his back-forty shooting and four-wheeler riding, Thomas got in his share of fun. He especially liked to drive into harsh terrain, where he'd invariably get our four-wheeler stuck: he relished the challenge of extricating it, especially if this involved attaching a chain to the buggy and yanking it out. All of this was good therapy, his way of learning more about nature and machines, about what he could and couldn't do. He was a gangly teenager, frisky and a tad uncertain in his movements like a colt. Every weekend he seemed to have grown a bit taller: his father was quite tall. His relationship with my dog was complicated: "I'm not Bear's favorite," Thomas sometimes said, a mature and accurate observation.

One weekend, he and I hauled down a rickety chest of drawers from the upstairs bedroom. This was but more of the detritus that Barry Helton, in his haste to leave the Ozarks, had left behind. Thomas and I put the chest out near the fire pit. It was odd to see a proper piece of furniture—its drawers all strewn about—sitting there amidst the sweeping backdrop of Dark Hollow.

"Turn that thing into firewood," I said.

"Really? Can I?"

I pointed at my maul, which Thomas seized with alacrity.

"And bust up all these drawers, too. Bust up the whole thing. But don't hurt yourself."

"I won't," he scoffed the way the young do because they think they're indestructible. "Let me at this thing. Stand back."

With his long arms, Thomas swung the maul as hard as he could, partly out of frustration with his situation back at home, partly as a test of his strength, partly for the pure joy of it. The maul, as he raised it over his head, moved in slow motion, yet as it fell the mere weight of it busted up the chest of drawers.

I left Thomas to his task and went inside. A few minutes later, I looked out the kitchen window and saw him, still engrossed, swinging the maul, pounding the furniture to smithereens. The joy Thomas brought to his task was in inverse relation to all of the times Susanne and I had earlier asked him to perform some less joyous though more constructive task. Finally, he had front-end permission from us to tear something up rather than what usually happened, which was he'd tear something up and then tell us about it, or not. Though, honestly, he didn't mess up as much stuff as I did. Susanne often came behind me, pointing out something I'd lost or having to fix this or that, which she was very good at, thankfully. My latest boo-boo: somehow losing the gas cap to our four-wheeler.

It was Saturday, and Larry Kirby was again at Hogback Mountain, this time to pick up his final check. His renovations had given our cabin and barn a mostly finished, though far-from-polished look. Larry was definitely a man who knew how to get things done up here in these mountains—one way or the other—and I could tell by his chipper mood that he was pleased with his results.

"These walls are just raw pine," I said to him. "You sure they don't need to be treated or stained *or something?*"

Larry rubbed his narrow, gray-bearded chin. "You can do that. Or you can just leave the walls natural. They'll slowly take on a pleasant yellow color." He led me out to the porch, where he tamped his foot on the recently laid planking. "But if I were you, I'd put a sealer on this deck in a few months, after it cures."

Despite a few rough spots, including the cheap-looking, composite-wood floors that Susanne and I had selected at a hardware store over in Batesville, Larry Kirby had indeed done some fine work. Our cabin looked better than we'd imagined it could. I especially liked the cedar-post railing along the front porch, the cozy back deck with its makeshift outdoor bar, the metal overhead doors on the barn, the sizable closets in the master bedroom. Most of all, with our carefully selected furnishings the place felt homey and genuine.

At our kitchen table, I wrote out Larry's final check, which he put in his shirt pocket without glancing to make sure it was for the right amount. He trusted me and no doubt hoped we'd work together again someday: I had hinted that Susanne and I might someday build a larger house—you know, *a real house*.

"Well, I reckon I've got to get back to town," Larry said as he looked admiringly around the cabin one last time. He shook my hand and, with a pat on the back, bucked me up. "You know," he added, waxing a bit philosophical about his labors on my behalf, "it's been a lot of work over the past month or so. But overall, I'd say that what you've got yourself here is a decent little ole cabin."

I smiled at the way Larry had said *decent little ole cabin*, as if referring to anything of a middling, serviceable nature. His down-home, countrified phrase could refer to practically any or all of the Ozarks, as in, "It's a decent little ole place."

"Thanks for everything, Larry," I said with a nod of appreciation. "And let's keep in touch."

5.

The Essential Four-Wheeler

Life in the Ozarks has its dangers, some in nature and some manmade, and as our Ozark odyssey progressed, I found myself susceptible to both. After I bought a chainsaw, I read the poem "Out, Out," by Robert Frost in which he describes a boy who severs his hand and bleeds to death. (*"The saw snarled and rattled, snarled and rattled...As he swung toward them holding up the hand, half in appeal, but half as if to keep the life from spilling..."*)

Other menaces up in these hills included four-wheelers, the all-terrain vehicles that, with their many uses for transport, are the modern-day equivalent of a horse. But like any horse, the four-wheeler, if not handled by an experienced rider, can behave erratically.

Seated high in the saddle of my recently repaired rig, all I wanted to do was to back up: a simple maneuver. I cut the wheels, looked behind me, and shifted into reverse. Suddenly, as if spooked, my four-wheeler revved, lurched, and spun backwards in a tight circle. Frantically, I clutched at the brakes, yet I felt the beast about to roll over, so I pushed off and propelled myself into the air and landed flat on my back.

What the heck just happened? More importantly, had anybody *seen* what just happened? Machinery of all types—boat motors, lawn mowers,

Weed Eaters, chainsaws—had pretty much always defeated me. Nothing ever worked when and how it was supposed to, and now my rebellious four-wheeler had unaccountably reared up and bucked me off. Why, oh, why had I bought this thing from Barry Helton in the first place?

An autopsy of my accident, conducted after my nerves had steadied a bit, revealed that the lever on the hand grip that I thought was the brake was in fact the throttle: in essence, I had frantically kicked the beast in the flanks instead of pulling in the reins. My error was only further proof that I was no natural hillsman and increased my conviction that I'd be fortunate to survive our adventure up in Ozarkland without being maimed or permanently injured. (Now where, exactly, had I put my newly bought chainsaw?)

The next morning, when I went to mount my four-wheeler, I discovered that it wouldn't start at all.

I pulled up in my fancy SUV with my ailing four-wheeler in tow. Seemingly on cue, Scott Hopper emerged from his pine cabin with his spunky terrier running ahead of him. Scott, wearing a cap and with an unkempt reddish beard, was burly and square-shouldered. His cowboy boots had tiny white crosses etched into them. He remembered me from when he'd replaced the head of the engine on my four-wheeler right after I bought the hexed machine from Barry Helton.

"I was thinking about that job recently," Scott said somewhat apologetically. "What's wrong with your four-wheeler now?"

"I don't know. The thing just won't start. Last time you mentioned the solenoid might need to be replaced."

My four-wheeler, which Scott helped me off-load from the trailer, fit in nicely with the other dozen or so sick four-wheelers on his gravel lot. They all looked the same. I didn't know how he distinguished one buggy from another.

A bucket filled with the severed head of a recently killed deer, an eight-point buck, guarded the door to Scott Hopper's quite palatial shop; the beast's dark, glassy eyes stared back at me. Scott took out a notepad, but declined my offer to give him the serial number off my four-wheeler, and, truly, this wasn't necessary: earlier, Susanne had written my name on the gas tank of my rig with a Sharpie, like a mother marks her kid's lunch box when she sends him off to first grade.

"How's your son?" I said. "He strikes me as a pretty smart kid." A few weeks after I'd first met Samuel Hopper, I ran into him at Walmart in Mountain View and he'd remembered my unusual first name, the first kid ever to do so after only a casual meeting: quite impressive.

"He's doing a lot better in school than I did," Scott said, and then with considerably more enthusiasm, he added, "He's also learning how to do a little trappin' out behind the house."

Scott's shop—with its full-sized bar, high-backed chairs, and flat-screen television—was a veritable Taj Mahal of engine repair. He'd cleverly designed a nifty fixture to raise and lower four-wheelers while he worked on them. "It's for my back," Scott said with a manufactured grimace. "I don't like to crawl around under four-wheelers."

"Of course," I conceded. On the floor, I spotted big glass globes filled with muscadine and persimmon juice—ingredients for homemade wine. When I asked if it was any good, Scott raised his nose in the air a notch, as if assuming the dignified air of a vintner. "I really enjoy making wine," he said. "I'd give you a bottle, but I'm out right now."

"Oh, that's quite all right," I demurred.

He pointed to an open box of coconuts. No telling what he could do with them, he intoned. It was going to be fun to experiment.

For ten days, I didn't hear anything from Scott Hopper, not surprising since he'd warned me that he was quite busy. Finally, he called.

"Got your rig ready."

"Was it the solenoid?"

"No, it was something else."

I pretended that I understood what he said he'd done to fix it—I did not want Scott to get the idea that he could just charge me for anything he pleased. He told me I owed an amount that was about what I had expected, though more than I'd hoped, and said to just mail him a check.

After I hung up, I realized I didn't have Scott's address and didn't know the name of his business either, which I soon learned was Hopper's ATV Shop. By all rights, though, his rather luxurious shop-cum-winery could have been called Scott Hopper's Kingdom of ATV Repair.

A few days later, I showed up at Hopper's ATV Shop. This time, Scott was hatless, and the knob of his bald white head looked like a nested egg perched atop his thick, reddish beard. After we loaded my four-wheeler on my trailer, he ushered me inside his palatial shop, where he wrote out a receipt.

"Did you ever make any wine with those coconuts?" I said.

"I did…It's a-bubblin' right now."

"I see you like Samuel Adams beer," I said, taking note of the many signs on the wall behind his bar. Apparently, this Boston-made brew was Scott's favorite, even though it wasn't easy to find craft beer in this part of the Ozarks, especially since over here in Stone County, as in numerous others throughout Arkansas including Izard County, liquor could not be legally sold.

"Did you name your son after Samuel Adams beer?" I inquired.

"No, I named him after Samuel Colt of the Colt revolver."

"Ahh, I see."

Atop Scott's long bar was the glass barrel full of fermenting coconut juice—the stuff he'd earlier said was "a-bubblin'." The juice looked like milky lemonade. Scott caught me eyeing it.

"It's not ready yet," he said possessively, as if this juice was the raw material from which precious Grand Crus Burgundy was to be wrought. He ushered me towards what he considered his properly aged stuff—several glass kegs of fermented muscadine and grape juice. When I asked Scott where he got his grapes, he said, "From Wilson," referring to a local grower. "He says that when the stems turn brown he can't sell them, so he always keeps a pile of them for me…Here, I'll give you some wine."

Scott pulled out a half-gallon jug of muscadine wine.

"Oh, that's way too much," I said, waving my hands.

Scott reached back into his cabinet and pulled out a smaller bottle of muscadine and a bottle of golden-colored apple wine too. He was determined to give me *something*.

"Let me pay you something for this stuff," I said as he handed over the bottles.

"Oh, that's all right."

"Okay. Thanks much," I said, figuring Scott Hopper's generosity owed to the fact that he'd realized that, given my obvious troubles with machinery, I'd be a good customer over the long haul.

"I sell some of this wine," he said, still peering with admiration into his cabinet full of hooch. "And the rest of it I try to hide from my alcoholic friends. It's the reason they come around here."

6.

Fortunes Built on Sand

A few weeks before Christmas, Dennis Gillian came up to Hogback Mountain with a gift wrapped in plain paper. It was a framed print of Norman Rockwell's *Stockbridge Main Street at Christmas*.

"I thought you'd like it," Dennis said with pride in his eye. "I framed it myself."

"Thanks much…You know, you didn't have to do that." Earlier, I'd mailed Dennis and his wife a fifty-dollar gift certificate to a farm supply store over in Batesville. But the Gillihans' gift was more personal, more thoughtful.

I asked Dennis what he'd been up to so far that day. He replied that he had risen at dawn to work several hours in his frame shop, fixed his commode (long overdue), fed his cattle, and then cooked a Crock-Pot full of chicken. When he returned my question, I offered that I'd slept late that morning, gone on a hike with Bear down to Little Grand Canyon, driven to town with Bear to eat lunch at the Rainbow Cafe, then come home to sit by the fire and watch a football game.

My lack of productivity was embarrassing. Then again, Dennis's work schedule was dictated by the task at hand, not so much by the clock or the day of the week. He was on seasonal, agricultural time and worked when and how he pleased, whereas my schedule was dictated by the demands of a corporation: I worked 8:00 to 5:00 during the week and had the weekends off. Even so, Dennis likely envied my leisurely weekends, while I was certainly jealous that he napped after lunch almost every weekday and took time off whenever he pleased—though he rarely did.

We decided to hang the framed Norman Rockwell print just opposite the painted disc blade of Hee and Haw, the housewarming gift from James Bell. Dennis hummed one of his little ditties as he hammered a nail into the wall. "I don't keep enough Kleenex around my shop," he said with a slight cock of his head to make sure the picture was hung straight. "I framed a painting for a woman this week, and when she saw the way I did it, it brought tears to her eyes."

Dennis's framing business—a side pursuit to his modest cattle operation—was his own personal declaration of independence. For years, he'd worked making airplane wings for Boeing in Melbourne, some twelve miles to the east. As part of his training in lean manufacturing, Boeing sent him to southern California a few times, the farthest he'd ever traveled from Izard County (and the source of his signature soul-brother handshake). Later, after Boeing shut down its factory, Dennis sought something over which he had more control, so he opened his Twin Creek Frame Shop, which he ran out of a small metal building behind his house.

Dennis was always looking for ways to make a dollar and, like many Ozarkers, he had a talent for small-scale entrepreneurship. A few years ago, when up on Devil's Backbone, a nearby mountain, he'd noticed odd pieces of wood lying around. An idea struck him: he gathered up the wood, loaded it in his truck and, over the next week, visited every taxidermist in the area. They eventually bought all his wood to use as bases for game mounts. Such resourcefulness, combined with simple living, bred a hard-won confidence in Dennis that he could survive damned near anything. In this regard, as a self-reliant man he was quite fearless—and had the right to be so.

"It'd be hard to starve me out," he said. "Somebody once told me, 'Gillihan, you're an opportunist.' At first I was offended, but then I realized it was a high compliment. Being an opportunist is one of God's gifts to me."

Even so, one-off opportunities like scrounging up scrap wood to peddle to local taxidermists were not where Dennis's heart was. Nor, really, was framing pictures. "Sometimes, I wish I hadn't worked for Boeing," he mused as we sat around the kitchen table. "It kept me from going into real estate. It's something I think I'm pretty good at, and you'd be good at it too. You have a vision for how to improve property."

"I guess," I said. "In some ways."

Vision was one thing, but trading was another thing entirely, and as a pure trader—a highly useful talent—few people I'd ever met were in Dennis's league. For years, he'd maintained an exhibitor's booth at an antique mall in Mountain View. His booth was stocked with items gleaned from area auctions and yard sales, where he always showed up wearing a policeman's hat, which he believed gave him an advantage. To Dennis, trading was a game and one he clearly relished, though he had no illusions about the small-fry nature of his wheelings and dealings. "Some people in big cities swap high-rise buildings," he said, "and some people like me just swap pots and pans."

We moved over into the living room, where I put a few more logs in the wood stove. On cold days, our cabin could get quite drafty despite Susanne's conscientious caulking of our windows.

Recently, I had learned of Dr. Jackson's plans to build a sand mine on his twelve hundred acres that adjoined my property and Dennis's property too. My neighbor, Ed Alexander over at Wildcat Mountain, had spotted geologists taking core samples on Jackson's land. Jackson's new company, Helios Mining LLC, had a jargon-filled website that touted itself as "a startup sand mine serving the oil and gas exploration and production industry with the highest quality proppants and other products. Our sand is a Northern White silica sand and comes from the St. Peters sandstone formation in northern Arkansas. We have access to all of the desirable sand sizes with high crush strength and meeting all 14 API specifications."

I figured Dennis knew all about what Dr. Jackson was up to—he and the good doctor had probably recently discussed it over supper—so as I poked at the fire, I said, "Have you seen or heard from our neighbor lately?"

"He was supposed to call me last time he came up," Dennis replied as he scooted closer to the stove, dragging his stiff right leg. "But I never heard from him."

This wasn't surprising. Around these parts, Dr. Jackson was as elusive, as enigmatic, as a yeti. I had never met him and did not particularly want to, for I feared he'd ask for access to his property via my Hogback Road, of which he owned a sliver (according to Dennis, who knew everything).

While it was possible for me to avoid meeting Dr. Jackson, I could not ignore his plans for his property. Three years ago, when he'd bought his tract of just over twelve hundred acres, he became one of the largest landowners in Izard County and a force to be reckoned with.

Not only was sand in evidence up here in this part of the county, but about seventy miles further south, around Guy, Arkansas, there was a considerable amount of oil exploration and hydraulic fracking going on—so much so that it recently had caused a swarm of earthquakes, the tremors from which were felt up here. The Ozarks have long been fertile ground for extractive industries like timber and lead, and our southernmost rim of Izard County was one of the only regions in this part of the United States that had silica sand. And lo and behold, it was of a texture and quality that was used in fracking—or so I'd been told.

But Dennis, ever pragmatic in his views and surprisingly centrist in his politics, was quite sanguine about what Jackson's grandiose plans meant for him. "I believe a man has the right to do with his property as he pleases," he said, referring to Jackson's land and no doubt to his own, should the opportunity arise for him to pull off a favorable trade.

"Me too," I said even though the prospect of this particular sand mine tested my deeply held beliefs in property rights and capitalism. At that moment, I leaned towards the more restrictive, not-in-my-back-yard (NIMBY) position.

"Who knows?" Dennis said. "Something good may come of this situation."

"We'll see."

"You know, there's a lot of mining that goes on around here. Some of my relatives have a sand mine over at Guion."

Lord only knew which of his many kinfolk up here in the Ozarks Dennis was talking about—or if any of his relatives once owned the sand mine. But the place he'd referred to was nowadays owned by a giant corporation. Many times, on my trips up to Izard County, I'd driven by the road that led to the sand mine, not far from Melbourne.

"If I was younger," Dennis said, still ruminating on the notion that Dr. Jackson was in on something really big—something that he could have been in on too if he'd just seized the opportunity a few years ago. "Agh, I'm still young," Dennis said with dismissive wave of his hand. "But I'm just crippled up."

All this intrigue over Dr. Jackson's land stirred my curiosity. Soon I read of new sand mines up in Wisconsin, which was described as the "new Saudi Arabia of sand." Was it possible that the southern rim of Izard County, Arkansas was about to become the new Bahrain of sand?

Of course Dr. Jackson was a dreamer. But the Ozarks have a long history of outsiders with big dreams about what can be done to improve the area, typically while making themselves tidy sums of money. Evidence of this was all around me: in the 1920s, a man from Ohio tried to develop a cave off of Highway 9 into a tourist attraction. Unfortunately, the Great Depression took him down. Just across the White River, there was once the Land of the Crossbow, where several businessmen in the 1950s envisioned building a medieval-themed bow-hunting resort. That failed too. Dogpatch, two counties over, was an

Ozark-related theme park based on Al Capp's *L'il Abner* comic strip that, after twenty-five years of operation, was shut down in 1993 after the owner inexplicably tried to graft a ski resort called Marble Falls onto it. The ranks of ambitious outsiders who dreamt of Ozark riches have even included a former President of the United States, Bill Clinton, and his wife, Hillary, who while he was governor of Arkansas rather foolishly became involved in an ill-fated 230-acre land deal further upriver known as Whitewater, a property once described by acclaimed financial writer James Stewart as "an undistinguished, second-growth scrub forest in the middle of nowhere."

Even with these impressive examples of local failure, I realized that Dr. Jackson's plan for a sand mine—while certainly ambitious—was also eminently practical, especially when compared to daffy ideas like the Ozark Medieval Fortress, a recently abandoned project hatched by some Frenchmen to build a replica of Burgundy's Guédelon castle in Lead Hill, Arkansas. The castle was to be hand-built using thirteenth-century methods to carve stone, make rope, and forge iron. It was to be forty-five feet tall with six-foot thick walls and take twenty years to complete, just as it would have in the Middle Ages. This starry-eyed project was a predictable disaster. The castle's limestone walls stood half-finished, like some fallen-down, twenty-first-century Roman ruin. Predictably, *The New York Times* had piled on with a snarky article titled, "Fixer-Upper. Ozarks Views. Vassals Welcome."

Granted, Dr. Jackson needed capital, but all that was required for him to pull off his sand mine, according to his prospectus, was a $60 million investment, a relative pittance in the go-go world of hydraulic fracking.

As the weeks passed and I hiked more and more on Dr. Jackson's land, I began to understand his dream of making a fortune off of a sand mine. What else could he do with this land for which he'd paid well over a million dollars? It was basically a series of ridges and hillsides pierced by a wet-weather creek. Granted, his property did include one of Izard

County's most secluded and beautiful spots: a gently terraced run of rippling water that eventually plunged ten feet into a deep, clear swimming hole. I wondered if Dr. Jackson had ever seen this spot—or if, for that matter, any other human being had ever happened upon it. The shoals and waterfall were in a place marked *Rattlesnake Hollow* on the framed topographical map that hung on a wall of our bathroom.

One day, when the winter sun emerged after a hard rain, my neighbor Ed Alexander and I hiked down to this waterfall. Tall with silver-blond hair and a Roman nose, Ed was bedecked in his professional hiking gear, including his North Face parka and GPS finder, while I wore knee-high wader boots, a jean jacket, and my new Stetson cowboy hat. As the water gushed, I sat on the ledge just above the spillway, with Bear at my side. Ed was across at the spot where a smaller creek spilled into the swimming hole. He took some photographs—his specialty, for he was among the best photographers of nature in the Ozarks, a veritable Ansel Adams of Ozarkdom. Over the roar of the waterfall, I shouted, "We should've brought some wine and a good book!"

"Right!" Ed said, and then he said something else in return, but we gave up talking over the rush of the water and just stared at it, mesmerized. Before long, lulled by the sound, we each found a place to lie down on the hillside in the sun and nap.

On the hike back to my cabin, Ed spoke of rumors he'd heard of Dr. Jackson's plan to buy a nearby cabin along Highway 9 and turn it into the worldwide headquarters for Helios Mining LLC. Ed had recently been interviewed by the *Arkansas Times* about the environmental impact of sand mines in Izard County. He of course had a plan to counter Dr. Jackson's plan, which was to find some little critter back in Rattlesnake Hollow that would be threatened with extinction by the appearance of the sand mine, and then invoke this-or-that clause of the Endangered Species Act (a scaled-down variation of the pecksniff strategy that environmentalists in California—invoking the Delta smelt, a three inch baitfish—were using to divert water from farmers in the San Joaquin Valley).

I wasn't an ardent environmentalist like Ed; nevertheless, I was all for his cause. It seemed as good a way as any to stop the building of a sand mine. Beyond this plan of Ed's—when it came to Dr. Jackson and the disposition of his land—all of us up in the lower half of Izard County stayed tuned and hoped for the best, which meant that we privately—and sometimes even publicly—hoped the worst for the good doctor.

7.

Wintertime Amusements

Already, Susanne and I had declared wintertime the best season in the hills, though we'd spent only an abbreviated fall at Hogback Mountain.

According to Ozarks folklore, the cut-open seeds of persimmons predicted the coming winter's weather. Pits shaped as knives meant an icy winter. Forked pits meant a mild winter. Pits cupped like spoons, as this winter's were rumored to have been, meant we'd soon be shoveling snow. Pray tell, what did the persimmon seeds show the year of the record low of twenty-four degrees below zero in Marshall, just two counties over?

As winter set in, it was our ambition to get stranded in a big snowstorm up at Hogback Mountain. This was not so easy. The most common precipitation in winter was a mix of rain and sleet. Any snow that fell typically didn't hang around longer than several days and could be overcome with only a modest exertion of will and want-to.

While back in the flatlands, we saw a forecast of a promising winter storm approaching. Finally, our chance! We bought groceries and packed our warmest clothes and headed for the hills, our thoughts on hiking in the powdery snow, sledding down our long driveway, huddling around the warm fire in our snug cabin.

Darkness fell as we drove the last twelve miles from Melbourne along Highway 9. Our car made fresh tracks in the sleet, and I dreaded the prospect of having to call Dennis Gillihan to come pull us out of a ditch—or even worse if we skidded off one of these mountains. The folks who lived up here full time—true Ozarkers—were home beside their glowing fireplaces. I could only imagine the eye-rolling if they learned about us flatlanders intentionally driving into the teeth of this snowstorm. *What is wrong with those people?*

We arrived safely and started a fire in our wood stove with bacon grease—a trick Susanne had learned from her father—and watched a late movie. As we got under our bedcovers, sleet blew against our windows in a steady patter of pinpricks. What did we care if the storm knocked down the power lines? We had no power anyway but for a small gas-powered generator to run our television, a few lights, and charge our cell phones.

The next morning, we awakened to a dreamscape of snowy white. We sipped hot cider and put extra logs on the fire and cooked turkey bacon and listened to classical music. Just outside the cabin's frosted windows, sparrows swarmed the bird feeder.

Around noon, the Gillihans sent us a text message: *The Dawsons' barn burned last night and they lost all animals: goats, rabbits, most chickens. Billy goat was in a different place so he is alive.* Apparently, the snowstorm had brought lightning.

Soon, in the Ozark tradition of a communal barn raising, we learned of other neighbors ready to help the Dawsons, who lived just up the road. But any aid to them would have to wait as the snow continued to fall in flakes as big as dimes. By noon, six inches had accumulated. I was ready to get out in the snow, as was Bear.

During wintertime, after all the leaves fall, the vast woods around Hogback Mountain open up, and this snowfall had opened them up even more. The landscape was soft, graceful, pristine, eerily quiet. Blanketed in white, familiar trails through the mountains took on a new dimension. Old logging roads resembled ski runs; other trails appeared that I hadn't noticed before.

The boulder-strewn West Twin Creek seemed lifted out of somewhere in the Rocky Mountains, and the rim of ice atop the limestone walls of Little Grand Canyon was like an eyebrow of white. Randomly, long icicles on the ledges broke off and crashed to the floor of the canyon. These noises startled Bear, already energized by the cold. He raced after a deer, then a rabbit, then several squirrels. Animal tracks were all over the snow. He and I hiked for hours through the glorious woods. What did I care if some saw briars scraped my skin, even through several layers of clothes? I did not see or hear a car on the highway all day long. Finally, just before dark I detected the sound of a lone truck—a road grader.

That night, temperatures plummeted to single digits. For dinner we had a pot roast of chicken, vegetables, and herbs; it had simmered all day on our wood stove. The full moon off the snow was so radiant that I didn't need a flashlight when, before bed, I went outside to make more yellow snow.

By the third day of fun in our winter wonderland at Hogback Mountain, we'd had too much of a good thing. We were certifiably stir crazy. Could we drive back to civilization—or at least get back to indoor plumbing and a hot bath—without skidding off the side of a mountain? I put on my heaviest coat and went out to check the highway, which, despite the diligent work of the road grader the day before, was still icy due to the base layer of sleet.

But in the stillness, from somewhere on the far side of the hollow, I heard the sound of a vehicle approaching. The car was traveling quite fast, judging from how high its motor revved. How encouraging! Maybe the roads weren't so bad after all. If this brave vehicle could make it through, why couldn't we?

Soon, a white pickup truck came veering around the bend and I saw, on its front grill, the Confederate flag license plate. As the truck passed, its tires as quiet on the thick snow as a horse shod in felt, the driver gave an abbreviated wave as though it was unsafe for him to unclench even one hand from his steering wheel. This driver looked to be barely old enough to shave.

Following this young man's courageous example, we hurriedly packed up our car and headed out. After we drove the treacherous twelve-mile stretch to Melbourne, the roads eastward were better—I relaxed a bit and looked at Susanne, over in the passenger seat.

"Your hair," I said with a wince.

"This is my cabin hair," she said, pulling on a stray strand of her long caramel-blond mane. "What do you expect after three days with no running water?"

"I know. Tell me about it."

"You don't look so great yourself."

We crossed the Black River, marking where the flatlands of the Arkansas Delta began. This was also where, as best as I could figure, the colloquial use of the word *y'all*, as said by flatlanders like me, transitioned to the word *you-uns*, the old patois as said by hill people like Dennis Gillihan. This nuance of language was but one of many distinctions between these two peoples, who remain as different from one another as Southerners are from Yankees.

As we crossed over to the pancake-flat terrain of the Mississippi River Valley, we received another text message from the Gillihans: *Dennis is on his way to the Dawsons with hay and food for the chickens and the billy goat. Fire burned up all their feed.*

For a town of only 1,673 residents, Melbourne, Arkansas had more activity on a Friday night than one might imagine.

At the entrance to the All You Need store, I was greeted by a young man cradling a Chihuahua puppy in a blanket. At first, I mistook the beady-eyed dog for his pet coon.

The young man asked if I had stopped by for the weekly meat auction. Swept up by the lilt of enthusiasm in his voice, I nodded. This must be some meat auction indeed, I thought, for there were at least twenty-five cars out in the parking lot, practically a traffic jam for Melbourne. Were they selling live cattle at the back of this building? Perhaps prime cuts of beef fresh off the hoof? After all, this was cattle country, sort of. Maybe area ranchers brought their best meat to town on Friday nights to sell to the locals?

For several months now, on our way up to Hogback Mountain, we'd driven past the flashing arrow sign advertising the weekly OLD COWBOY AUCTION. This sign had always intrigued me; now I was about to see what the fuss was all about.

From the back room, beyond my view, I heard the chattering voice of the auctioneer, then the authoritative rap of his gavel. I was close. But to reach this back room, I first had to wend my way through a front room that was a veritable obstacle course of random, oddball merchandise: a life-sized, blow-up Santa Claus and several reindeer, shelves filled with black sneakers and old books, several kids' bikes, a telescope, a puke-green colored velour couch with matching chairs. Amidst the bric-a-brac, marked *Not for Sale*, was a ball cap with *Jesus: God 'Er Done* on its front bill. I felt a rush of cold air as the front door opened, and a woman wearing a gray and white chinchilla coat sauntered through the room. She looked as if she'd been mugged by a pack of skunks.

Finally, I peered around the corner into the back room, where a crowd of some forty people sat, facing towards the auctioneer in row after row of old church pews. I might have thought I had wandered into a Baptist revival were it not for the short man in a straw bowler hat, who, like a carnival barker, walked the aisles pimping each new item up for sale. What was in those small boxes he held up in the air? Did the auctioneer just say that the bidding for three boxes of iodized salt started at two dollars? On and on this went, with a twelve-pack of apple juice and a host of other bulk items of packaged, non-perishable food falling under the auctioneer's gavel.

Plainly, there were no choice cuts of beef being sold at this auction. In fact, there was not much protein for sale here at all, unless one counted the beef stock in the family pack of Campbell's French Onion Soup. Regardless of the humdrum nature of the merchandise for sale, there was no doubt the merchants who ran the Old Cowboy Auction played for keeps. *Caveat emptor* signs were everywhere: ALL SALES FINAL WITH NO GUARANTEES OF ANY KIND.

I felt a bit sorry for the audience, a rather hardscrabble, downtrodden group—though for their benefit, the auctioneers also ran a concession stand that hawked reasonably priced nachos, hamburgers, Frito pies, and "pickels."

Out in the parking lot, I waved goodbye to the young man still swaddling his Chihuahua in a blanket.

"Come back next week," he said. "We're here every Friday night."

"Yes, I know. Thanks. See ya."

A quarter-mile down the highway, I passed the new Dollar General store with its freshly laid asphalt parking lot and well-lit storefront. Compared to the All You Need store this place seemed like Neiman Marcus. This new store was a welcome sight in Melbourne; although it was the seat of Izard County, the town wasn't even big enough to warrant a Walmart.

I drove on towards Hogback Mountain and stopped by the Rainbow Roller Rink, four miles outside of town. When I came in the front door, John Byler, the owner, recognized me. He was a well-built fellow with a wide face that was as weather-beaten as an old baseball glove. John was quite proud to own one of the few skating rinks within a hundred-mile radius. It was a simple metal building ringed by limestone boulders that he'd set in place to keep lost truck drivers from turning around in his parking lot.

"Wow! Look at this!" I said over the blaring music. From the tone of admiration in my voice, you'd have thought I'd just wandered into a bustling nightclub in West Hollywood. To my astonishment, twenty or so people skated around John's rink. "Your place is really crowded tonight! Isn't it? Huh?"

John shrugged, unimpressed. "There's not much else to do around here on a cold winter night."

"That's a fair point." I leaned in closer so John could hear me without me shouting. "You look like you've got a tan. Your face is kind of pink."

"Oh, I've just been outside a lot lately cutting a bunch of wood around my house."

John Byler was as handy as I was unhandy, and I had lately come to rely on him. Our regular phone conversations typically involved him informing me of recent weather conditions along Highway 9—as if my other home in the flatlands were two time zones away—and then inquiring if I'd thought of chopping down a splintered tree up at Hogback Mountain, or cleaning out the gutters on my cabin, or laying in an extra cord of firewood. Then I would invariably reply that his idea—whatever it was—sounded good to me and to go ahead and do the work.

Then, a few days later, John would call me back in the flatlands to report how many hours he'd worked, and I'd send him a check, making sure to pay him promptly. The quality of John's work was very high, and he always did what he told me he would, on the schedule he promised.

A few days later, Susanne and I went to the Gillihans' house for dinner. While Dennis and I cooked rib eye steaks out on his grill, I asked him about the Old Cowboy Auction. He shook his head and tried to suppress a laugh; when it came to what went on in Izard County, he was loath to criticize because, after all, a fair number of the people who lived around here were somehow related to him.

"I call it the Potato Chip Auction," he said with a titter. "It's pitiful."

I laughed too, relieved that Dennis found some humor in it all. "Yeah, boy, it was a pretty rough crowd in there."

At this, Dennis bowed up a bit: "You'd be surprised about the money some of those people have."

It would've been snobby of me to press him over his assertion, even though the facts were against him: the per capita income for Melbourne was just over $14,000 per year, and almost twenty percent of the population was below the poverty line. All of Izard County pretty much was—when it came to the relentless economics of Ozarks marginality—ground zero.

In an effort to keep our conversation on the light side, I said, "Who was that funny-looking little dude at the auction who wore the straw bowler hat?"

"Oh, that's Lee." A look of bemused concern had overtaken Dennis's face. "You know, many of those men who work there at the auction were once in prison. It's a place that's basically run by prisoners."

"Really," I said, unsure of his seriousness. "What were they in for?"

"Stealing."

8.

Power and Water, Please!

Into late winter, our only source of power was still our small generator. This was fine as long as the weather stayed cool—we had plenty of firewood to keep our cabin warm. But as spring progressed and the temperatures rose, we would need air conditioning. We were on the clock to get electricity up to Hogback Mountain.

In the meantime, we also had our solar system, which Barry Helton had left behind. One Saturday evening, Robert Herbstreit, an electrician, came to our cabin to look at it. The solar system didn't work very well, but, if properly hooked up, it could supply at least a few hours of power. Susanne envisioned it as our backup power source in the event of a cataclysm that led to the-end-of-the-world-as-we-know-it. This could be brought about by an earthquake. A solar flare. A comet. Nuclear attack. The Second Coming. Regardless of the threat, with my wife unquestionably in charge of preparedness, we were going to be more than ready.

Robert was a lean, flashing-blond fifty-five year old who wore his black cowboy hat low on his brow. I'd heard some of the locals call him Cowboy; figuring he wasn't much of wine drinker, I offered him a pour of Jim Beam whiskey.

He waved it off. "If I have one of those I'll wind up riding my horse naked through the streets of Melbourne."

"Fine," I said. "I'll take your word for it."

Robert went into the closet off our living room, where he flipped some switches and fiddled with several wires as Susanne looked over his shoulder. Inside the closet was a bank of car batteries, where the power generated by the solar system was stored, plus a fairly sophisticated controller—the brains of our system. Unfortunately, up on our metal roof, there were only two solar panels, about one-tenth of the number required to fully power the cabin for any length of time. It was like having a head yet no body.

Until the 1940s, when the hydroelectric dams were built, electrical power up in the Ozarks was a precarious endeavor. These dams were a game-changer, as were the railroads when they were constructed back in the late 1800s. But the electricity-generating dams did not address the subsequent challenge of running power lines to all of the hills and dales and hollows across the Ozarks. And it was over this so-called last mile that Barry Helton had quarreled with the power company. He thought their price to run the power line from the nearest pole up to the cabin he'd built—now our cabin—was a bit high. He had a fair point, for I too had recently called the power company about this and almost choked on the price.

But I knew better than to get into a quarrel with a monopoly power provider. I absolutely had to have air conditioning for the summer, and this little stillborn solar system of ours would hardly do the trick.

"I've unhooked your system so that nothing will blow up when you finally get your electrical power," Robert said as he dusted off his black hat. He and Susanne had the solar system all figured out, apparently. She undoubtedly knew a lot more about it than I did—and probably more than Robert knew about it, too. At the very least, she had read the instruction manual.

"You sure you don't want a shot of whiskey?" I said before Robert left.

He hesitated, but then said, "Nah," and went out the door.

That week, while we were away in the flatlands, the power company ran the lines to our cabin. When we returned to Hogback Mountain the next weekend, I could scarcely believe my eyes.

The desolation was shocking. In rural America, the sanctity of power lines is beyond dispute. Everything within a twenty-foot radius on either side of the lines must be cleared to ensure that not a single tree falls on the precious lines—at least not in our lifetimes. And if there is any doubt as to whether or not a particular tree should be cleared, the power company doesn't waste time making judgment calls. They just go Neanderthal and cut down everything in sight.

Now, like my predecessor Barry Helton, I too wanted to fight the almighty power company. But my beef wasn't over the expense. I was mad about my trees! I was particularly incensed that, along our driveway, the crew had cut down a thirty-year-old cedar. It had been the perfect adornment for our front gate.

But the damage didn't stop there. For weeks, Thomas and I had labored to carve out Brandenburg Trail, a path through the woods at the corner of our property closest to Brandenburg Mountain. This picturesque trail led to a circular turnaround, which I'd named, not surprisingly, Brandenburg Turnaround. The trail was another interesting facet of our land, a fun place to hike or ride our four-wheeler.

Now Brandenburg Trail and Brandenburg Turnaround—and the surrounding woods from which they were carved—were gone. Flattened. As I stood in the driveway, I called Thomas to report what I was seeing.

Over the phone, he optimistically replied, "We'll fix it."

"You don't understand. It's as if the entire area has been cleared for a giant parking lot. It can't possibly be fixed, ever."

The carnage of trees notwithstanding, we now had electrical power, plus plenty of downed trees for firewood for next winter. A major obstacle towards a more refined existence at Hogback Mountain was overcome.

For months now, Dennis had generously offered to bring his bulldozer up to Hogback Mountain. I finally paid to have it trucked up from his house. (Even in the Ozarks, a bulldozer can't be driven on the highway.)

With the arrival of the bulldozer, our thoughts turned to how to use it to improve our property. I wanted Dennis to clear some trails before the woods greened with the coming of spring. But he too had his own ideas about what should be done. "I always like to have some yard around my house," he counseled. "I could clean up this area for you around your cabin, and then you could put out some grass seed and just smooth it over."

I hesitated—Susanne also desired to groom the hillside that was covered with waist-high brush, saplings, and patches of tall golden sage grass. But the last thing I wanted at Hogback Mountain, my weekend retreat, was any sort of yard to mow. "I think I'll just let it go natural," I told Dennis. "I like it kind of like it is—you know, wild."

"All right," he said with an air of mild regret.

I feared that I was being too hardheaded. There was my wife to consider, after all. So I pointed at the gray-white limestone boulders, the rocks so pale that they seemed to glow on moonlit nights. "Well," I conceded, "I guess you could clear out a few of those large rocks."

"What about the area below the rocks?"

"Okay, go ahead and clear that out too. Who knows, maybe we could have picnics down there this summer."

Dennis hummed one of his ditties as he climbed up onto his dozer, maneuvering his stiff right leg over the seat and settling in. "I just love working this dozer," he said with a touch of veneration. "I got inspired when a neighbor of mine once brought his dozer over to my house, and after he left, I said to myself, 'If he can afford a dozer, then I can afford a dozer.' Even today, ten years later, it's worth more than I give for it."

Indeed, I thought to myself, for it was seldom that Dennis got the short end of any stick.

The old contraption belched black smoke when Dennis shifted it into gear. As it burrowed into the hillside, it moved with all the dexterity of a World War II tank. Eventually, the dust cleared to reveal Dennis's handiwork. As I'd feared, he was creating even more yard around my cabin. But it wouldn't matter anyway. When summertime came, all the saplings and underbrush he'd just flattened would grow back thicker than ever. I wouldn't have to mow it.

Dennis stopped his dozer, finally, and a blessed silence came over the hillside. He reminded me of a sculptor who rests his trowel. He seemed quite satisfied with what he'd accomplished so far. Before he dismounted, he said, "You wanna drive this thing?"

"Heavens, no."

"You sure?"

"Positively."

I knew that if I even so much as touched the dozer's steering wheel, one of its huge metal treads would surely come off, or break, and I'd have to fix it, which I couldn't even begin to do, or pay to have it fixed.

From atop the hillside Dennis and I gazed down upon his ranch and the surrounding area known as Twin Creek, so named because it was nestled between East Twin Creek and West Twin Creek.

"I wish I could see what went on down there in that valley a hundred years ago," Dennis said. "Wouldn't that be a sight?"

I wondered what in the world he was talking about? *A hundred years ago? Why?* But then I realized Dennis was speaking of a time when Twin Creek had a relatively large population of several hundred people, a general store, and three school districts so that no child had very far to walk to get to their one-room schoolhouse.

Usually, only oppressive government or a war can depopulate a region. In rural Ukraine, Stalin burned the crops of farmers who wouldn't willingly collectivize their land according to communist doctrine. The ensuing famine was so awful that mothers, fearing cannibalism, warned their children not to leave their houses. Then, not long after this manmade ideological catastrophe, the Nazis had invaded.

By comparison, all it took to depopulate the Ozarks and empty out hamlets like Twin Creek was the Great Depression of the 1930s and the construction of decent highways that led to places with better opportunities like Little Rock or Springfield or Batesville or St. Louis. Life could be hard in these hills, a reality with which Dennis was well acquainted.

Longingly, he said, "A relative of mine named Clint Gillihan lived down at Twin Creek back in the olden days. I heard he went under financially and had to move out, but he just moved somewhere else further down the creek. All that's left of his old home place is a grown-over pile of rocks.... You know, on cold winter nights, I've stood out on the ridge where his house once was and wondered how he ever managed to survive up here."

Dennis sipped a cold soda and turned his gaze towards Brandenburg Mountain, just to the north, a sight that triggered another of his memories of those he reverently called "the old timers." "My uncle Dwain Ponder lived up there," he said. "He was Cherokee, or some sort of Indian. He had a red face and short-cropped black hair. He may have been a paw paw, I don't know. His wife was a Gillihan. Her name was Elzorie."

"Elzorie?"

"Something like that. Anyhow, back in the nineteen thirties, one of my uncles' nephews came to live with him after he'd killed a black man with a knife over in Newport."

We heard the pealing call of Dennis's peacocks from his ranch down in the hollow. "Wigalaars," he said matter-of-factly. "Wild creatures that jump on your face and suck your innards out through your nostrils."

Only when he smiled was I sure that he was kidding.

"They're monsters, as my dad used to say." Dennis chuckled at his recollection of his father's endearing mispronunciation. "My dad once told me that I'd better learn to like to work because I was going to be doing a lot of it. He was a great man."

"Speaking of work, you ready to clear my trail?"

I had already named it Dark Hollow Trail because this was the name of the hollow on the topographic map on the wall of my bathroom. On many days, when I hiked these surrounding hills, I consulted this map to figure out where I was going, or where I'd been.

Dennis remounted his dozer, his pride and joy, and drove down the hillside, then through a meadow while I followed like a foot soldier. The dozer made an awful shirring noise and I saw the bobbing white tails of three deer when they darted off in fright. We curved back up the hillside into the dense thicket, and the bulldozer swerved to avoid two tall trees, a spot I later named Cedar Twist. (In all my naming on Hogback Mountain, I was admittedly quite literal minded.)

"Where are we going?" I called out in Dennis's direction.

"There's an old road up here somewheres," he shouted back from the driver's seat. "We'll find it! We'll find it!"

Though I had no idea where Dennis was headed, I was nonetheless thrilled with our progress. It wasn't worth owning the land unless there were trails on it for me to hike. The hillsides were so steep, the limestone bluffs so severe in places, that I was willing to accept any path I could get. It seemed a minor miracle merely for Dennis to get his bulldozer through these dense thickets.

The old road that Dennis was looking for led deep into the woods, to places I'd never seen. Obviously there once were homesites somewhere back here. To now, I'd thought of this land of mine and all that adjoined it as a relatively untouched wilderness, but signs of earlier habitation were now in evidence: old rutted wagon trails, unexpected clearings amidst the trees, the outline of a shallow root cellar, the last brittle strands of a rusted barbed wire fence.

After our trail clearing was finally done, Dennis and I sat on the porch of my cabin, sheltered from the chilly breeze. I petted Bear for a spell and noticed that the metal ID tag I had bought for his collar was gone. The tag had my phone number as well as Dennis's on it, just in case Bear got lost. I asked Dennis about it.

"Well, Bear got into a fight with a coyote," he said, not pronouncing the *-e* in coyote. "They were out in one of my fields. I swear that coyote swallered his tag. Ole Bear's had a tough week or two. One of my cows kicked him in the head, and after that he walked sideways for about an hour or so."

"He looks to be okay," I said, rubbing the dog's head tenderly like a concerned father.

I offered Dennis another cold soda, but he turned it down: he didn't need any more sugar. By his own admission, he'd been reckless with his health. He had a touch of diabetes, and years ago he'd tried everything he could think of to quit smoking. Finally, he got down on his knees and asked God for help. "I used to sit by the stove in the early mornings and drink coffee and have my first cigarette of the day," he noted. "As they say of scratching poison ivy, it's better than sex."

We watched the shadows of the clouds move across the rugged landscape and stared into the vast expanse of barren hills surrounding East Twin Creek. I wondered aloud who lived in the white house atop the distant mountain. Aside from a faraway cell phone tower (and thank goodness for it!), this house was the only scar of humanity on the otherwise pristine horizon. I had taken to calling it Big Sky because I'd heard Robert Herbstreit, the cowboy electrician, once call it that.

"I've never heard it called that," Dennis said, as if offended. "My cousin lives up there. It's his land."

It certainly did not surprise me to learn that someone named Gillihan owned the place.

"My family owns around three thousand acres up in this area," he added. "All of it paid for by selling timber off the land. The original Gillihans included three brothers who all got along because each of them agreed that the elder brother was in charge and went along with what he said."

Given the famously combative nature of Scots-Irish settlers like the Gillihans, I doubted this was entirely true. Dennis, for his part, had long marinated in the oils of hating the English, his passions stoked by a book he'd recently pored over that chronicled the potato famine and resulting devastation of the Irish population back in the 1840s. Then again, if Dennis's recollection was that the three Gillihan brothers, his forefathers, had gotten along just swimmingly, then it had to be true.

We watched a hawk soar below us, riding the winds that swirled down in the hollow. Recently I'd bought an adjoining thirty-six acres, which lay between our cabin and Dennis's property. I rationalized the purchase by declaring to Susanne that I didn't want any close neighbors, though it wasn't exactly the choicest parcel of land. Truth was, as a habitually acquisitive Baby Boomer, I just wanted to own more property; I was, by golly, up to sixty-three acres! And still, there was the hope of buying sixty more acres from the lady in Dayton.

To Dennis, I said, "I saw the fence you're putting in between my new land and yours."

"We want to keep our cows from getting out."

"Who's doing the work?"

"Me and my wife. It goes pretty fast if we stick with it. You know, farmers like us basically just grow grass. Then the cattle eat the grass. It's pretty simple. I just love foolin' with them cattle."

The sudden appearance of the fence didn't seem very neighborly. Why on earth would Dennis's cattle wander up our steep hillside, where there was nothing to eat but brush and saw briars and mint weed? Had Susanne or I done or said something to offend the Gillihans? Then again, perhaps they were wise to worry about their cattle roaming up to Hogback Mountain—without a fence of some sort between us there was nothing to keep their cows from wandering for miles in a westerly direction. Recently, I'd seen where, in one spot, Dennis had installed what he called an "Arkinsaw gate," his name for his somewhat crude, handmade barrier.

Before Dennis left, he parked his bulldozer along our driveway. He planned to come back later and move more of those gray-white boulders up near our cabin: Susanne wanted them all cleared out. But a few days later, Dennis told me the boulders were merely the tips of icebergs. Beneath them, buried underground, was an unseen mass of rocks as big as Volkswagens. He couldn't budge them.

Getting well water up to Hogback Mountain was a stiffer challenge than was running the power lines for electricity. For one thing, there was the question of where to dig our well. Perhaps down in front of the barn, near where Susanne wanted to eventually plant some fruit trees? Or maybe behind the cabin, closer to a future homesite? Or, to save money on pipes and pumps, was it better to drill the well as close as possible to our cabin and barn?

Yet all such practical considerations begged the ultimate consideration—nature's consideration, which was, just where, oh where, beneath this nearly one-thousand-foot high mountain was the water?

To help answer this all-important question, Susanne fashioned two coat hangers into makeshift divining rods and showed me how to use them. I walked all around our property, engaging in a bit of backtrails well witching. It was a fool's errand, I knew, even as I dutifully held the rods in front of me to see if, and where, they crossed. I was skeptical of such a crude method—it seemed an old wives' tale, like the sentiment that a whippoorwill singing downhill from you was bad luck, yet one singing uphill was good luck. But with thousands of dollars on the line with the drilling of a well, I was willing to try anything to gain an edge.

As I stood in my driveway with the bent-up coat hangers in my hands, Shane Moser, professional well driller, arrived in his black pickup truck. His wife, who wore an AC/DC sweatshirt, held their infant son on her hip. Shane had spent the morning hunting for coyotes with some buddies. He'd had no luck, he said, mistaking me for someone who knew about—or cared anything for—coyote hunting. Though with my fancy SUV parked nearby, Shane no doubt quickly surmised that I was no true hillsman.

I informed him of my discovery—the location I had just divined as the best spot for my well was behind the cabin.

"Show me," Shane said crisply.

We walked up the hill and stopped at the spot where my coathanger rods had earlier crossed. Though I still had my rods in my hand, I did not see fit to take another reading: Shane would just have to take my word for it.

He cast his eyes toward my cabin, not too far away, and said, "Where's your septic tank?"

"In the front yard."

"It's illegal to put a well within three hundred feet of a septic tank."

"Oh. Sure. That I can understand."

"Is this more than three hundred feet from your tank?"

"I don't know.... More or less."

"I'll probably only have to cut down a tree or two to get my truck back here."

"You will?!" I was still tender from the destruction the power company had wrought when they'd run their precious electrical lines.

"To be anchored properly, it's got to go this way." Shane signaled with both hands that his drilling truck would need to be angled in perpendicular to the hillside. "It's a big-ass truck."

From down the hill, I heard Shane's infant son crying and his wife calling. By now, confronted with Shane's well-digging expertise, plus his talk of where he'd place his big truck, I was having further doubts as to the scientific validity of my well-witching methods: the spot I had divined was at the very crest of Hogback Mountain. In the slanted late-afternoon light, the view from here was indeed fantastic. But that of course didn't mean that it was necessarily the best spot to dig a well.

"How deep do you think you'll have to go with the well?" I said.

"Won't know until we start drilling."

"What's the deepest you've ever had to drill around here?"

"Twelve hundred and four feet," Shane said immediately, as if his labors to drill that particular well were forever burned into his memory. Likely, he was also smiling inside as he pondered the sum of money he'd made from digging it.

As Shane and I walked down the hill, I multiplied this depth of more than twelve hundred feet by the per-foot cost of drilling he had mentioned earlier: it was big number, more than I'd expected to spend for a well.

"But that well was across the river," Shane said in a belated attempt to soothe me.

"Exactly how far across the river? Like, was it pretty far over into Stone County? Aren't the mountains a little bigger over there? They look bigger anyway. Right?"

Frustrated with my nattering questions, Shane reached into his pickup truck and handed me a ball cap with *Moser's Well-Drilling* and his phone number stitched on it, his gesture a way of encouraging me not to back out now, no matter how deep he had to drill on my mountain to get water. Soon, he was off in his pick-up truck with his wife and young child.

The next week, Shane called to report his progress.

"We've gone down eight hundred feet, and I'm getting two to three gallons per minute," he said. "It's not enough."

I didn't know whether this was true or not, but I certainly did not want a well that was too shallow. As with the power company, I was at the mercy of the experts, which, when it came to well digging, was indisputably Shane Moser. "Keep going down then until you get plenty of water," I said. "I don't want to have to come back later and re-drill it."

On our trip up to Hogback Mountain the next weekend, I saw Shane's drilling rig wedged into a clearing. To make room for his giant truck, he'd cut down two mid-sized oak trees, but compared to the devastation the power company had earlier wrought, I considered this no big deal.

Later that week, when I was gone, Shane called me from up at Hogback Mountain and said he was now down to 1,040 feet and the flow rate, at eight gallons per minute, was acceptable. It seemed that my backtrails well witching was fairly accurate after all. Though, who knew? Shane could've drilled at another spot a few hundred feet away and hit ample water at eight hundred feet. Or not.

Immediately, I called the pipe layer to tell him we were ready for him. After he whistle-marveled at the depth of my well, he noted that oil prices were up lately and consequently the cost of the plastic pipes used in the well was also higher. The price he gave me to run the pipe and install pumps was higher than I expected too.

"Well, do your thing," I said grumpily. "And the sooner the better. My wife and I are tired of not having any running water. We're about to go nuts out here."

"Hey!" I called out from the shower. "Hey! Hey!"

Susanne came rushing into our steamy bathroom. "What is it? What's wrong?"

From behind the shower curtain, I said, "This hot shower sure does feel great! The water pressure is fantastic, and it's good hard water, too."

"I know," she said. "What a blessing it is. Woo-hoo!"

"It's a good thing I'm such an excellent well-witcher."

"Yeah, right. We got lucky."

I pulled back the shower curtain so that I could see Susanne's face. "Seriously, this is the most expensive shower I've ever taken. Counting the electrical power and the well and the pumps and the hot water heater—just add it all up. It's shockingly expensive."

"Right…This shower cost almost as much as what we spent to buy the original cabin, barn, and twenty-seven acres of land," she said before she closed the bathroom door and left me to my long, hot shower.

The well water, due to traces of sulfur, smelled a bit like rotten eggs, especially after a hard rain. Nevertheless, our water problems at Hogback Mountain were over for good. Moreover, our indoor commode was up and running. We'd never realized how much hot-and-cold running water and a flushable toilet mattered until we had gone without them.

It was Saturday, a day for chores and repairs at Hogback Mountain, and just before lunchtime Robert Herbstreit, the cowboy electrician, came up our driveway. He sat so low in the seat—his black cowboy hat barely visible over his steering wheel—that his truck appeared to be driverless.

Robert slowly got out, unfolding his slight, angular frame. A few weeks ago, he'd been hit in the groin by a falling tree. Susanne had suggested that he see a doctor, but he hadn't seen one in years. He didn't trust them, he said, and no amount of pain—or not-so-gentle persuasion—could make him think otherwise.

Robert crept gingerly up the stairs to our porch. He disappeared into the tiny closet just off our living room, where he again futzed with our solar system, trying to hook up the wires he'd disconnected weeks ago before the electrical power was turned on.

After a spell, I stuck my head in the closet to see how he was doing.

"Where's your wife?" Robert said as he went on studying the control panel.

"She's underneath the house looking at the foundation with Dennis Gillihan." I tapped the floor with my foot to indicate approximately where they were.

"Tell her to come see me when she gets a chance."

By now, Robert of course knew that our solar system was a thorough mystery to me. Frankly, the threat of the-end-of-the-world-as-we-know-it notwithstanding, I considered it redundant: our cabin was forty miles downstream from one of the largest hydroelectric dams in this part of the United States. Over the last seventy-five years, heaven and earth had been moved—and billions spent—to make sure folks like us who lived in remote areas had plentiful, reliable electrical power.

While Robert continued his work inside our tiny closet, I went out to the porch, where I overheard voices underneath the house—Susanne and Dennis were discussing how to fortify our foundation. It was obvious that, despite all of Larry Kirby's good work to overhaul our cabin, our foundation still lacked. Only so much could be done without starting all over. Susanne was particularly concerned about the weight of the bank of car batteries in the tiny closet off our living room.

Thankfully, she knew a bit about foundations—as a teenager, she'd helped her father build a house—and accordingly, she feared our cabin could collapse. We had to be careful about the weight of the furniture in certain rooms. We also couldn't have too many people in the cabin at one time (at least until the liquor flowed during our dinner parties and such precautions went by the wayside). Already, we'd had trouble shutting the door to our bedroom, a telltale sign of a sagging floor. Somewhere back in Texas, Barry Helton—one-time owner of a company that built foundations for homes up here in the Ozarks—was laughing at us.

"What do you want me to do?" Dennis said to Susanne when they emerged from underneath the cabin. From the porch, I was gazing down upon their heads, eavesdropping on their conversation.

"Nothing," Susanne said to Dennis. "I'll get my husband to help me put some more cinder blocks underneath the house. At least he can do that."

"I'm listening," I said accusingly.

She looked up at me. "You can start putting the cinder blocks underneath the cabin tomorrow morning."

"All right."

As our life at Hogback Mountain evolved, I was walking a fine line. It was difficult for me to work every weekday at my managerial job in the flatlands—my real job—and then also do chores every weekend around our cabin up in the mountains. At first these tasks were fun, even somewhat therapeutic: cleaning up trash, chopping wood, marking trails, hauling water and firewood. But when it came to more complex tasks, I wasn't so enthusiastic or so well qualified. I had approached burnout. Susanne, though, had no day job per se, so between us, a pattern emerged—she worked like a pack mule on the weekends at our cabin and recuperated the rest of the week back in the flatlands, while I worked at my real job in the flatlands and then did the best I could with chores up at Hogback Mountain. Every week, we repeated the cycle.

Our talents, while complementary, were a classic case of role reversal: I, the man of the cabin, could fix nothing, while Susanne could fix anything. She had grown up on a farm in the Arkansas Delta and from an early age could repair her bicycle, assemble her younger sister's new baby bed, tear apart and put back together a clock—the list was endless. Certainly, she would have been handy on the arrested frontier of the Ozarks back in the mid-nineteenth century—and she rightfully took pride in her skills.

I was thankful to have Susanne as my partner: I'd heard that Dr. Jackson's wife, upon seeing the rather luxe cabin he'd bought over on his property, had turned up her nose and told the good doctor that he'd have to spend $50,000 on the place before she would even spend a single night there.

By comparison, all Susanne wanted was a cabin with a foundation that wouldn't collapse and a working solar system to provide backup power—if and when the-world-as-we-knew-it came to an end. It wasn't so much to ask.

9.

Enter the Land of the Preppers

Susanne and I pulled up to the Dawsons' house, on an errand to buy some of their eggs. Both Bill and Cody—father and son—wore knee-high mud boots as they cleared the charred ground where their barn had burned a month earlier. They put down their shovels and came over to greet us.

"Our new barn is going to be ten feet bigger," Bill said with pride.

"How nice," I said distractedly as I fended off the Dawsons' dog.

"Oh, that's Harley," Bill noted. "My wife said I'd always wanted to have a Harley in the front yard, but this dog is all she had in mind."

I smiled wanly at Bill's joke, which he'd obviously told more than once, and then turned to Cody. Though shorter than his dad, he had a bigger belly and looked to be generally the same age. Cody worked at a hardware store in Mountain View, the one somehow surviving even with the giant Walmart next door.

"What does *Begin Curtilage* mean?" I asked, curious about the words on the two signs I'd seen posted at both entrances to the Dawsons' half-circle driveway.

"It's a Latin term that's stronger than *No Trespassing*," Cody explained through a beard so thick that it was crimped like the hair on the back of a woman's head. "It's means private sanctum. We learned about it at a Tea Party meeting over at Calico Rock."

"It's a legal term—Latin, I think," Bill chimed in. "It gives us an extra layer of protection. You know, if something happened...."

The woe-unto-thee tone with which the Dawsons spoke made it sound as if their posted signs, which also bore the address of a survivalist-oriented website, gave them carte blanche to wreak havoc on any poor soul who happened to step onto their property.

I was a bit taken aback. "Does anybody really know what *Begin Curtilage* means? Until you just told me, I had no idea, though I admit I never took Latin in college."

"Yes, well, that is a problem," Bill conceded as he smoothed his lush gray mustache. "Nobody really knows what it means."

Susanne and I gathered up our eggs and said our goodbyes.

"Don't forget our get-together in two weeks," Bill said, referring to the upcoming meeting of our prepper group.

"Oh, yes!" Susanne said. "We're looking forward to having everybody over to our place now that we have electricity and running water. Yippee!"

On a Saturday night, our group of twenty or so preppers gathered at our cabin on Hogback Mountain. The kitchen table was laden with cheese and crackers, pretzels, potato chips, a veggie tray. Before our meeting started, we took some time to socialize, an important aspect of prepping since it gave the Ozarkers who otherwise led relatively isolated lives a chance to mingle with like-minded folks. Among the preppers, I detected a fair amount of interest in how Susanne and I lived. As relative newcomers to this group, we were being sized up.

Mark Richardson, a retiree from Navistar up in Illinois, had an ardent interest in solar power and spoke of noncrystalline solar cells and photovoltaic feed-in tariffs. I nodded my head as if I too was an expert, then ushered him into our tiny closet to inspect our stillborn solar system and left him to it.

Back in the kitchen, I noticed Esker Brown, a gray-haired retired telecom engineer, studying the bottles in my wine rack. He was an intense, intelligent fellow who excelled at practically anything he took on: electronics, scuba diving, woodworking, wine making, squirrel hunting. Like many Ozarkers, he was intimidatingly self-reliant, and to top it off, he was even a darned good oil painter.

"Do you make wine?" he said as I approached.

"Hardly," I replied, suppressing a laugh. The longer Esker stared at my modest assemblage of wines—mostly middling California wines bought at a package store two counties over—the more pretentious I felt. In an effort to distract him, I said, "You been doing much deer hunting?"

"Not this year, but last year I hunted every day of the season, from early October until the end of February."

"Every day?"

"I wanted to see if I could do it," Esker said. "It's something I always wanted to try."

"*Every single day? For almost five months?*"

"You'd be amazed at what you hear and see in the woods."

"That's some serious dedication." I soon learned that many years ago, when Esker was in the Navy, he'd won national titles in rifle shooting as well as in pistol shooting. "I guess you got your limit of deer, huh?" I added.

"The limit was five," Esker said, "and I killed my last one in the last hour of the season, right before sunset. Every day, I'd see at least six deer, some so close to me that I could've touched them." He shook his head, as if he knew his quest—this obsession of his—was over the top. "Hunting every day would've made more sense if I could've killed more deer."

Our leader, the venerable Bill Dawson, called our meeting to order. I was pleased to see that one attendee from our last meeting had not shown up: the portly lady who had rambled on about "harps"—some sort of sinister devices the federal government controlled that were capable of manipulating earthquakes and volcanoes. Her paranoia was too much, even for the staunch libertarians amongst us.

With his white hair and careworn eyes, Bill Dawson had a calming, grandfatherly manner, yet he also conveyed a folksy gravitas appropriate to the seriousness of his subject matter. Most of us would have followed him across the parted Red Sea.

Bill noted that his son, Cody, was featured in *American Frontiersman*, a magazine for those who prefer to linger in the frontier lifestyle. A copy of the publication circulated around our living room. Cody was also a member of a group called the Early Arkansas Reenactors Association (EARA), which "specializes in the activities and concerns of the 'common folk' who populated this area before Arkansas became a state in 1836."

In 1803, with the Louisiana Purchase, the Ozarks had opened to the world. It was a crucial time in the development of humankind. In *The Birth of the Modern*, historian Paul Johnson writes, "The years 1815–1830 are those in which the matrix of the modern world was formed." Maybe so. But EARA members such as Cody Dawson took pains to avoid anything modern during their periodic campouts and reenactments at state parks across Arkansas. They wore their deliberate anachronism as a badge of honor.

Like the EARA members, many of our preppers also resisted certain aspects of modern life. Something in the air and water of the Ozarks nurtured this mentality. In an era when President Obama ridiculed those who "cling to guns or religion," prepping had become a way of life for many people up here. The prepper's mindset was that we must always be ready to live out in the woods by our own wits and do everything for ourselves. This mentality runs counter to every trend in modern life, which steadily moves toward an increasing specialization and division of labor, combined with ever broadening patterns of consumption.

This specialization is what it means to be a part of the global economy. Consider a New Yorker who works in something esoteric like arbitrage in a Wall Street investment banking firm: his highly specific work is largely an abstraction, yet he consumes goods and services from all over the world. The truly modern man works narrowly and consumes broadly. The world, literally, is his oyster.

Conversely, the traditional, old-time Ozarker of the 1800s—and even beyond the Depression years into the 1940s—worked from sunup to sundown to provide his family with daily essentials such as food, shelter, and firewood for fuel. Mountain women cooked, made soap and candles, and washed and sewed clothes. The old-time Ozarker trekked to the nearest town once or twice a year to buy sugar and salt and perhaps purchase a pair of thin-soled boots. Indeed, these Ozarkers of bygone days worked as broadly and consumed as narrowly as perhaps any subculture of humankind since the Middle Ages.

This was why, nowadays, Walmart was a boon to any community in the Ozarks fortunate enough to have such a store. It gave previously isolated people broad access to a wide world of previously unavailable goods. For modern-day Ozarkers, a trip to Walmart was a treat in the way that a visit to fancy-food emporium Dean & DeLuca so delights certain Manhattanites.

Yet the true prepper isn't seduced by Walmart. She uses it merely as a place to buy the supplies and provisions necessary to survive when the fateful day comes that Walmart is no longer around due to a catastrophic earthquake, the collapse of the power grid, or bioterrorism. Today's prepper yearns for simpler, bygone times when no division of labor defined society and everyone, by necessity, worked broadly and consumed narrowly. And so, in the name of surviving a disaster, the prepper draws on this heritage and, well, prepares, all the while pushing back against the encroaching world. And what better place to do it than up here in the Ozarks?

After Bill Dawson's introduction, Susanne followed with an extended description of what had been going on lately in the heavens, especially as it related to some potentially menacing incoming comets. For sure, the near future was not going to be pleasant. Then, a female therapist among our group asked us to consider the psychological impact of enforced communal living in a cave or rock shelter in the aftermath of the-end-of-the-world-as-we-know-it. Our group really needed to think hard, she said, about the lack of personal space, especially as it affected women and their "hygiene."

This was followed by a quick demo on making a filter from a tin can and piece of wire, plus a refresher in how to properly use a whistle. A book, titled *Mushrooming Without Fear*, was passed around. A report was given on the latest from the local Patriot meetings, followed by head-shaking over betrayals by the local politicians, chiefly for taking corporate money. (True prepping calls forth the most hackneyed tropes of the political left, as well as the right.) There was some hand wringing about the possibility of the federal government attacking its own people.

To conclude, Bill Dawson passed out copies of the much-coveted, long-anticipated Red Book. Inside was the all-important phone chain—the list of whom each prepper was to contact when a prepped-for event finally happened. Our preppers were organized into chains of three—thus, no member had to call everyone and no one was left behind.

Inside the Red Book was more—much more. For each attendee, there was a typewritten page titled "Your Skills and Knowledge." Collectively, our group offered an impressive range of know-how: butchering, goat raising, dehydrating, small engine repair (before the computer age), firefighting, carpentry, canning, gardening, nursing, herbal medicine, hunting, fishing, trapping, foraging, lumber sawing, beekeeping, cheese making, self-defense, crisis intervention, disaster response, wood-stove cooking, shooting (concealed permit), map reading, plumbing, piloting, tractor driving, fire building, hypnosis, grief counseling, and prophecy.

My! Any group as skilled as this could definitely tote its own load!

On my page, my list of prepper-worthy skills was limited to a short description of the distribution company for which I worked. As for me and my talents, that was pretty much it. As these preppers saw things—and with some justification—my master's degree from an Ivy League university was utterly useless. I was tolerated at these meetings because my wife's talents as a nurse practitioner were especially useful, if and when the hammer finally came down. I was consoled somewhat by the fact that at least my phone number was listed correctly, though I wasn't sure why anyone would call me except to get in touch with Susanne.

To close our meeting, and to send us preppers off on an upbeat note amidst an evening filled with some rather ominous forebodings, Bill Dawson rose from the couch. "Don't miss our next meeting," he said. "Cody and I will demonstrate how to gut a hog and make sausage. I certainly hope you can be there."

10.

Clinging to Religion

The hymn dragged on and on: "*So I'll cherish the old rugged cross, Till at last my trophies I lay down. I will cling to the old rugged cross, And exchange it someday for a crown.*" Among the thirty-two congregants, only a few could carry a tune; indeed, the music at the Mount Olive Cumberland Presbyterian Church was beyond lackluster. But one of the many charms of this house of worship was that it was the polar opposite of an urban megachurch. Neither Susanne nor I were Presbyterians, but there were few churches around Hogback Mountain to choose among.

Outside, the cold spring wind blew hard. I was thankful we were inside where it was warm: one church member had told us that last summer his son had shot an armadillo with a rifle but then couldn't find it. The varmint had crawled up under the church and died, the smell so vile that the following Sunday's service was held out in an open-air pavilion.

"What a blessing!" Pastor Steve Moon said after the hymn concluded. With his thick hair, rotund bearing and Fu Manchu mustache, he called to mind Craig Stadler, the golfer affectionately known as the Walrus. Steve wiped his watery eyes with his hand towel, gathered himself, and bragged that Wisconsin, his home-state team, had won yesterday's basketball game. Then sensing he'd overstepped, he chuckled and added, "What's worse than a car with a Yankee license plate and a U-Haul attached to it?"

Pastor Steve had his quirks, no doubt. Then again, so did his predecessor, who'd delivered his final sermon with his hand wrapped in a blood-soaked bandage. He'd cut his thumb down to the artery the night before with what he'd repeatedly referred to as a "tater knife."

The little church at Mount Olive—mother church of the Presbytery throughout the White River Valley—was a two-room, white-painted structure, about the size of a large two-story house. The pews were rough-hewn and worn, and near the front door, a rope from the steeple bell hung down. The altar was simple, furnished with only a lectern, a big wooden cross, a picture of Jesus, and an American flag.

Pastor Steve picked up the church bulletin and started down the prayer list, an entire page filled with local names like Aiken, Barrows, Hicks, Jeffery, and Oldham. Sprinkled throughout were afflictions such as Brain Tumor, Car Accident, Scerocis [sic] of the Liver, as well as dreaded occurrences like Upcoming Travel and big-picture concerns such as Our Country & Leaders, Law Enforcement, and Middle East Peace. This prayer list was ever so tenderly updated and amended in the typical way Ozarkers look after one another. From the first time Susanne and I stepped through the church's front door, the embrace of this small congregation was so hospitable that we felt we'd joined an extended family.

A man in a front pew rose to thank the congregation for its help with the previous day's bake sale at the Ruthie Mountain Volunteer Fire Department. Then, from the rear of the church, a heavy-set older lady called out with enthusiasm, "The desserts were fantastic! And I know, because I tried 'em all!"

A stooped elderly gentleman came forward carrying an old-style cassette player. We were about to hear a part of the history of Mount Olive, he said. It was the sound of a train passing, recorded back during the so-called White River Heyday when this town, founded by pioneers in 1816, swelled to one thousand inhabitants and served as a stop for trains on the new railroad that began service in August of 1903. The sound of the choo-choo gathered, eventually so loud that the fake red roses atop the piano wiggled slightly as if ruffled by a wind.

This little history lesson was the kind of thing lost on younger people—*That just sounds like any old train to me*—but the effort was appreciated by this congregation, which trended elderly if not downright ancient. At fifty-something, Susanne and I were considered young-adjacent. Young families around Mount Olive were rare, and the children who grew up around here typically left for better opportunities elsewhere. The low point had come just after World War II, when the town withered to less than twenty residents.

On this day, Pastor Steve's sermon was necessarily abbreviated, though he once again reminded congregants that 7,487 promises were made in the Bible, and he gave his usual altar call for us to accept Jesus into our lives. We sang another hymn, and the pastor was nearing the end of his send-off prayer when Bear pushed in through the church's front door:

"...And thank God for this dog!" Pastor Steve said without missing a beat.

As Bear raced for the altar, I shot up from my pew and grabbed him by his collar. He barked and barked while I wrangled him back outside.

After the service, the heavy-set, dessert-eating lady came up to me. "That dog was determined to be saved today," she said with all due seriousness. "He was not to be denied."

"I'm so sorry. I didn't think he would try to get inside. I guess the front door was slightly ajar."

"You should just let him come in and sit by you during the service. It would be just fine."

"Oh, I don't think so." I imagined a congregation full of unruly dogs sitting on the pews alongside their owners.

The heavy-set lady pulled me closer and whispered, "Well, that dog's more lively than the old people around this town." Then, half-smiling, she stood back to gauge my reaction.

Soon, out in the anteroom, I found Pastor Steve and apologized to him for Bear's behavior. But the preacher just laughed it off. Invoking one of his favorite tropes, he said, "That's why I get paid the big bucks."

With spring coming on, Susanne wanted to put in a garden. Unfortunately, the thin, rocky soil up at Hogback Mountain supported only the hardiest of trees, the scraggliest of brush. So we had two truckloads of rich dirt brought in from the river bottom, and soon Dennis was up at our place, working his magic with his old bulldozer.

I framed the garden's perimeter with wooden beams, while Susanne plied the rich loam: a fourth-generation farmer's daughter, she relished having her hands in the dirt. All we needed was warmer weather for her plantings to flourish. Using his ever-trusty dozer, Dennis even managed to cover with dirt the green top of our septic tank, which protruded from the ground like a giant bottle cap.

Our work done, Dennis and I sat on the porch to spit and whittle, as they say. Our relationship, around six months old now, transcended the typical flatlander-versus-hillsman, city-boy-versus-Ozarker dichotomy in which one side puts on an act for the other (while sometimes transmitting a low-level hostility). Dennis not only had an impressive native intelligence—I always needed his help, it seemed—yet I also felt important to him. Perhaps because people were scarce up in Izard County, or because he had more tranquility to ponder such matters, he placed a high value on our friendship. He genuinely wanted to get to know me, and with his mastery of neighborly conversation, he often revealed himself in ways I could never predict.

"Do you play golf?" he said, perhaps anticipating better weather in the months to come.

"Sure," I said skeptically. "But do you?" Truly, I'd never imagined Dennis as a golfer.

"I used to play sometimes," he said. "Me and my sons. I set up a course down at my place, with several holes. We had a fun time. It was a really nice course to play as long as you kept your ball out of the cow manure."

I laughed—though not so hard as to offend Dennis, who somehow made his cow pasture golf course seem as much fun to play as Augusta National. The porch of my cabin was cantilevered towards Dark Hollow, and as we looked down upon his ranch along East Twin Creek, we heard the distant mooing of his cows. I petted Bear and wondered what the dog's life was like before he'd shown up on our deck last fall. Had he been mistreated? One clue: Bear was very skittish about gunfire. Another clue: he didn't like cars. I figured he'd either been run off by somebody with a gun, or loaded into a car and dumped, or both. Regardless of his past, between me caring for him on weekends and Dennis caring for him during the week, Bear had a great life now.

"I've got a bull with an injured pecker," Dennis said, his mind never far from his herd. "My wife is one fine cattle woman, I'll tell you that. She got that bull moved and got him a shot of the medicine he needed."

The previous year, with its ample summer rains, had been good for raising cattle. Dennis and his wife ran about fifty cows; over the years they'd used the earnings from their cattle operation to pay for their 220 acres of land. Dennis was understandably proud of what he'd accomplished, but he expressed little of the dreamy grandiosity typical of outsiders like me. "You can't run too many cattle," he intoned. "They'll just eat a pasture down to its root, and then you can't sustain a larger herd."

While Dennis had wise a sense of his limits, he hardly lacked for ambition. Whenever he and I got together, the subject of Dr. Jackson came up, and once again he said that he wished he'd bought all that property— some twelve hundred acres—before Dr. Jackson had bought it three years ago. *I don't want to own all the land; I just want to own all the land that touches mine.* Dennis speculated that Jackson had acquired his land for just over $1,000 per acre, maybe even less. His tone of voice registered disappointment over the once-in-a-lifetime opportunity he'd missed to wheel and deal in a big chunk of real estate that adjoined his property.

But in the main, Dennis was quite content with his life. He'd attended college in Jonesboro, my hometown, and worked there for a time for a grocer, then for a seed company. He'd also traveled enough when he'd worked for Boeing to know how good he had it up in these hills. He had a zest for the life he'd created for himself, and he woke up every morning looking forward to what his day would bring. "It's great," he often said. "I get to do a little bit of everything. I just love living at Twin Creek. Love it!"

Indeed, Dennis's affection for this little lost corner of the Ozarks manifested itself in many ways. He had some pull in Izard County, and earlier that week he'd somehow arranged for twenty men from the state prison up at Calico Rock to clear the brush and cedar trees around the lookout on the highway above his ranch. To show his appreciation, he'd wanted to take the entire gang of prisoners to lunch. But, for reasons of security, this was impractical, so in the end he took them five boxes of Little Debbie snacks. "You'd have thought I'd brought them Christmas dinner," he said with a sparkle in his gray-blue eyes.

With Susanne's garden readied for planting, Dennis's dozer work at Hogback Mountain was finished. While we sat on my porch, he decided he'd try to somehow drive his contraption home through the woods. To me, this sounded like a great idea, since otherwise I'd have to pay for a flatbed truck to come haul his dozer back to his ranch. "But I can't drive my dozer home this afternoon," he added. "I need to feed my cows. I'll do it later in the week."

I walked with Dennis out to his truck. Typically, whenever we talked at any length I learned something from him that made me shake my head in wonderment; sure enough, before he closed the door to his truck, he passed on another snippet of his vast and somewhat quirky local knowledge.

"You know," he said. "A few days ago, a train derailed back by the White River, not too far from my house. A portion of the track just collapsed due to the heavy rains."

"Hmm," I said. "Does that kind of thing happen very often around here?"

"No, but it's about the most exciting thing to happen around here in a long time. And the thing is, I'm not sure anybody even knows the wrecked train is back there."

When I returned the next weekend, I walked to the back of Hogback Mountain and eventually found another path that Dennis had cleared further into the forest with his dozer. Then, at the end of this new path, amidst a stand of small trees—and just onto Dr. Jackson's adjoining property—I spotted Dennis's abandoned contraption. Apparently, he had not been able to drive home through the woods after all.

Eventually, Dennis called in a flatbed truck to haul his bulldozer back down to his ranch, and I paid him back for the cost.

"The lady from Dayton wants us to have the land," Susanne said when she got off her phone. "She just took our offer!"

"That's great!"

"We've got it! We've got it!"

I gave her a celebratory kiss, while Bear jealously barked. He didn't like for anybody to touch me or for me to touch anyone else, even my wife. My only hope was that the Dayton lady didn't come down to Izard County before our deal was final—if she saw the three waterfalls and Sandy Wallow Cave, she would seriously reconsider. In our minds, Susanne and I had cut such a good deal that, as our penance, we decided to pay the seller's legal costs.

It was weird to think that we owned three waterfalls and a cave. How does anyone own a wonder of nature? I ordered up engraved wooden signs to post on trees near each waterfall—I'd long ago named them Switchback, Maidenhair, and High Twin—and I ruminated on what we could do with our new cave besides marvel at it and, when necessary, use it as a tornado shelter.

Soon—and I'm still unsure what triggered this—I came up with the idea of showing summertime movies down in the cave. By gosh, we'd have a cave cinema! The cave—deep inside—was a constant fifty-eight degrees, the perfect place to escape the oppressive Arkansas heat. Even though it was only early springtime, we couldn't wait for July to get here. It wouldn't be long.

While we were positively giddy over our new property, not everyone was so smitten with it all.

The Dawsons, our neighbors and fellow preppers, came over one Sunday afternoon, and naturally, Susanne and I just had to show them our newest possession. We could hardly contain ourselves.

I helped Cindy Dawson navigate the crease between the giant limestone boulders that lined the narrow path down to Sandy Wallow Cave, while Bill and Cody trailed dutifully behind. With all of our earlier excited talk about the cave, I felt as if I was leading them to some long lost city of gold.

But when we got down to the cave, the Dawsons stopped before they went in. As if pausing to critique a giant painting on a wall, they backed up a few steps to survey the dark recess from the proper perspective. They noted a crevice in the ceiling and the water that seeped down through it. They wondered how the cave would hold up during an earthquake. When the Dawsons finally deigned to enter, they expressed disappointment with the unevenness of the floor and the way the sand was piled into undulating mounds. There really wasn't anywhere on the cave floor for anybody to lie down perfectly flat. If and when it came to the-end-of-the-world-as-we-know-it, and they had to take shelter down here in Sandy Wallow Cave, they weren't sure exactly where they would sleep.

All in all, the Dawsons were more interested in seeing one of our newly purchased waterfalls. Who could blame them? Outside our dark cave, it was a cool but sunny day. Cody walked ahead on the trail. When the rest of our group caught up to him along the ridge above West Twin Creek, he pointed down at a baby copperhead he'd just smashed with a rock.

I was alarmed. I had hiked this trail for months and never seen a snake, and now Cody, within minutes of setting foot in these woods, had killed a copperhead. *Was I this oblivious?* What else was out there in this vast expanse of forest that I wasn't seeing?

Cody, however, wasn't much concerned with the dangers posed by any poisonous vipers; he more feared any potential backlash to his act of snake-killing from the agencies of the federal government and the animal rights activists. "Be careful," he said in warning to us all. "The EPA will be out to see you. PETA will come calling."

Taking a more pragmatic approach to the situation, Bill intoned, "There's always more than just one snake around."

"The waterfall is just down here," I offered in an effort to move our group along.

A few days later, we took Dennis down to the cave, not to gloat over our new ownership of it—he'd tried for years to get in touch with the previous owner of this acreage—but rather to share its glories. Susanne showed him the All-Seeing Eye of God and talked on about what a great shelter our cave would be in the event of an end-of-the-world cataclysm. When she finished with her dead-serious explanation, Dennis pulled me aside and, with a snickering laugh, said, "I reckon we can come down here and eat each other."

This of course was hardly Dennis's first visit to Sandy Wallow Cave. He took my flashlight and walked us further back, where he explained that when he was a boy the cave had been much deeper and had another entrance that slowly collapsed when the highway was built over it. While in this darkest part of the cave, Dennis also suggested that we plant a set of eyes of some sort back here so as to freak out any visitors, invited or uninvited. They'd shine their flashlight into the blackness and see two big shiny orbs staring back at them. The mere thought of the panic that would ensue brought a devilish smile to Dennis's face.

11.

Hanging Out with Dennis

Dennis had long desired to take me on a tour of Lower Izard County, and I was eager to go. I knew it would be a tour like no other. So one cloudy afternoon we headed out in his pickup truck with Bear in the back seat. We passed the lookout over Dark Hollow and saw his ranch below, nestled into the hills surrounding the hamlet of Twin Creek.

Down one of the many godforsaken gravel roads off of Highway 9, Dennis, with me serving as his straight man and Bear as his four-legged prop, commenced: "Hurley Morehead was raised right in here and owns this land, and now he's got a bunch of toothless cows." He turned to the back seat. "Bear, get back and settle down. Sit! Sit!"

Satisfied that Bear was under control, Dennis continued, "Hurley's kind of an unusual guy. He's never worked for anybody that I know of. He cuts a few logs and some hay in the summertime. I don't think he's on any kind of disability or government aid. He was married, and then his wife died. There's a lot of Moreheads in Izard County."

"Surely, there aren't as many Moreheads around here as there are Gillihans?"

"Nah, everybody's related to the Gillihans. We're heavy breeders."

I chuckled at this, for Dennis, with his endearing naturalness and lack of pretense, had made it sound like he was describing a bunch of highly procreative farm animals.

"Heavy breeders," Dennis repeated slowly. "The Smiths were catching up with us, but we finally married into them."

"You overtook them, huh?"

"Yes, overtook 'em! You see a name in the phone book around here and it looks like there's a lot of 'em, but they're all married into the Gillihans."

We circled back towards Highway 9, and for this I was grateful; the dirt road was so rough that the front of Dennis's pickup truck seemed as if it was about to rattle apart. "All Gillihans live on gravel," Dennis noted. "Usually if you've got land, you'll be out in the middle of nowhere. My Uncle Kenneth, who lived up near Melbourne, once said, 'I wish they'd take up this asphalt—there's too many people living back here that I don't know.'"

On Highway 9, we drove through a short stretch as curvy as a snake—it was as if the road crew that built this highway years ago had intended some sort of everlasting practical joke.

"There's a big cave just up the road," Dennis said as if this just had to be seen. "I never took you to that cave? Well, I won't take you to it today. I don't want to get you dirty."

"Now, I don't mind getting a little dirty," I said defensively. I didn't want Dennis to think that I was too pampered, though by his lights I most certainly was. He hummed another of his happy-go-lucky ditties, and when we came upon a run-down house that I knew something about, I dared to trot out one of my rare triumphs of local knowledge: "The man who lives there calls himself Big Danny. He came up to Hogback Mountain a while back to fix one of our backup generators. He has no teeth—or none that I could see."

"I don't know him," Dennis said. "But that guy—Big Danny or whoever he is—bought that house he lives in from a Gillihan whose wife had died."

Dennis of course had just one-upped me. *Well, I wandered into that one, didn't I?* I thought to myself.

We passed a tall, metal gate with the word Gillihan atop it. The gate looked like something out of the Wild West. "Now, that's the road that goes up to Big Sky," I said, referring to the white house on the mountaintop that could be seen from the deck of my cabin.

"Naw," Dennis corrected. "That's Junior Gillihan's son's place. The place you're thinking of is Shelby Gillihan and his brothers."

Again, I'd been one-upped, and by now my head was spinning: I needed a map or a program—preferably both—to keep up with all the Gillihans, present and past, who lived around here.

We came upon the outskirts of Melbourne where, thankfully, the highway wasn't so crooked and steep. "My aunt lives right there," Dennis said. "My cousin over there…. From Twin Creek up to here, us Gillihans have pretty much sewed it up. You make one of us mad and we'll all be mad by nightfall."

"Thanks, I'll remember that," I replied with a wink, to which Dennis responded with a smile and a tip of his head as if tickled inside.

Now that we were in Melbourne, I assumed our tour was winding down, yet we'd merely transitioned from the hills and hollows, where some of the Gillihan descendants lived, to the little town where Dennis's brother Roger and his mother resided. We drove past Ozarka College, a two-year institution with programs in disciplines like automotive service technology, culinary arts, and criminal justice.

Dennis admitted he sometimes still called the school by its old name. "I know some people who work there," he said. "And they get real mad when they hear me call it the vo-tech school. Boy, are they touchy about that. *Really touchy!*"

Our trip through Melbourne prompted tales about a former schoolteacher of Dennis's who'd been robbed by her grandson; about a man who for some reason still owed him a hundred dollars; how, as a boy, he and his mother got trapped in a root cellar with an angry rattlesnake; about a former sniper in Vietnam who, in warning to a man he didn't like, bouced bullets off the rooftop of his passing car with a .22 rifle. Dennis had so many stories that it seemed he'd lived three lives, all of them around this part of Izard County. His mind was like a wonder box full of oddball Ozark tales.

"We're just country people," he confided. "I grew up poor and backwards. But I've got a smart dog." He glanced back at Bear and gave a big round-faced smile.

We were on the eastern edge of Melbourne when, out of the blue, Dennis said, "Here's Steve's place. He once had all his cattle killed."

"All of them?" This didn't seem possible—I was looking out onto a huge pasture with hundreds of cows scattered about.

"Yeah, when a tornado came his cows gathered up there on that hill in a tight circle. That storm killed most of Steve's herd, so he brought in Merle Haggard."

"Merle Haggard?!"

"Yeah, they had a Merle Haggard Festival over in this field," Dennis said, motioning to the other side of the highway. "Thousands of people showed up to help pay for Steve's new cattle. It was kind of a charity thing. Merle came down and played one or two nights. I've got a framed poster advertising the concert at my house."

"Did you go to the concert?"

"Naw, I was too busy working.... Merle's got a house not too far from here, over at Guion. He and one of the Coopers are good buddies. They had a lot in common and just hit it off, so the Cooper guy called him up and said, 'Merle, a friend of mine lost his cattle, so can you do a concert to help him out?' And Merle did it. Now, that's a true story, that really happened."

"Oh, I believe you," I said, persuaded by Dennis's mention of the advertising poster, a telling detail.

He went on: "You know my favorite song by Merle? It's a poor person's song—for people who are struggling—and it's called 'If We Make It Through December.' It's about a guy who can't do much for himself or anybody else for Christmas, but promises to do better come January."

"I haven't heard it," I mumbled. As we drove on, I remembered that some years ago Dennis had lost his job when the Boeing factory had moved out of Melbourne. That had to be a very scary time for him and his family: a blow to his pride, as well as to the community he so loved.

"That song brings a tear to my eye every time I hear it," he said.

I was touched by Dennis's confession, at how he'd let me even further into his unique world. To ease the awkward silence, I said, "My favorite song of Merle's is 'Pancho and Lefty.'" I'd only thought of this song because I'd recently heard it played at a bonfire near Mount Olive. Truth was, I didn't know any other Merle Haggard songs, which were mostly about country people who were down and out.

Just up the road, Dennis, his tone now cheerier, said, "See that house on the hill? The guy who lives there is called BB. He's got two or three relatives named after ammunition. There's Twenty-Two, BB, Magnum, and such as that. I can't remember them all."

"Good lord, what's their last name?"

"I can't remember that, either. But BB's a good guy. He makes a lot of money."

"I've never heard of anybody naming their kids after ammunition," I said, stating the obvious.

"That's what I was told."

"Then it must be true."

"Must be," Dennis said with a half-laugh. "But don't quote me. It's just something I hear. But I know his name is BB, for sure. He makes a good living clearing right-of-ways for the power companies. He's got the experience and knowledge to do it, until that one time when he was cutting a line with a welder and started a fire that burned up about twenty acres. After that, the power company didn't let him do anything for quite a while."

We turned off onto another gravel road and the dashboard of Dennis's truck again vibrated and squeaked. I was getting queasy but tried not to let it show, for I wanted Dennis to keep on: Izard County was a place that didn't easily yield its charms, such as they were.

"When we was kids, they had lots of quail back here," he continued. "And we'd drive along and shoot them out of the back of our old Dodge truck. We'd take a twenty-two rifle, and next thing we'd know we'd have a mess of quail. We weren't bothering nobody.... Bear, you're passing gas! I can smell it! Get that grin off your face!"

He pointed towards another mountain. "Martin Miller lived over here. His dad, G.H. Miller, was baling hay one day, and after a while the fellow raking the field with him noticed G.H. was missing—he couldn't find G.H. nowhere. His tractor was just sitting there with the motor running, and the baler was running too. So he walked over and hit the trip hammer that throws out a bale and there was G.H., up inside the baler... True story... He'd been walking behind the baler and started kicking up stuff into the back of it with his foot and somehow something grabbed him by his breeches leg and pulled him up into the machine and crushed him."

"Oh my," I said. This was a doozy of a story, for sure.

"Yeah, that's horrible, just horrible," Dennis said, his voice trailing off with heartfelt remorse over the fate of a fellow Izardite. "That's the way ole G.H. died."

Beyond Lunenburg, we stopped at the intersection of Highway 9, whereupon Dennis decided to take the long way back to Twin Creek, so we turned down yet another meandering dirt road. "It's been so long since I've been back here that it's new to me," he said as we crept along. "That's Ethyl Robinson's old place over there."

"Wow!" I said. The sprawling multi-story, log cabin-style house was the nicest I'd seen in Izard County.

"I knew you'd like that house a lot," Dennis said. "Her dad owned the sawmill back there. Some people can manage money, some people's good at it. He'd buy and sell land."

"Do you know who lives there now?"

"Yeah, but it's a terrible story and I'd hate to tell you about it. It's pretty bad, pretty bad."

If the story of the present occupant of Ethyl Robinson's old house was worse than the tale of the crushing of G. H. Miller up inside his own hay baler then, truly, I did not want to hear it.

Around another curve, we came upon a run-down shotgun house.

"I know who lives there," Dennis said. "That's the home of Chief Dancing Ghost.... It is, I'm serious!"

"Chief Dancing Ghost?"

"He calls himself Chief Dancing Ghost," Dennis confirmed. "He keeps a lawsuit going all the time. I researched him, and found out he's no more an Indian than I am."

We laughed at the absurdity of Chief Dancing Ghost. Then, in an effort to include Bear in our fun, I poured some water into a cup. He lapped it up, splashing water all over the armrest of the truck.

Ever since we'd started down this particular never-ending dirt road, Dennis had been in search of a place once owned by Dr. Gray, a man he admired. Finding where he'd lived had somehow become our quest. Meanwhile, along one of the few straightaways, Dennis said, "Have you ever been down to look at the grave in the cemetery where—let's see, it wasn't Davy Crockett's brother who's buried there."

"I think it's Sam Houston's brother," I replied, trotting out another of my paltry nuggets of local knowledge.

"Yep, that's who it is. We'll be going by the cemetery where he's buried. I think we'll be passing by it, but I'm not sure. I'll have to think about that."

John P. Houston, brother of Sam Houston of Texas, was the first clerk of Izard County. According to one account, he was "an educated man of extensive reading and intellect, amply qualified to occupy the highest office in the United States had he not been shipwrecked by drunkenness." John P. Houston had lived and died in a little town along this road called Athens, which, despite its civilized Hellenic name, was a rough place: it was reported that Houston, contrary to all his supposed learning, "spent a great deal of his time thinking about killing somebody or keeping somebody from killing him."

We were on the roughest stretch of this dirt road yet. To calm my stomach, I took deep breaths.

"Dr. Gray lived up here just a little ways," Dennis said with anticipation. "Now, I just can't imagine how he drove this gravel road every day. You know, we've had a lot of doctors and educated people that live up here in the hills where we're at, you being one of them. Dr. Gray lived down in here. Doc Milam lives somewhere around here too. Doc Tatum lives on Highway Nine. You got your therapist that lives up on top of the mountain up there. There's a chiropractor that lives toward Mount Olive somewhere.... You sure you got me on the right road?"

"Don't count on me to navigate back here," I said. "I'm completely lost."

"I'll see a landmark here pretty soon. I ain't seen it yet. I think we take a left here in a minute."

I turned to the back seat. "Bear, we're getting close. Just hang on." Like Dennis, I'd begun to talk to the dog as if he were a child.

"Now I know where we're at!" Dennis pronounced. "Ole Doc Milam's place is just ahead. These hills up in here were just full of people at one time. People were everywhere. Hear the train coming? Hear it, Bear? What is that, Bear?"

Finally, we came to the prize of Dennis's scavenger hunt along this particular godforsaken gravel road. "This was Dr. Gray's farm here on the right," he noted.

"It's nice," I mumbled, feeling obliged to praise the doctor's old place, though all I could see of it was a meadow and a copse of trees in the distance.

"This is where Dr. Gray used to live before he became a grown-up doctor," Dennis added. "When he lived out here, he was just a baby doctor."

As we drove on down the rough, potholed road, I pondered on Dennis's riddle—his line of loopy meaning worthy of Yogi Berra. I finally decided what he meant to say was that Dr. Gray had started as a pediatrician out here in the boondocks, but later moved into town—probably due to a lack of newborns as this part of Izard County emptied out—and had then gone into family practice.

In twenty minutes, Dennis and I were back at Twin Creek. His one-of-a-kind tour was over.

12.

The Many Uses of a Cave

One Sunday, after church in Mount Olive, Pastor Steve Moon and his wife, Harriet, came up to Hogback Mountain. That morning's service had been highlighted by the singing of old Southern gospel songs by a quartet who ranged from tall to short, bald to long-haired, wraith thin to potbellied, young to old; their only visual bond was that each of the four men wore similar wire-rimmed eyeglasses. Finally, better music at our church!

It was a gorgeous early-spring afternoon, and the four of us all sat in the sunshine and drank iced tea. The Moons had been married a few years earlier, and Harriet believed she'd found the perfect man in Steve, who'd been single almost two decades. "Full of pride and stubborn," he admitted. Steve had played semi-pro football over in Europe, where he claimed to hold twelve records of some sort.

"I didn't know they played much football in Europe," I said. "I thought they just played soccer, or what we Americans call soccer."

"Oh, they love football," he said. "Real football. I played for Heidelberg."

Steve didn't much look like a former football player: medium height, pudgy, bespectacled.

Over our iced teas, along with a bag of barbeque potato chips, Susanne persuaded the Moons to come see our new cave. She even mentioned it as a place where the following week's sunrise Easter service could be held. So, despite Steve's professed aversion to caves, we drove to the other side of the hollow, near Panther Ridge, and pulled our car over onto the side of the road.

When we got out, I spotted beer cans on the ground—they'd been tossed out by motorists along Highway 9, who littered way too much as far as I was concerned. Then again, these cans could have been left behind earlier by some of our guests. In any case, as discreetly as possible, I kicked the cans behind a tall clump of brush.

Susanne and Harriet walked ahead on the trail that led down to the cave, while Steve and I hung back and talked more about his athletic career. Steve was also a track star in high school and set state records in Wisconsin and Arkansas. He spoke of how he'd disappointed his father—a hard man with whom he'd clashed—by eventually being beaten in a race by a black man.

After Steve and I walked down the trail, we stood out by the empty fire pit—he was still uncomfortable with the notion of entering the cave—and got down to matters of a more spiritual nature. "I believe in the early and mid-times Rapture," Steve said. "Your wife believes in the mid- and end-times Rapture. I've studied Revelation a pretty fair amount. Do you believe in the Rapture?"

I was not aware that the Rapture could be so divided like the sequels of some blockbuster movie, but anyway, I said, "I'm a searcher," and then mumbled on about Hal Lindsey of *Late Great Planet Earth* notoriety and all the false prophecy he'd espoused when I was a teenager back in the 1970s. Truthfully, some of the most spiritually ecstatic moments I'd spent so far up here in the Ozarks were on my long walks with Bear around Hogback Mountain.

From inside the cave, Susanne mentioned the All-Seeing Eye of God, and with these words as an enticement, Steve relented and went in. As we stood under the Eye, Susanne described how the Easter service would unfold: it would be at sunrise, torches would light the cave, the congregants would stand in a circle, and so on. Steve was warming up to the idea, I could tell, his eyes riveted on Susanne, who could be quite persuasive and sell about anything when she got going.

"Who should we invite?" he said.

"Only church members," Susanne replied sternly. She didn't want other people to know where the cave was lest it be later overrun during an event that led to the-end-of-the-world-as-we-know-it. Accordingly, any Easter service held down at Sandy Wallow Cave was to be conducted with a secrecy befitting a high-level military operation.

"Certainly we can trust the church members," I said.

"Yes," Harriet helpfully chimed in. "For sure."

"But a lot of the older members won't be able to get down here to the cave," Steve said, concerned like any good shepherd about every sheep in his flock. "Or once they get down here, they won't be able to get back out."

"Good point," I conceded. Our new cave wasn't exactly compliant with the American Disabilities Act. "We'd probably have to try to carry some of them in and out, and that might really discourage attendance."

Later, it was decided that due to such complications—not to mention Pastor Steve's aversion to caves—it wasn't such a good idea after all to have the Easter sunrise service down in Sandy Wallow Cave.

13.

Schemes and Dreams

I knew the hillbilly life was penetrating deeper into my soul when, on a trip to California, much of what I saw and did seemingly tied back to the Ozarks.

In Los Angeles, I shopped at Barneys on Wilshire Boulevard where I bought a pair of double-sided camouflage pants. I'd surely be the only resident of Izard County who ever wore a pair of Japanese-made camo jeans advertised *For the Denim Purist. Just the best fabric in the world combined with modern fits. Printed Different Base Color Inside and Outside so you can flip up the leg opening and rock a cuff or a roll.*

My new camouflage pants were hardly the homespun, dyed-with-black-walnut-hulls, cut-by-guess breeches that Ozark mothers made for their sons and husbands back in the era of the settlers. Then again, I wasn't the first Ozarker to fall for slick fashion. In *Life in the Leatherwoods*, published in 1974, John Quincy Wolf, Jr. wrote of his father's life, circa 1880, when a "shrewd peddler" came to his cabin over in Stone County and sold him a pair of moleskin pants imported from England. The fabric—literally made from a mole's skin—was rank. But aha, noted the shrewd peddler, the foul smell was proof of the authenticity of the garment.

On Rodeo Drive, I felt like a real Beverly Hillbilly when I visited the mansion-like Ralph Lauren store. After a lengthy search, I bought a long-sleeved denim work shirt, perfect for keeping chiggers and ticks off my arms when summertime arrived in the Ozarks. Then, at a secondhand store on Melrose Avenue, I purchased a buckskin coat fringed with long tassels. Daniel Boone himself would have been proud to own this jacket. I couldn't wait to wear it on chilly fall nights up at Hogback Mountain.

Headed north along the California coast to Big Sur, matters totally careened out of control when I stopped at a resort and saw something called a "human nest," a twelve-foot high structure built of sticks of eucalyptus wood. This so-called nest was accessible by a ladder, could sleep two people if necessary, and had a glorious view of the vast blue expanse of the Pacific Ocean.

I wondered: what would it be like to have a human nest at Hogback Mountain? I wasn't at all interested in the New Age transcendentalism associated with a place like Big Sur—such spacey thinking had no place in the ever-practical hills of Arkansas. Yet this human nest intrigued me, if for no other reason that it would, on dry, temperate nights in the Ozarks, provide us with a place to sleep more people at Hogback Mountain.

When I returned to Izard County, I went to see Ben Harvey, the furniture maker who lived along Highway 9. A transplant from Chicagoland, he had a rambling shop up on a hill where he made Adirondack chairs, cabinets, armoires, picnic tables, credenzas, planter boxes, and outhouses. Really, Ben Harvey could build darned near anything, most of it fashioned from cedar. In this, he was typical of the area's woodworkers who, going back over a century, found cedar easier to fell and haul than hardwood trees. Ben had built our cedar outhouse, the one I'd bought from Barry Helton.

At his shop, Ben Harvey was nowhere to be found. I honked the horn of my SUV, and soon he walked down from his house further up the hill. He was a lanky man in his mid-sixties with dark hair and a tight-lipped expression that, while not exactly grim, could in no way be interpreted as customer-friendly, either. I shook his hand and told him my name, which for some reason upset him.

"I don't do names," he said with a firm wag of his head.

"Well, I like your Adirondack chairs especially. You've got some nice stuff around here. You really do. You do nice work." I gathered my courage and handed Ben one of the photos I'd taken of the so-called human nest out in Big Sur. "Do you think you could build something like this over at my place?"

Ben adjusted his Coke-bottle-thick eyeglasses as he studied my photo. "I don't know," he finally said, as he regarded me over the top of his glasses. "I think I'd just rather stay around here."

Obviously, Ben was a homebody, so to accommodate this preference of his, I said, "Maybe you could build my nest here at your place and then we could truck it up to my place?" I showed him another of my photos of the human nest. "See, it's basically just two pieces. You could build the nest and the stand separately. That might make it easier."

"I don't think so."

"Okay," I said, giving in. "Then, can you just hold six of these Adirondack chairs for me? I'll come back later with my trailer to get them."

I paid Ben for his chairs—his prices were quite reasonable—and figured the next time he saw me, after he cashed my check, he'd probably take more of an interest in my name.

Rebuffed in my quest to find a builder for my Big Sur-inspired human nest, I mailed John Byler the same photos I'd shown Ben Harvey. My hope was that John, while perhaps not a furniture maker of Ben's caliber, would take on my project. So far, he'd been willing to do anything I'd asked, and he was quite resourceful. He'd even built a nifty mount for the windmill that helped power our backup solar system. In my enthusiasm, I could envision John making a business out of building human nests for clients all over the Ozarks. I imagined him one day—after this trend really caught fire—thanking me profusely for bringing him such a brilliant money-making idea.

"I don't know about this," John said, when I called him to ask what he thought of my photos. "It looks like they use a lot of eucalyptus wood. There's definitely not much of that around here."

Stung, I said, "I think you could make the nest from trees found up here in the Ozarks. Surely, there's something we could use."

"Willow vines, maybe."

"Yes, well, we'll just have to get creative. It's kind of a crazy idea, I know. But it would be really cool to have a human nest, wouldn't it? Huh?"

"It's different, that's for sure."

I waited, hoping John would fill the silence with some expression of his further interest. Finally, I said, "Do you know of anybody else around here who might take on such a project?"

"No," he said. "Not really."

My fixation with Frank Lloyd Wright was entirely predictable. It took firm root one day at High Twin Fall as the glistening water spilled over the ledge. A trio of us sat in the springtime sunshine in my new Adirondack chairs—built by Ben Harvey—and sipped beers. At some point, one of my well-educated sisters-in-law said, "This would be a perfect place to build something like Fallingwater."

Of course, Fallingwater—the holy grail of organic architecture. Ever since this magnificent house was built over Bear Run, a stream in western Pennsylvania, in 1939, no telling how many people have sat at a waterfall—*any waterfall*—and said something similar. So, on cue, I too began to wonder if something similarly fabulous could be built at Hogback Mountain.

Frank Lloyd Wright died in 1959, though one of his most successful apprentices had been Fay Jones, a resident of Fayetteville, only 150 miles away. I soon learned that, unfortunately, Jones had died a decade earlier. Seeking one of his disciples, I called Maurice Jennings, who had worked with Fay Jones for twenty-five years.

Mr. Jennings told me that he was available. Apparently, the demand for high-end houses and grand chapels—his specialty—had cooled since the onset of the Great Recession. A week later, I received a nice letter from Mr. Jennings, along with a snazzy portfolio of his work, which I pored over like a sixteen-year-old drools over a copy of *Playboy* magazine. Immediately, I started to scheme on how to build Frank Lloyd Wrightesque structures at various places throughout my property: down at one of our waterfalls. Nestled into a south-facing ridge with a view of nothing but folds of mountains. Even tucked into the gorge that I called Little Grand Canyon. Every day it seemed, I had another brainstorm for a house, a pavilion, a swimming pool, a barn, a small chapel of some sort.

I had gotten way ahead of myself. My architectural ambitions had outrun my financial means.

Since I couldn't have Frank Lloyd Wright's architecture—or anything generally approaching it—I began to collect tchotchkes and geegaws derived from the master himself. In no time, our decent little ole cabin was filled with Wright's Indian-patterned coasters, his stylized placemats, the Whirling Arrow salt-and-pepper shakers in his signature color of Cherokee Red, a pillow embroidered with his Celtic cross, a trivet made in a Tulip-pattern of his design …

I couldn't stop myself. (Though my wife could, and eventually did.)

My favorite was Boulder Man, a replica of the statues that guarded the entrance to Wright's studio at Taliesin. It was an earth-toned figure of a naked man sitting on his haunches with his knees raised, one hand over the back of his head, his other hand gripping his lower leg. Wright thought this statue represented the creative man striving to throw off the shackles of society and conventional thinking. But Boulder Man could also be viewed as a dude cowering in anticipation of his imminent doom.

"It's TEOTWAWKI man," I said to Susanne to justify placing the statue in a prominent spot on our back deck. "See, he's hunkering down, getting ready for a comet to strike the earth."

"I hate it," she said.

"Just think of him as a forward-thinking prepper."

"He's naked. Look at him."

"Use your imagination—he's awaiting a calamity, just like us."

"That statue is just awful."

My thwarted architectural ambitions notwithstanding, there was no reason for us to be discontented with our decent little ole cabin. Granted, it lacked the genius of Frank Lloyd Wright's organic architecture—in fact, pretty much everything about it was precisely the opposite. But we'd done a fine job resurrecting our cabin, which, as it stood, was a unique combination of civility and barbarism, the essence of the arrested frontier. Think Martha Stewart meets Grizzly Adams.

On Martha's side, the side of civility, were our oriental rugs, an antique chest of drawers, an Arts and Crafts desk and bookcase, an Indian-patterned couch that my mother claimed cost as much as a small automobile when she'd bought it thirty years ago, a well-stocked wine cabinet, and of course, our indispensable cast-iron wood stove. Often, on Sunday afternoons especially, Frank Sinatra music played over our speakers.

On Grizzly's side, the side of barbarism, was a bleached deer skull mounted outside our front door, an antlered deer's head over the hearth, my coonskin hat and several wall-mounted bows and arrows, a back scratcher fashioned from the claws of a turkey we'd struck one night with our car. There was also a well-stocked ammo box near the back door and, typically, atop our bedroom dresser, next to a Russian jewelry box that I'd purchased on a trip to Kiev, a few spare bullets lying around, just in case.

This juxtaposition of civility and barbarism carried forth into our yard with a life-sized fake deer that served as target practice for aspiring bow hunters, a skeet thrower, a crude fire pit fashioned from the rim of an old tractor tire, and—until recently—hanging down from a tall oak tree, two ropes used for stringing up a dead deer. But Susanne, ever handy, had used her miter saw to make a wooden seat and then fashioned the long ropes into a swing for our nieces.

Of course, the rub was that the barbarism could overwhelm the hard-won civility, and the entire enterprise could descend into a kind of unkempt white trashiness or just plain hillbilly slovenliness. Sometimes, when we came up the driveway, I winced when I caught sight of our cabin and barn. An old saying from the Mississippi River Delta came to mind, which was "It just ain't fittin'," a phrase mumbled when standards need to be raised by somebody with the wherewithal, or inclination, to make it "fit."

Though my architectural dreams were dashed for now, up in the fresh air and natural beauty of these hills, my imagination soared on undeterred. I, as a dreamy Ozarks tastemaker, was going to make this place better, dammit, whether it needed bettering or not. I would leave my mark, somehow.

One day I thought I should build myself a library. It would be a library tower, not unlike that of Michel de Montaigne, the sixteenth-century French essayist. I had the perfect spot for my skybrary—a promontory behind our cabin, just above the rickety scaffold over our reserve tank of water. That eyesore could be moved somewhere else.

I envisioned a tall, round structure of native stone built to my unique specifications, as Montaigne had erected when he retired from public life and began writing. I would, like Montaigne, adorn my library with paintings and Greek and Latin quotations that inspired me, though my proverbs would be rendered in English—I was, after all, monolingual—for example, Shakespeare's *One touch of nature makes the whole world kin*. I would sit up in my stone tower, gaze out over the Ozarks, and dash off essays filled with timeless wisdom.

And why not me? For as Montaigne wrote, "Every man has within himself the entire human condition." Though in a less high-minded moment, he also called his essays "some excrements of an aged mind." And when I tired of writing, I would descend to the bedroom on the second floor of my tower to nap. But instead of a chapel, which Montaigne built on the first floor of his library tower, I would instead build a man cave where I could watch football games in the fall. And what about a wine cellar underneath? That too was a good idea.

No telling what all I could do with my skybrary. The sky was literally the limit. All I needed was a history-minded architect willing to play along with me, some skilled stonemasons, and gobs of money.

14.

Further Explorations

It's nice to live in a gorgeous place like the Ozarks, but it can be difficult to enjoy if you are trying to scratch out a living. Dennis Gillihan wasn't much of a sportsman and usually didn't take time off to fish or hunt or hike. There were areas near his property—notably the beautiful shoals and waterfall back at Rattlesnake Hollow—that he'd never seen. But one day he invited me to go hiking over at Devil's Backbone Natural Area, so designated because of several rare plant species that grew on the saddle of land that joined two mountains. He knew I hadn't hiked over there and figured I would enjoy seeing it.

Dennis wore a work shirt, blue jeans, and his Red Ball work boots, and when I asked if he'd brought along any water, he said he had a can of tomato juice in his truck. I had on my new hiking boots and quilted down jacket, as well as my backpack (when it came to hiking gear, I'd recently upped my game). In essence, I looked like a wannabe Alpine hiker, while Dennis looked like the Ozark rancher that he was.

Soon after we started down the trail, Dennis interrupted one of the ditties he habitually hummed to note that his right knee, his bad one, was mostly just gristle. He was worried about his ability to sustain a reasonable pace—or worse.

"If you fall, I'll try to carry you out of here," I said, only half in jest.

"Aw, just dangle some food in front of me. I'll eventually get back to my truck."

As we made our way through a dense glade of Ashe juniper trees—a rare species known for its wide, multi-growth trunks—Dennis said, "Cows like to get in a cedar grove like this on a cold winter day. It's like a blanket to them."

I looked around for cows—or something that had prompted Dennis's comment—but none were around. It was just that his mind was still on his cattle back at his ranch at Twin Creek. "This is my kind of land," he said, speaking of the Ozark hills in general. "People make fun of this land. I know it's not cattle-raising land, but you can raise whatever you've got a mind to."

While we hiked, Bear stayed close to me. When choosing between following me or Dennis—the dog's two masters in our unusual co-parenting arrangement—Bear always chose me. Basically, he followed me everywhere I went. Dennis sometimes teased about this, but nonetheless the dog's obvious loyalty in my direction hurt his feelings, I could tell.

We came upon a Chinquapin oak that hung menacingly over the trail. I sped up for fear the tree would fall, but Dennis walked underneath it at his usual gimp-legged pace. "I just dare God to kill me," he said as he eyed the huge tree trunk, inches above his head. Just ahead we found a cave, its mouth only a slit in the limestone bluff. Coming upon any cave in the Ozarks was the equivalent of, when in Europe, visiting a great cathedral. Dennis hunkered down, but before he went inside he looked back warily. "If I don't come out of here, you can donate my body to science, if anybody'll have it."

"Go on," I said with a motion of my head. "I'll come in after you've had time to clear out any coons." The modest proportions of this cave and its irregular rock floor made me appreciate Sandy Wallow Cave all the more.

Back out on the trail, we heard the coo of doves as they took flight. Along the ground were patches of a red wildflower called

Indian Paint Brush, which the Indians rubbed on their cheeks to impart a reddish, coppery hue. At an overlook, Dennis took out his small camera: "I bought this for fifteen dollars at the auction in Melbourne last Friday night," he said.

"At the Potato Chip Auction, huh?" I said, teasing him.

"Boy, I got a great deal! Somebody was asleep. I bought two of these cameras, and I'll sell them in my booth at the arcade in Mountain View for forty dollars apiece. It's all just a game, just a game."

We watched Bear chase a squirrel up the ridge, then after we thought we'd lost him, he came charging back down the hill. He was panting and looked slightly crazed, slobber all over his face. Dennis petted the dog's head to calm him. "You know, I take ole Bear with me when I go to the farm supply store in town, and I tell the fellas there that he's a world champion cattle dog and how he's won a bunch of prizes. They just marvel at him and say, 'Can I pet him?'" Dennis laughed. "Truth is, sometimes Bear does genius things and sometimes he's useless. I wish I had more time to work with him and train him."

As we climbed another ridge, outcroppings of limestone and dolomite on the surrounding hills came into view. "There was once a shallow sea here," I said, trotting out my amateur's knowledge of geology. "If you look closely you can follow the line along the mountains that marks the level the water once was. Perhaps this area was much further south at one time but slowly moved north due to continental drift."

I sounded like a college professor, I realized. But Dennis wasn't listening anyway. He'd earlier admitted that while hiking, his thoughts often wandered to practical considerations like trying to calculate how much timber the land on which he trod could yield.

We descended the ridge and walked through a meadow, one of the few flat areas around.

"This looks like a spot where Indians once lived," Dennis said.

"How do you know?"

"I can just sense it."

I wasn't feeling it—but Dennis clearly was. He said, "The best way to look for Indian artifacts is get a whip antenna."

"Whip antenna?" I figured I'd slightly misheard Dennis's reference to some sort of specialized equipment used on scholarly archeological digs, but, unfazed, he replied, "Yeah, you know, one of those long metal antennas they used to put on old cars. I call 'em whip antennas."

"Oh, okay. Now, I understand."

He instructed, "You get a whip antenna and weld an X on the tip of it and use the tip to probe the soil. You might pull up a shard of pottery or an arrowhead or a piece of bone…. It wasn't easy on the Indians when they lived back here."

Even when walking with his stiff leg, Dennis moved quite well. I had no concerns about his overall fitness. He could outwork me at practically any job, if he had a mind to. I always enjoyed hiking—the fresh air, the views, the vitalizing sense of movement—and Dennis seemed to be enjoying his hard-earned leisure as well. "I love this trail right here," he said. "It's fairly level. I'll sleep well tonight."

We passed an old home place that fascinated him: who once lived at this dilapidated old cabin, how they lived, what they'd left behind that he might find useful. Unfortunately, he didn't have his metal detector. "Places like this always have a dump nearby," he said as he nosed around. "That's where you find glass and pottery and metal. I once found a gold cross."

The prospect of finding some rusted junk or lost trinkets at this old homesite prompted a story from Dennis about something horrible that happened long ago on Devil's Backbone: "There was an old refrigerator up here and it was just laying down on a ledge. I saw it for years, but nobody ever done nothing with it. But one day somebody was walking around up here and they opened up the refrigerator, and there was a human head in it."

"*A human head!*"

"Yep, so they called the police and that night I heard them talking about it over the scanner down at my house, and I said to my wife,

'Let's go up there and talk to the police,' so we went up there and saw two cops." Dennis went on, speaking of the disembodied head as if it had a life of its own: "The head had been dead a long time and it belonged to one of two boys who lived down there, just off the bluff where you and I were sittin' a while ago and lookin' off down into that ridge right there. There were two boys who lived down in that holler and they were gay."

"Really," I said in a neutral tone, for I wanted to see where Dennis was going with his latest revelation. Though he lived in a region not known for its open-mindedness, I'd never detected any bigotry in him.

"Those boys were in their early twenties. Nice boys, nice boys."

"Did they ever find out who killed the boy who lost his head?"

"The police investigated, but how would you determine whose head it was? It takes a lot of money to investigate, but things have a way of turning out. They don't know what really happened. I only learned about all this years later."

Despite Dennis's murky conclusion to this particular story, when it came to Lower Izard County, he was a walking, talking encyclopedia (though he wore his knowledge lightly). When he was gone—when his memory was gone—this area of the Ozarks would suffer a blow comparable to what the ancient Egyptians suffered when the library at Alexandria burned to the ground.

Near the end of the trail, I asked Dennis if he'd heard from Dr. Jackson, the local land baron aiming to raise $60 million to build his sand mine.

"No, but one day last week I drove around with some men from Searcy."

"Searcy?" I said with a touch of alarm. The small town over in White County, seventy-five miles southeast, was hardly a mecca for the oil-and-gas industry. "Were these men looking for land on which to build a sand mine too?"

"They just wanted me to show them around. They asked a lot of questions. I don't know what exactly they were looking for. Anyhow,

I'm sure I'll hear from Dr. Jackson soon. He still wants to get access to part of his land by going through my back gate."

Dennis was as independent as a pig on ice, and accordingly I was still unsure of his attitude towards Dr. Jackson: friend, enemy, frenemy? This whole matter of the good doctor's sand mine was a cesspool of rumor and dark possibility.

By the trail's end, I was ready for another drink of water from my canteen, and so was Bear. Dennis too was thirsty for his can of tomato juice in the back of his truck. We'd hiked for almost two hours, and I was flattered he'd taken time out of his busy life to do something I enjoyed. Our most unlikely friendship was further cemented.

We piled into his truck with Bear, and as we headed towards Twin Creek, Dennis's thoughts circled back to the familiar:

"I know of a man who had several of his cattle shot," he said.

"Around here?"

"Yep. And he knows who did it. People are crazy."

"People are mean."

"Well," Dennis said. "I'm glad you're my neighbor."

On a Saturday, I went for lunch at the Rainbow Cafe. I tied Bear's leash to the newspaper stand and told him to sit on the wooden bench and stay. Inside, I sat at my usual table and tapped on the front window to make sure he knew where I was. Out on the sidewalk, everyone who passed by wanted to pet Bear, and a few of them, the more cautious ones, made eye contact with me through the window as if to say, *Is it safe to pet him?* and I typically nodded yes.

Bear was quite the crowd pleaser.

I wasn't in my seat long before I had to go the bathroom, this stirring in my bowels a Pavlovian vestige from last winter—before we had a functioning indoor toilet up at Hogback Mountain—when I came here not only to eat lunch but also to use their facilities. I'll forever have fond memories of the Rainbow Cafe's cozy, golf-themed bathroom with its clean commode, ample toilet paper, and hot running water.

When I got back to my table, I ate my usual plate of pinto beans, beets, fried squash, glazed carrots, and Texas toast while I read the *Stone County Citizen*. I glanced over at the jukebox and noticed that Matthew Arnold's round-topped hillbilly hat was not where he usually put it. Nor was Matthew anywhere to be found: rather unusual. Allison, my usual waitress, soon informed me that after Matthew's wife had recently died he had moved back to upstate New York.

Though Matthew was gone, he was hardly forgotten. A grainy photograph of his gray-whiskered visage—sans his hillbilly hat—was emblazoned on the napkin dispensers atop several tables throughout the cafe. The pictures of Matthew recalled those black-and-white photos of missing children they used to put on the backs of milk cartoons.

It was the weekend of a mountain bike race at Sylamore, and the cafe was full of biker-yuppies from Little Rock, where I'd once lived. I probably should've tried to make conversation with them, but they seemed out of place here. One reason I enjoyed being in the Ozarks so much was because few city folks were around. Except for me, of course.

Pat Maheny, owner of the Rainbow Cafe and eternal Elvis fanatic, hovered near the biker-yuppies, refilling their coffee cups and chitchatting, occasionally laughing with a cackle. Apparently, Pat didn't much like to work back in her kitchen for on the front cash register was a bumper sticker that read, *If God intended for me to cook and clean, I'd have steel wool for hands.*

Allison brought me an iced tea to go and also—inside a little Styrofoam box—the hamburger patty I'd ordered for Bear. I cut up the meat and took it outside, where the dog scarfed it down, along with a little piece of the white box too.

I crossed the street to the Woods Old Time Soda Fountain, a local landmark. I sat at the counter and had a strawberry milkshake, made with Yarnell's, an Arkansas-made ice cream. Sitting at this soda fountain was like going back in time, to the days of the TV show *Happy Days*, which depicted the 1950s. I half-expected Fonzie to walk in any minute.

But I couldn't stay here long—Bear was still tied up to the newspaper stand across the street. Nonetheless, afterwards, I hustled over to the thrift shop and bought two pairs of secondhand pajamas, even though the pants and the sleeves were too long for me. After all, they were one hundred percent cotton and cost only five dollars. Further up the street was the Arkansas Craft Gallery, where the local crafters sold their wares, but Bear—straining at his leash—was ready to go back to Hogback Mountain and so was I. So we headed back to take a nap, followed by a long hike.

For both me and for Bear—whose idea of great fun was just to hang out with me all day, going wherever I went—it was a good afternoon.

On our weekends at Hogback Mountain, Susanne busied herself with cooking and cleaning, and according to her telling, doing my job, which was to fix things around our cabin. She had better things to do than go hiking. But one early May afternoon she joined me and Bear, though she had a higher utilitarian purpose in mind: she'd taken an interest in wild crafting and wanted to forage in the woods for foods to eat.

Susanne had been inspired by Billy Joe Tatum, a fellow resident along Highway 9 who'd recently died. Unfortunately, this was a case of us appreciating someone after reading her obituary. Upon her death President Clinton had declared, "Billy Joe was an extraordinary woman with an unmatched generosity, warmth, and charisma—she truly was our ambassador to the world."

Ambassador to the world? A woman who'd lived just a few miles away from us on Highway 9? *Really?*

We'd heard old stories about Billy Joe foraging in the local forests with a turkey feather in her hair, a handmade basket under her arm, and trailing behind, several book editors from New York. She was once a guest on *The Tonight Show* with Johnny Carson. Never mind ambassador to the world, how did a woman from Izard County wind up appearing on the most popular late-night television show of her era?

Weeks before, Susanne and I had sought to pay our respects. Within days of Billy Joe Tatum's death, we pulled into the Tatums' driveway. Her husband, Doc Tatum, was just leaving, and he waved wanly as he passed by in his car. His trilby hat called to mind a natty gentleman who lived up in the Swiss Alps. His eldest daughter, Angel, greeted us at the front door. Our conversation was perfunctory until I mentioned that my neighbor was Dennis Gillihan, whereupon Angel proudly declared that he was the first boy she'd ever kissed.

The Tatums called their house Wildflower, a name that appears in *Billy Joe Tatum's Wild Foods Field Guide and Cookbook: An Illustrated Guide to 70 Wild Plants and Over 350 Irresistible Recipes for Serving Them Up*. Published in 1976, the book included a "Foragers Field Guide," for as Billy Joe wrote, "After you have foraged for a time you become more aware of your surroundings, more knowledgeable about ecology and the needs of the environment, and I promise that you will develop greater sensitivity in many areas of life."

Wildflower was a rambling house on a craggy point that overlooked fold upon fold of hills that evinced scarcely a trace of man's presence. The decor reflected the Tatums' interests: writing, woodworking, natural foods, medicine, basketry, and puzzles.

With Billy Joe Tatum still in our thoughts, Susanne and Bear and I set off on our hike around Hogback Mountain. She'd brought along several plastic sacks and had a gardening spade stuck down in the top of her boot. I wasn't so gung ho on foraging. Last fall, soon after we'd bought Hogback Mountain, I sought to learn more about the plants of the forest and, on one of my hikes, I'd picked and then eaten some interesting-looking red berries: it turned out these were sumac berries, certain varieties of which can cause severe allergic reactions when ingested. I'd endured some anxious moments after Susanne pointed this out.

We ventured deep in the woods, back on Dr. Jackson's property, following an old, rutted wagon trail that eventually dissolved into the trees. Somewhere back here was a settler's homesite, but damned if I could find it again. I kept my eye out for a turkey feather for Susanne to put in her hair. All along our way, she picked up some lime-colored moss, trout lily, fern fiddle, flox, goldenseal, and wild hydrangea. Susanne's plastic sacks hung from the crook of her arm, as if she toted groceries.

Back at our cabin, it got chilly after the sun sank below Panther Ridge. In the gloaming, the wind kicked up and a storm rolled across the mountainscape. I sat on the porch and heard the rolling thunder and saw flashes of brilliant lightning as clouds of rain swept by.

After this spectacular show of nature's power, I was hungry yet also quite curious about what we'd have for dinner after Susanne's afternoon of foraging. Billy Joe Tatum's cookbook included recipes for Dandelion Broth, Spanish Cat-Tail Bud Pie, Persimmon Chews, Amaranth Greens with Brandied Orange Sauce, Prickly Pear Pads with Yucca Seeds, Sweet Goldenrod Soup, and on and on for pages. The first line of Billy Joe's book—*"Each of us are many in one"*—was appropriate for a woman who quoted Milton and Virgil while dispensing recipes for Spiced Nut Nibble and Glazed Burdock Slices.

When I came back into the kitchen, Susanne said, "Let's just cook some steaks. I've already thawed out the meat."

"Huh? What about all that stuff you gathered out in the woods?"

"It will take me forever to make a meal out of any of that stuff, and even then…"

We built a charcoal fire in our grill and prepared a dinner of New York strip steaks, brown rice, salad and red wine—all of this utterly conventional and all of it, except the red wine, purchased at Walmart in Mountain View. It was a mighty fine meal.

15.

Springtime Rites

On our drive over to Ruthie Mountain for the fire department's bake sale, we saw a bald eagle soaring against the blue sky. It was unusual for an eagle to be up this way, several miles off the White River where the trout were easy prey.

The Ruthie Mountain Volunteer Fire Department served the hamlets of Mount Olive, Boswell, Piney Creek, and Twin Creek. As area homeowners, Susanne and I were wholehearted supporters, even though the best they could do if our cabin caught fire was to prevent the blaze from turning into an all-consuming forest fire. In any case, the presence of the local fire department helped lower the cost of our homeowner's insurance.

The bake sale, a twice-yearly fundraiser, was held inside a metal building with its doors opened wide to the warm breeze. To make room for three long dining tables, the fire trucks were parked out near the barbecue grill, which puffed white smoke. Amidst the crowd of fifty or so attendees, Cody Don Dawson, fourteen-year-old son of fellow prepper Cody Dawson, sought me out. He was a cherub-faced, upbeat youngster with a bemused grin that made it seem as if he was always about to spring something on his elders.

"Did you enjoy the Rendezvous?" I said, noting his T-shirt, which advertised last year's Rendezvous campout over in Leslie sponsored by the Early Arkansas Reenactment Association. While most kids Cody Don's age were innately future-minded, his parents took him to camps that recreated the living conditions of fur trappers back in the 1830s.

"I love those reenactments!" he said, beaming. "Those campouts are my main source of income. I put up tents for people. Last year, I made sixty-five dollars in one day."

I nodded appreciatively at Cody Don's hustle. The kid had a future. "It's always a pain to put up a tent," I said. "Most of them have so many poles and stakes and stuff like that."

"I know, especially some of the old tents at the reenactments. One guy only paid me four dollars after I put up his tent. He had a hundred dollar bill, and I'd have taken that. Who wouldn't take a hundred bucks for putting up a tent? It wasn't a big tent."

In the buffet line, Susanne and I got a hamburger and then sat down at one of the long tables across from Morgan and Mary, a young couple who lived nearby in a trailer with no running water or electricity. Mary had unruly brunette hair and seemingly hadn't bathed in quite a while, and Morgan, with his thick beard and long hair down his neck, for sure hadn't shaved in forever. Both were transplanted Yankees—Mary from Michigan; Morgan from Washington, D.C. "But I tell people I'm from Maryland," Morgan noted. "It's provokes people less than when I say I'm from Washington."

"I hear you on that," I confirmed.

Nowadays, these two Yankee lovebirds spent a good bit of their time fetching water from the spring at the Blankenships' farm just up the road in Mount Olive. How they'd survive the upcoming summer heat and humidity without air conditioning was completely beyond me.

"How do you like living here?" I asked Morgan.

"I did a study of the best place to live in the United States considering natural beauty, clean water, fresh air, safety, low cost of living, the hospitality of the people," Morgan intoned. "And I wound up here."

"Interesting," I said, feeling a bit remiss, since the main reason I'd wound up in Izard County was because about a year ago, entirely by fluke, I'd picked up a brochure at a convenience store that advertised Bear Gap, a bed-and-breakfast over on Highway 9. I guess, per Morgan's strict and rather exhaustive criteria, that I'd just gotten lucky.

Mary and Morgan ate their hamburgers with such greed that I was relieved to hear them say they had plenty of potatoes and pasta and beans back at their trailer. The subject of solar power came up, not surprising since without electricity of any sort, these two basically rose with the sun and went to bed when it got dark.

Morgan and Mary had met in Washington, where he'd been a chef. Then they followed the culinary trail down to New Orleans. But eventually Morgan decided they needed to move to the mountains. Via the Internet, he'd met a friend of David Blankenship's and discovered that David, now part owner of a successful wholesale spice business in Melbourne, needed help on his farm. All in all, the reason this young couple moved to Izard County sounded more like Morgan's spontaneous response to a chance online encounter than to any methodical study he'd undertaken of the best place in America to live. In any case, Morgan and Mary evoked the youthful back-to-the-landers, the hippie sorts who came to the Ozarks in the 1970s and most of whom, when faced with the choice between country life and city life, gave up and left.

But perhaps Morgan and Mary would stick it out. Their wanderlust quelled for now, they seemed to be enjoying themselves so far. "Just chillin'," Morgan said, flashing some of his East Coast big-city lingo when someone down the long table asked what he'd been up to. Later, someone else asked how he was doing and he answered, "Awesome good," in the run-on cadence of a hipster.

The crowd here at the bake sale brought together various threads of the life Susanne and I had created for ourselves up here in the Ozarks: neighbors, church members, fellow preppers. The cavernous metal building was abuzz with homespun cordiality. Up in these hills, it was wise to be civil with those who might be able to do you a favor. If you couldn't count on your neighbors, you were basically on your own.

The attendees soon heard speeches from two women running for the state legislature, one for the House and one for the Senate. These women lived one county over, which, from the way the blond-haired senatorial candidate spoke of it, cast her in the role of a long-shot outsider. "Look, I want your vote even though I'm not from around here," she said apologetically. "But I've got to lay my head somewhere."

Then, to the audience, the dark-headed lady said, "I ran for office because I was just fed up," as she clutched the tiny hand of her daughter. These women, with their tough-love conservative values, were a kind of hill country incarnation of Margaret Thatcher. Also in attendance, seated at one of the long tables, was a candidate for sheriff of Melbourne, as well as the town's justice of the peace.

"He's a good boy," Dennis said confidentially, speaking of the young justice of the peace. "You know, stuff like justice of the peace, constable, county judge—that's all easy work until there's a controversy. A road will get real bad, or a sand mine will want to come in—something will happen—and then you'll have people calling you day and night."

I went from table to table, talking with folks while Bear followed me around, scouring the floor for something to eat. Our dog was familiar to those who attended church with us. One of them had gone so far as to refer to him as a "sacred dog." Even amongst our friends who didn't attend our church, stories about Bear's repeated intrusions during Sunday services had become a running joke.

Dennis pulled me aside to tell me how, the week before, he'd taken Bear with him when he went to visit Esker Brown, the avid deer hunter and mutual friend who lived just up the road. The dog was certainly familiar to Esker, but he couldn't quite place him—Esker had never seen Bear with Dennis, his other co-parent, only with me. "I know that dog from somewhere," Esker had said, puzzled. *"Somewhere?"*

"Oh, you know him all right," Dennis had deadpanned. "He goes to church with you."

Soon, the auction cranked up, with a birdhouse and a cedar chest and other trinkets up for bid. Then came the main attraction—the sweets, including pies, cakes, fudge, candies, cookies, and peanut brittle.

While this went on, Esker Brown's wife, Charlotte, whispered to me about some property down on Piney Creek that had recently been auctioned off at what she thought was a low-ball price to a man from Hawaii. She implied this was a juicy land deal that I shouldn't have missed out on. Then she asked if Susanne and I would ever retire to Izard County.

"I don't know," I said. "We're a long way from that, believe me."

I expected Charlotte to regale me with the joys of retirement up in the Ozarks and all that I had to look forward to during my golden years, but ruefully she said, "We work all the time. Every morning, my husband gets up at sunrise and says, 'What's the plan for today?' It's exhausting. Esker just works all the time. The only difference now is that we don't get paid."

At last, the auctioneer held up a carrot cake covered with thick white icing. He handled the plate with some effort, as if it was loaded with lead. Since we'd arrived, I'd had my eye on this particular dessert, and after my winning bid, the auctioneer delivered it to me. On the edge of the plate, I spotted a handwritten note: the cake had been baked by Jeannette Gillihan, wife of George Gillihan, a distant cousin of Dennis's.

I should've known.

From behind me, I overheard Morgan say, "Let's bounce," to Mary, his hipster way of saying he was ready to leave.

Susanne and I, and Bear of course, followed the young couple out into the bright sunshine, and soon we were off too.

The weather was warm and wet. My thoughts turned to kayaking on the Buffalo River, a wild river that flowed according to the seasonal rains. Late springtime was typically the best time to float. Timing was everything.

I called an outfitter at Ponca—west of us, further into the really, really dark heart of the Ozarks—to inquire about the conditions up near the river's headwaters. The outfitter warned me—no, he flat-out told me—that I was not to come float this particular stretch unless I was experienced at kayaking in whitewater rapids. I didn't bother to add that Thomas, my fifteen-year old nephew, was coming along with me for his first trip on the Buffalo. (I'd also considered bringing along Bear; we'd even bought him a doggie life jacket since he didn't like deep water.)

"We can't be responsible for you," the outfitter added with a weary tone. No telling how many phone calls he had recently fielded from casual kayakers like me, checking on the river's conditions. He continued, "Understand that if something happens to you, we don't have any one to send to come help you. You're on your own, man."

"Okay, I gotcha," I said, sharply. The guy was really beating a dead horse. "I'm not coming, don't worry."

I set my sights further downstream where the Buffalo River broadened and the waters were calmer. I also gave up on bringing Bear along—life vest aside, I couldn't image him sitting still for a three-hour float. What was I thinking?

This kayak trip was to be a break for Thomas from his tough situation back home in Little Rock, where his father was still sick. On our outing, he and I could talk about his plans for the summer, what we'd cook on the grill that night for dinner, corny lines from country music songs, St. Louis Cardinals' baseball. Basically, we could talk about anything but his father's condition. For months now, he'd been coming up to Hogback Mountain on weekends, and he and I had grown close. He was coming to rely on me as a father figure, a new and growing role for me. The father of my two stepchildren, John and Emily (both off at college), had died of a heart attack a few years ago: he was two months younger than me. I found this sobering, to say the least.

Early on a sunny morning, Thomas and I headed out for Marshall, about thirty-five miles away. We drove in the old white van that for months now I'd occasionally used to haul stuff up to Hogback Mountain: Thomas called it the "child molester van," as in, a van a child molester would drive. It was not a comfortable ride. To entertain us, Willie Nelson blared on the radio.

The two of us had no kayaking gear except for our bathing suits and sandals. We showed up at the outfitter, just north of Marshall, where they rented us kayaks, paddles, life vests. We also purchased sandwiches and cold drinks and then loaded into the old school bus that transported us, and about thirty other kayakers, upriver to Woolum, the drop-off point.

Our trip downstream started out uneventfully. Mercifully, the Buffalo River was not nearly as cold as the White River, which was fed by water let out from the bottoms of Lake Norfork and Bull Shoals Lake. I could actually dip my foot into this water without it going numb. With the recent rains, the water flowed fast but not too fast—at least not here. The paddling was hardly strenuous.

After a time, Thomas and I stopped at a sandbar to eat our sandwiches. We scouted around in the surrounding woods and kept an eye out for bald eagles.

Further downriver, in a particularly choppy spot, I took a diversion around an island in the river. Thomas, unfortunately, decided to follow me. In the rippling water, our kayaks got turned sideways. Eventually, we each capsized and floated on as the water deepened, holding onto our respective upside-down kayaks. Thomas tried to aright his kayak, but the current was too strong, his arms too young, to flip it over. I was having the same problem with my kayak.

"Just swim it down!" I shouted in surrender. "Swim it on down!"

We finally managed to escape the strong current and pull our kayaks onto a sandbar.

"You all right?" I said.

"I lost my favorite T-shirt," Thomas noted.

"Maybe we'll find it downriver."

"I seriously doubt it."

"You're right," I said, acceding to Thomas's candid wisdom, uncommon for his age.

We floated on downstream yet saw only a sliver of the immense majesty of the Buffalo National River. For months now, I'd heard my neighbor Ed Alexander talk about spots further upriver like Hemmed-in-Hollow, Lost Valley, Roark Bluff, and Boxley. There was so much to explore. Ed often hiked into the wilderness of the Buffalo and camped out for days by himself. He loved the beauty, the solitude. It was a photographer's dream. His deceased father, a naturalist who's been called "the father of Arkansas conservation," had passed down his love of this unique area to him.

On the drive back to Hogback Mountain, Thomas and I speculated about elk hunting over near Jasper, just southwest of us. Once native to Arkansas, the last elk were seen around here around 1840, but in recent years some determined conservationists had reestablished a herd of almost five hundred. Of course, Thomas and I had little chance of getting a highly coveted elk-hunting permit: statewide, only twenty or so were issued each year. Still, it was fun to think about hunting elk and to know such beasts roamed not far from here.

"Thanks for taking me to the river," Thomas said as we sped along in my so-called child molester van. "I've always wanted to float the Buffalo."

"It was a lot of fun," I said. "Sorry you lost your favorite T-shirt."

"Oh, it was well worth it."

We drove on in silence, the late-afternoon sun still bright, and then in violation of my unsaid rule of not speaking of his father's illness, I gave in. "Listen, as far as your situation at home, there's nothing that's going to come your way that you and I can't handle."

Thomas didn't say anything, and I tried to imagine what was going through his head, the trepidation he felt as he watched his father wither. My parents, both pillars of my life, were in their early seventies, vibrant and healthy.

"We'll get through it, you know," I added, my words inadequate.

"Yeah," he said, flatly. "It'll be okay."

About all that, there was nothing else for either of us to say.

We were hungry again and stopped at a family-run restaurant for hamburgers, French fries, strawberry milkshakes. We shunned the picnic tables out in the courtyard and sat inside, near the window-unit air conditioner. Already, we knew we'd gotten a lot of sun out on the river.

A shapely young lady walked by our table, and after I cut my eyes at Thomas to see if he'd noticed her, he just shook his head. Having turned fifteen, he was becoming more interested in the opposite sex; accordingly, over the course of his regular visits up to the Ozarks he'd become convinced that there were no good-looking girls up here: not any that he'd seen anyway. Once, as we stood in the checkout line at Walmart in Mountain View, he'd commented, "You know, the people around here are sort of ugly." This, a sharp-eyed teenager's take on a region of the Ozarks that certainly not many so-called beautiful people called home.

The next morning, just how much sun Thomas and I had gotten while floating the Buffalo River was painfully apparent when we awakened with sunburns in the reverse shape of our rented life vests. Even our knees were a scalded red. We looked as if we'd been blow-torched while seated in our kayaks. I felt bad about sending Thomas home to his parents in Little Rock. Some father figure I was.

It would have been most helpful if the day before, when he and I had shown up at the outfitter up near Marshall to rent our kayaks, someone there with a head on their shoulders had sternly said to us, "You two don't even think about going out on that river unless you put on plenty of sunscreen!"

But, alas, no one at the outfitter had thought to do so.

One by-product of our weekends at Hogback Mountain was that Susanne and I could drink rather freely, if so inclined. Certainly, drinking and driving was not an issue because there was no place to go. Too, with all our weekend chores around our cabin, we typically needed a little something to take the edge off.

Mostly, we drank like the locals: beer and middling wines purchased at a package store two counties over, where liquor could be legally sold. For harder-drinking guests, our bar included a bottle of Jim Beam whiskey, if for no other reason than I was lately amused by that Hank Williams, Jr. song with the line, *"I have loved some ladies and I have loved Jim Beam, and they both tried to kill me in 1973."*

But last year, I'd turned fifty years old. My tastes were evolving. I was coming to fashion myself as a hillbilly gentleman, if such a thing was possible. I didn't anymore want to drink like the hill people drank. I wanted to drink better than them.

So, I began to bring finer wines up to our cabin, notably reasonably-priced Bordeaux and Rhone wines from France, enjoying their subtlety and finesse amidst the rusticity of the Ozarks. This became my thing, my private compensation for being so radically unhandy and un-self-reliant that any true hillsman considered me an embarrassment. One night, for our guests, I even attempted to hold a wine tasting, but their attention wandered and our gathering devolved into an all-around drink fest.

Beyond my fancier wines, our weekend life at Hogback Mountain was full and surprisingly stimulating. Fifty years earlier, access to the world beyond the Ozarks had been severely limited. There were only a few TV channels, at best. To get even a mediocre local newspaper required a drive to town. On the radio one found only gospel or country music, if you were lucky. And forget about buying a newly released book.

In fact, the further back you go back in time in the Ozarks, the worse life got. From 1840 to 1902, the principal civilizing force in the White River Valley was the steamboat, some of which had dining rooms and dance halls and even staterooms. Back then, news spread mostly by word of mouth, if at all. Things were pretty darn dull. In *Life in the Leatherwoods*, John Quincy Wolf, Jr. tells about his family's purchase of a freestanding clock back in the 1880s. Lo, the excitement this created! His neighbors came over just to watch the clock for entertainment. They would sit around their cabin for hours just to watch it chime *cuckoo*.

Nowadays, though, it was encouraging to ponder all of the technology we had access to at Hogback Mountain. Susanne and I weren't exactly roughing it. Via satellite television, we watched some 250 channels and ordered movies-on-demand. Our choices of music were endless, thanks to satellite radio and music-sharing services. Via my phone or tablet, I could read practically any newspaper in the world or download virtually any book.

Back in the 1990s, I'd found that one of the benefits of living in Manhattan, as opposed to the flatlands of eastern Arkansas, was that I could buy *The New York Times* every morning. When I'd come in late on Saturday nights, I'd purchase a copy of Sunday's paper and have it sitting at my bedside when I woke up the next morning. Such worldly conveniences made the hassles of living in the city worthwhile.

Now, though, on any ordinary day in the Ozarks, I sat on my front porch and looked out over the blue-hazed hills and read *The New York Times* cover-to-cover on my tablet. Fantastic! Why show up at a grubby kiosk at two o'clock on a Sunday morning on the corner of Sixth Avenue and Fourteenth Street to buy a world-class newspaper? After decades of New Yorkers making fun of Arkansans—*Nothing down there but a bunch of hillbillies*—the joke was on them.

None of this is to say that Izard County, Arkansas was now the garden spot of America. But with all the worldly connections that technology made possible, places like the Ozarks or the Appalachians, while not exactly regions that are loved to death, are hardly lost-in-time backwaters anymore either (perhaps to the detriment of the uniqueness of these places). In fact, our current situation up in Izard County approached the best of all worlds: modern technologies of all types had found the Ozarks, but, fortunately, not very many people had found the place at all.

16.

The Two Dannys

To go with our four-wheeler, we'd also purchased a previously owned two-seater utility vehicle (UTV) made by Honda. Inevitably, our rig broke down and needed repair, so one day a man named Big Danny came to pick it up. Big Danny had been to Hogback Mountain before to repair our backup, backup generator, the second unit Susanne had procured as part of her ongoing preparations for the-end-of-the-world-as-we-know-it.

This time, Big Danny arrived with another beefy-looking fellow, the driver of their truck and trailer. Both men wore dark shirts and were middle aged, tallish in height, and mostly bald: they could've passed for twin brothers.

"That's Little Danny," Big Danny said with a nod towards his sidekick.

"I'm glad you came out here with me," Little Danny said in Big Danny's direction. "I'd never have found this place in a million years."

The two Dannys positioned their trailer, communicating via mumbled utterances. Big Danny in particular spoke as if he had a wad of cotton in his mouth. He didn't have many teeth that I could see—not in the front of his mouth anyway.

"Are you two related?" I said.

"We're just business partners."

I was relieved to hear this, for it would've indeed been a cruel joke by their parents to name them both Danny. The Dannys' company was called East End Small Engine Repair, headquartered on the eastern end of Melbourne, which apparently was not to be confused with the west end of Melbourne.

While Little Danny positioned the ramp for their trailer, Big Danny came over and inspected my utility vehicle. It took him a while to locate the engine—it wasn't in back of the UTV, he noted, and it wasn't in the front either. When Big Danny bent down to look underneath, I saw the curlicue tattoo atop his head.

"The engine must be underneath," he concluded when he rose up.

I was a bit troubled that it had taken Big Danny so long to locate the engine, so I said, "Have you worked on Honda engines before?"

"I went to Honda School to get certified. They're fine, fine engines. We'll haul this thing back to our shop."

Following Little Danny's emphatic hand signals, I drove my sick utility vehicle up onto their trailer. With a winch, Big Danny secured the front of my rig.

"Now," said Little Danny with a sense of foreboding, "I've got to figure out how to back out of here." To give himself more room to maneuver in our driveway, he asked me to move our old, beat-up Land Rover, which was parked on a patch of gravel near the barn.

"That's just a dummy vehicle," I said. "It won't start."

"A dummy vehicle?" Little Danny replied, as if offended by the very idea of such a thing.

I didn't think it wise to further explain to either of the Dannys that our vehicle—basically a decoy not unlike the dirigibles the Allies had used to fake out Hitler during World War II—was only there to make it look like Susanne and I were at Hogback Mountain during those times when, really, we were not. To reveal such information would only have defeated the purpose of using our vehicle as a feint in the first place.

Little Danny and Big Danny conferred, considering several scenarios for backing up their truck and trailer. As a show of sympathy for their predicament, I blurted out, "I can't back up a trailer either; I usually have to get my wife to do it." At this, Big Danny cut his eyes at me, and feeling a bit unmanly, I added, "Well, I can back up a trailer a little ways. I'm just not very good at it."

While Little Danny backed their trailer down the long driveway—he was doing a masterful job thus far—Big Danny and I stood in the high grass, out of his way.

"Are you from around here?" I said to Big Danny.

"I'm from Texas."

Some Arkansans, like me, have a reflexive hostility towards Texans, so with a hint of accusation, I said, "What the heck are you doing up here?"

"I've been here three years. Before that, I was a meth addict for twenty-seven years, but I've been clean for the last three years. From Tyler, Texas. Had my sister come down there and pick me up. Used to, I didn't think I could get out of bed without smoking meth. But I'm clean now."

"Good for you, man."

"I wanted to live so that I could see my kids get old and my grandkids grow up. I feel great! My work is great!"

"Way to go!" I gave Big Danny a fist bump, and he returned a mush-mouthed smile.

We gazed down the driveway where Little Danny, after backing down the truck and trailer, was now trying to turn around. He didn't dare back out onto Highway 9; to do so was to invite death, for the entrance to my driveway was on a nasty blind curve.

"Did the meth cause you to lose your teeth?" I said to Big Danny.

"Most of them." He stuck his forefingers into his mouth to widen it. He had only a few teeth on his top jaw and those on his bottom jaw were broken and discolored. "I can only chew on one side," he said after he took his fingers out of his mouth. "But I can chew."

"You can always get dentures when you get older."

"I not sure I've got much longer to live. I'm sixty-two."

Having turned fifty not so long ago, I was somewhat rattled by Big Danny's talk of an abbreviated future. Then again, by his own admission he'd lived quite a hard life.

Down the driveway, Little Danny had finally positioned their truck headfirst towards the highway. The two Dannys were set to head back to Melbourne. I stood and watched as they drove off. I could only imagine their conversation as they made their way back towards Melbourne, and I had no idea if they could fix my utility vehicle—I'd only sought their services because Scott Hopper did not repair UTVs down at his Taj Mahal of ATV repair in Mountain View. Too, as the Dannys pulled away, the possibility crossed my mind that I might not ever see my UTV again.

Basically though, for some reason—perhaps foolishly—I trusted these two Danny characters almost completely.

A few days later, I returned a phone message from East End Small Engine Repair in Melbourne. "Is Danny there? I just missed his call."

"Big Danny or Little Danny?" the receptionist said.

I was surprised to discover that East End Small Engine Repair had a receptionist at all. *Were these guys really too busy to answer their phones?* Nonetheless, to this pleasant-voiced lady, I said, "I need to speak to Big Danny, I guess. But either Danny will do. I'm hoping one or the other of them has some good news on my UTV."

Big Danny got on the line and told me that he couldn't service the Honda engine in my rig because it was fuel injected. I started to remind him that he'd told me he'd gone to a Honda school of some sort to get certified to fix their engines. But I let it pass and instead asked if he could deliver my utility vehicle back to our place the next time he came out this far on Highway 9, no quick or easy round trip from Melbourne, for sure, and a delivery he'd have to make at his own expense.

The next weekend, when I arrived at Hogback Mountain, I was relieved to see that my UTV was there, beside the barn, just as Big Danny had told me it would be.

17.

The Chicken Bandwagon

Being a sucker for high design, one day, on the Williams-Sonoma website, I showed Susanne a picture of a chicken coop featured in their curated line of products aimed at yuppie homesteaders. The ever-so-cute coop was made of red cedar from a family-run sawmill in Washington State. "Isn't that something?" I said.

But my ever-sensible wife declared the price, which included a hefty shipping charge, to be confiscatory. Even so, I had unwittingly stoked Susanne's lifelong love of animals, even for lowly birds like chickens. So we took the picture of the high-dollar coop to Ben Harvey to see if he could make one like it, but only cheaper.

Since we'd begun buying furniture from Ben on a fairly regular basis, he'd warmed up to us, going so far as to regularly call me by my first name as if we'd been high school chums. Yet, because Ben had spurned my idea for building a human nest, I didn't know what to expect when I asked him about building us an over-designed chicken coop. Actually, I did know what to expect: Ben was going to say that this project was out of his comfort zone, which seemed about as wide as the pointy end of a nail.

Ben held the picture of the chicken coop close to his Coke-bottle thick eyeglasses for a long time. I did not know if this was good or bad.

"I can make that," he pronounced.

"You can?" I said, sounding more surprised than I'd intended.

"It'll take me about a week."

"How much will it cost?" Susanne interjected.

Ben's price was one-third of the fancy Williams-Sonoma coop.

A week later, I got a call from Ben, again warmly calling me by my first name: Susanne's coop was ready.

My wife was giddy when she saw it. I'd seldom seen her so happy. The coop had cedar shakes on its roof, plus a well-built run and a nifty little door over the nesting box to retrieve any newly laid eggs. The coop was painted forest green to blend in with the landscape—the architecture of this glorified birdhouse was dutifully organic in that sense.

We placed our coop next to a cedar tree out by our barn. Susanne set down slabs of limestone rock around the coop, installed a solar light, and put a tarp on its roof to protect the chickens from any harsh sunshine. Alas, but for now, we had no chickens.

Therein ensued a discussion over what breed we'd buy. My only request was no roosters. There would be no crowing at sunrise to disturb my late-morning sleeps on our weekends at Hogback Mountain. A week later, we had procured two Orpingtons and two Easter Eggers.

Around this time, I read news stories about "the poultry bandwagon," citing "a growing number of suburbanites and weekend farmers [raising] poultry for fun, not just food." For me, as a prototypical Baby Boomer, this was no surprise: across the arc of my life I had dabbled along the edges of virtually every cultural trend—good, bad, or indifferent. I was like a poster boy for those who blew along with almost any prevailing societal wind. But hey—in my defense—wasn't our sudden chicken fetish all part of being Ozarkers? Chicken raising was common in this region. Nationwide, the name of Tyson Foods over in northwest Arkansas was synonymous with retail chicken products. But of course, with our four chickens, Susanne and I were hardly in danger of becoming what one left-leaning magazine called "The Serfs of Arkansas" who raised thousands of chickens for big integrators like Tyson Foods.

Admittedly, it was satisfying to see our hens running around our mountain. I was curious why these birds could not fly for more than a few seconds. Why were their eggs different colors? Why was one hen smarter than the rest of the flock? More pressingly, what would we name our chickens?

"How about Thelma and Louise?" I suggested, thinking of the movie by the same name. "At least for two of our hens."

Susanne shook her head emphatically: "Those girls drove off a cliff!" She decided on Miss Scarlet and Prissy, both names from *Gone with the Wind*. The other speckled hen was named Pebbles; the coppery-brown one was Penny.

Shortly though, I gave in to Susanne's plea for a rooster. A friend from central Arkansas had told me that he liked having a few roosters around his hobby farm. They added to the atmosphere of his place, he said.

We brainstormed on what to name our new rooster. I suggested the name Hefner, noting our lucky bird had a ready-made brood of four hens, as well as a mansion-like coop. Susanne had always liked the warrior named Maximus in the movie, *Gladiator*.

Our rooster, named Max for short, had a beautiful red crown and layered feathers of golden brown and stark black. A cocky, dominating little dude, and a bit of a showboater, he was immediately preoccupied with his gaggle of hens.

Inevitably, Dennis Gillihan, knower of all things local, came up to survey our new coop and the precious contents therein. As always, he wore his work clothes—jeans, long-sleeved cotton shirt, rubber-soled boots, his cap slightly cocked as if he'd been too busy laboring all day to fool with straightening it.

"It will take about three days for the coons to figure out how to open that latch," he said.

"*They can open a latch?*" I said.

"Sure." Dennis told us how some coons once found a weakness in the roof of his wife's coop—or the coons had made the weakness—

and bit the heads off seven chickens before order was restored. "Coons are wily critters," he confirmed.

"Obviously. But I just never thought—"

"Everything eats a chicken," Dennis declared while Susanne worked with renewed diligence to coon-proof her coop.

Dennis was in a hurry to get back home. In an effort to lower his heating bills during winter—months away as we were barely into summer—he'd spent his day blowing insulation into his attic. He said he'd hired somebody to help him, but the fellow hadn't shown up, so his wife Carol had crawled up into the attic, something Dennis couldn't manage because he couldn't bend his gimp right leg. "She did an awesome job!" he told me before paying his wife his ultimate compliment: "She did it better than a man."

Even now, in these early days of our ownership of chickens, I knew where Susanne's ride on the chicken-raising bandwagon was headed: we were to get so many birds that, to take care of them, we'd be required to come up to Hogback Mountain every weekend, no matter.

But, heck, we were already doing this anyway.

18.

Sacrament on the White River

Susanne was highly intrigued when Pastor Steve Moon informed the congregation of his plan to baptize several church members down at the White River. So after the service, we followed a caravan of vehicles along a bumpy dirt road to a sandy landing on the shoreline.

This baptism intrigued me too. For one thing, I wanted to see who had the guts to go through with it. The tailwaters of the White River are artificially frigid due to the power-generating dams some forty miles north of us. Only trout can survive it, though the water typically isn't quite cold enough for these fish to spawn: ergo the necessity of upstream trout hatcheries to stock the river. All of this was quite complicated. Suffice it to say, the White River was damned cold, even on a sunny afternoon in June.

When we got out of our SUV, Susanne went straight for Pastor Steve, who'd already rolled up his pants and donned a royal blue robe. My wife had been baptized as a child, but this setting on the river spoke to her. We were at Split Rock, where her father had taken her fishing many times as a girl. Back in those days, she'd risen at first light and, with her sisters, piled into a flat-bottomed boat. The morning air was cool and fog hugged the river, and it was here, at Split Rock, where her father always killed the boat's motor and they began their drift, fishing for trout all the way back to Jack's Boat Dock (nowadays going by the more high-falutin' name of Jack's Fishing Resort), a round trip of some ten miles.

Susanne's father, Hays Sullivan, first came up to these mountains back in the 1950s, lured to the region by the hill folks who came over to the Arkansas Delta during harvest season to pick cotton for wages. Years later, Hays served under then-governor Bill Clinton on the Arkansas Game and Fish Commission, which put him in good standing with Jack Hinkle, owner of Jack's Boat Dock, who needed to keep the river stocked with hatchery-raised trout for his customers. So Hays had made sure Jack's customers had trout to fish, and Jack made sure Hays and his daughters were well cared for at his boat dock-cum-resort.

Hays Sullivan always said, "It's not what you know, it's who you know." A longtime FOB (Friend of Bill), he once took a cooler full of duck breasts to the White House, where he'd pulled up to the front gate. His beat-up cooler was covered with duct tape and somewhat resembled a homemade bomb. The Secret Service agents went nuts and pointed their guns at him. But eventually one of the agents—a fellow who'd once duck-hunted with Hays back in the Delta—recognized him and commanded the other agents to let him in the White House gate. The last time my father-in-law was up at Hogback Mountain, he pulled out a business card he'd gotten from Bill Gates's personal assistant (or so he said). The connection? Well, this woman used to work for Hillary Clinton. Hays said he'd sent this assistant two big sacks of Arkansas pecans, one for herself and one for her boss. *Who knows?*

I lost track of Susanne as I mingled with fellow church members on the riverbank, where a potluck lunch was being set out. Eventually she came towards me, her eyes teary, her face determined. "I want to do it," she said. "I want to be baptized here."

"Haven't you already been baptized?"

"I have, but not here."

I mock shivered and said, "The water will be cold."

"I know. It won't matter."

"It won't? Nobody dares to swim in that river."

"I've just got to do this."

For Susanne, this place held a significance beyond her memories of trout fishing with her sisters: just as Mount Olive evoked the Mount of Olives in Jerusalem, Split Rock evoked the miracle Moses had worked in the desert when he struck a boulder with his staff and produced water for thirsty Israelites.

Susanne held onto Pastor Steve's arm as they waded out into the river, both now dressed in knee-length blue robes. Steve's robe was completely soaked, for he'd already baptized two other people. From the waist down, he had to be as numb as a mummy.

The two of them, the shepherd and his sheep, went out at least a hundred yards. Watching them wade out whetted my appetite to go fishing—something I had not done much of since we'd bought Hogback Mountain. They got on their knees in the cold, clear current. Then Steve held Susanne's head as she leaned back and went under. *Completely*. From the shore, I imagined the chill, while Bear barked and barked in their direction. He was very protective of Susanne; I practically had to muzzle him.

When Susanne returned to the riverbank, her hair was a waterlogged mess, her mascara runny. She looked like a drowned raccoon. My wife was the type who always wanted to look her best when out in public, but as witness to the strength of her faith she had given herself over to the frigid baptismal waters.

"You know about the story in the Bible?" she said. "About Moses and the split rock?"

I said yes, but she told me the story again anyway.

During our potluck lunch, I chatted with John Kushmaul, a retired high school chemistry teacher. John's daughter had attended Middlebury College in Vermont, where he'd once lived. His wife, who'd traveled the world, was a renowned expert in fruit trees. John had a big garden at his place just downriver and always brought some of his produce to church for sharing—potatoes, beans, tomatoes, squash—all of it piled in the back of his truck, a veritable farmer's market on wheels.

I pumped John for information: a few weeks before, 150 people from as far away as Minnesota had gathered just downstream at Sparkling River Farms, which he co-owned with five other families, for the fortieth annual celebration of The Rites of Spring, a days-long camp out and pop-up music fest. It was reputed to be a toned-down Woodstock for hillbillies.

Susanne and I mingled for a while with our church friends: people who cared for us and whom we'd come to care for as well. With her impulse baptism, my new wife and I had gotten to know one another even better. We were as opposite as could be, but we'd known this before we got married. As they say, opposites attract. She had her strengths and I had mine, such as they were. So far, through our first year of marriage, we'd discovered that we made a good team. Our love was deepening, thanks in no small part to the time we were spending here in Izard County.

Into summer, Susanne's garden grew like kudzu in the topsoil we'd hauled in earlier in the spring. We sat in our rocking chairs on our porch, admiring her handiwork. "I want us to be self-sufficient," she said. "I want to be able to come up and have a salad and eat out of our garden."

I sensed Susanne was exhausted from all of her labors at Hogback Mountain, so I said, "I know you enjoy gardening, but it's a lot of work. We can buy anything we need to eat at Walmart."

"What would I do on the weekends if I didn't have my garden?"

Susanne, like me, was transitioning from a divorce to remarriage in middle age and, with her children in college, an empty nest. She too was on a journey of self-reinvention. For so long, she'd felt undernourished by her city life and by pressures to live in ways that didn't entirely suit her nature. She was a far more natural and talented Ozarker than I'd ever be. "I feel more alive when I'm up here," she went on. "It's good for my soul."

It was remarkable what a few truckloads of topsoil and some planted seeds had yielded: knockout roses, red gladiolas, white daisies, zinnias, moonflowers, sunflowers, and mums. Our garden, adorned by our cedar outhouse, was full of vegetables with fanciful names like Straight Eight Cucumbers, White Half-Runner Pole Beans, Red Burgundy Okra, Long Island Brussels Sprouts, April in Paris Sweet Peas, Detroit Dark Red Beet, and my favorite, Forellenschluss, a tasty lettuce from Austria with a roll-off-the-tongue name that means *speckled like a trout*. I ate every leaf of it that Susanne could grow. We also had medicinal herbs like chamomile, hyssop, Solomon's seal, wild yam, evening primrose, mint, and mullein. What a bounty!

To somehow assist Susanne, I'd discovered a website with gardening tools for Englishmen and purchased a hand cultivator, a set of blackboard garden markers, a dibber, gardener's kneepads, pruners, and a nifty basket in which to tote around all this stuff. Certainly, it wouldn't do for my wife to work the Ozark soil with anything less than the implements used by an eccentric British gardener.

Inevitably though, a problem arose. In our absence from Hogback Mountain during the workweek, deer and coons ate what we grew. When would we ever pick a homegrown tomato?

Susanne went on the attack. More solar lights were installed. Wind chimes went up. Chicken wire was brought in. To scald the delicate mouths of any invasive animals, bitter herbs were planted around the garden's edges: lemon balm, mint, thyme, oregano, and jalapeños. Another weapon in her arsenal was to get Bear to pee in our garden to scent it. He proved quite capable of the task.

But there was another threat: our chickens. Typically, they stayed in their coop when we were away, but some days our neighbors came over, collected the eggs, and let our chickens out to roam until sunset.

"I just know they're eating everything out of my garden when we're not here," Susanne said as we sat on the porch. "It's frustrating. I can't talk anymore about my garden."

She went out to the barn, just down the hillside. I had a good idea what she was up to. Like any hobby pursued wholeheartedly, gardening reveals personality, and sure enough Susanne and I had hit upon a philosophical difference over the use of weed killer. She was an aggressive user of the poison, but I wanted only a minimal amount applied, if any at all. Her justification was that she had to kill the grass in order to keep it out of her garden and also to help control any snakes around our cabin. My reasoning was that I did not like the scorched-earth look the weed killer left behind.

Every time I turned my back, Susanne sprayed more weed killer—or so I imagined. Did she hide her pump-spray jug from me, like an alcoholic tucks away a bottle of hooch? I had tried, with limited success, to make sure her weed killing did not extend too far beyond the cabin. It was like trying to keep water from running down a mountain stream.

Late that afternoon, I hiked down to West Twin Creek with Bear. When I looked up in the direction of Hogback Mountain, I noticed a haze of smoke just over the tree line. Holy cow! Our cabin was on fire!

I broke out into a trot, with Bear behind me, but as I got closer to our cabin, I saw that it was only the hillside that was on fire: Susanne had started a controlled burn. It was nearing dark and the long rope of fire slowly, inexorably crept down the slope below our cabin. The golden sage grass crackled as tuft after tuft went ablaze.

"A rain's coming in a few hours," Susanne said casually. "But I got out the water hose just in case the fire gets out of control. Here, take it."

Before I took the hose and assumed the role of a fireman, I went up on the porch and turned on some loud music: "New Year's Day," by U2, the Irish band's anthem to the Rapture. Then I returned to the hillside and grabbed the water hose from Susanne as I listened to the moody music and watched the fire continue its creep down our mountain. I still wasn't too happy about this—the fire was scorching the slope far worse than any of the weed killer she'd ever sprayed—but the whole glowing scene was quite atmospheric, I had to admit.

After dark, we cooked hamburgers on the grill and ate a salad of Forellenschluss lettuce. Susanne, at one point, said, "This is a pretty good supper."

"A decent little ole supper," I quipped.

A few days later, back in the flatlands, John Byler called me. He'd just returned from Hogback Mountain where, at his suggestion, he'd cut up for firewood one of the many trees the power company had felled last spring.

"It looks good where you burned the hillside around your cabin," John said. "That was a smart thing to do."

"Thanks," I replied. "But it wasn't my idea. All credit goes to my wife."

19.

Fishing and Fishy Stories

With the onset of hot weather, the White River beckoned with its water so clear the early French explorers felt as if their pirogues floated on air. Thomas and I were going fishing, and on this particular trip I was glad Dennis Gillihan was along because he knew how to handle a boat.

Two weeks earlier, Thomas and I had foolishly launched from the shore before we started our boat's motor. As it happened, the motor never started—a rookie mistake, for sure. As the adult, I should've known better. Then, to add to our woes, when Thomas and I got around to fishing, we discovered there was no line in our rods. We had drifted downriver for miles, steering with only a tiny trolling motor and one paddle. The tricky part was to hit the takeout ramp at Sylamore Creek. If we missed, we'd have drifted another twelve miles down to Guion or, if we'd so desired, eventually floated all the way to the Mississippi River.

Years ago, Dennis had worked as a fishing guide on the White River, and on this trip he aimed his helpful instructions on boatmanship at Thomas. I guess he figured there was no point in trying to teach me. I just sat in the front of the boat and poured cold water on Bear's black-furred head.

"Do you know what's the most important thing about running a motor?" Dennis said, pointing down. "This switch locks the motor in place. No telling how many boats I've seen ruined by not knowing how to lock and unlock the motor."

Thomas nodded as we idled in the current. Like practically any fifteen-year-old, he was itching to rev the engine. "Whatever you do, don't get into a hurry," Dennis counseled as we approached a half-submerged tree limb. "Don't get the boat hung in the middle. If you're going to hit something, hit it on one end of the boat or the other and the boat will spin around. You're cooked if you hit it in the middle."

We hit the tree limb on one end of the boat and, just as Dennis had predicted, the boat harmlessly spun around. At last, Thomas revved the motor and we sped up past Split Rock, where he cut the engine. The three of us took out our rods while Dennis carried on:

"I was on this river one time with a guy who was driving in the fog, and after we told him to slow down he told us that he knew this dadgum river like the back of his hand. Then, seconds later, he ran the boat right up onto the riverbank. We all just sat there and laughed."

The trees along the river swayed in a wind so stout that it slowed our drift southward. I'd brought along my new Orvis fly fishing rod, as well as some store-bought, hand-tied flies including woolly buggers, zebra midges, sow bugs, prince nymphs, pheasant tails. But fly fishing can be a lot of trouble—not to mention require Job-like patience—so, like Thomas and Dennis, I baited the hook of my casting reel with whole-kernel corn from a tin can. Finally, we all had lines in the water.

Fishing on the White River can be tricky. Are the fish biting up towards Norfork Dam or down towards Mountain View? Is frozen shrimp the better bait? Another consideration is the water level, which has little to do with rainfall but rather when the generators at the dams upriver are running. It's thought that the trout bite more when the river is rising—the strong current kicks up more food. So the savvy angler knows how long it takes for the water released at Bull Shoals and Norfork to reach various points downriver—Calico Rock, Mount

Olive, Allison. Of course no one in our boat had bothered to check any of this beforehand.

"It's not easy to make a living as a guide on this river," Dennis said, speaking from his long-ago experience.

"So I hear," I replied. "The last time I fished this river, my guide said the only qualification for a job such as his was to be independently poor." I was referring to Jerry Clements, a white-haired, pink-skinned older fellow who lived up in Baxter County on ninety acres his grandfather had homesteaded. Many years ago, Mr. Clements and I had spent a leisurely afternoon filled with his crabby opinions (the Ozarks were too crowded to suit him); his crude jokes (most pertained to horny dogs); his contrarian preferences for lunch (he was sick of eating trout); and his unending instructions (damnit, I was holding my thumb the wrong way on my rod).

But at least when I was in Jerry Clements' boat, I'd caught some trout. All Thomas, Dennis, and I were doing was casting and reeling and drifting with the current. It was getting hot, but taking a swim in this frigid water was a no-go. As I poured more water on Bear's head, my mind drifted to what it was like on this river during the era of the steamboats—with their colorful names like the *Randall*, *Tycoon*, and *Quickstep*—when the kids along the shore yelled, "The *Queen*'s a-comin'!" as the *Ozark Queen* chugged upstream, loaded with its 260 passengers. In another era, locals dragged this river for mussels, the shells of which were used to make buttons: forty carloads of mussels made one carload of buttons. I thought too of my grandfather who'd fished this river for smallmouth bass, before the dams were built and the bass all died out when the water temperature dropped dramatically. Like a number of well-to-do flatlanders in eastern Arkansas, my grandfather subsequently bought a summer house on the newly-filled Lake Norfork, forty miles upriver, where I spent summer weekends during my youth.

From the back of our boat, Thomas spotted a bald eagle perched in a tree along the river. The eagle's nest seemed nearly as big as an army cot. The eagle took flight, circled, and finally dove into the shallow water for its prey—a silvery rainbow trout—then flew off with the glistening fish in its talons. As the three of us watched, longingly, Dennis said, "What's for lunch?"

Unfortunately, we'd only brought cold drinks.

With renewed determination to catch a trout, Dennis cast his rod with great effort, yet the weighted lure landed only a few feet from our boat. The lure sounded like a bullet when it entered the water.

"I once saw a man catch the biggest fish I've ever seen on this river right after casting his line straight down into the water, like a retarded cast. Just like that cast I just done." Dennis left his line in the water a long time in hopes of duplicating the fishing miracle he'd just described. "That's what I call it," he said belatedly. "A retarded cast."

We floated by the landing at Mount Olive, the sight of which prompted a story from Dennis about hunting, for he knew Thomas liked to stalk deer and, hey, we certainly weren't catching any fish: "There was a young man from here at Mount Olive who was determined to make a living down here on this river. But it's hard, really hard. One time, he came to my house, and while we were standing in my driveway, he reached into the back of his truck for his rifle and then shot a deer down by my mailbox. I didn't say anything about what he'd done, and finally the young man looked at me and said, 'I'm sorry, Dennis, but we're getting kind of hungry down at my house.'… He's the only guy I ever let shoot anything from my driveway."

I tried to make out Thomas's reaction to Dennis's deer-hunting story. But he was too busy trying to catch a fish to pay it much attention. We all thought we'd have more luck catching trout below Mount Olive. But we didn't. Meanwhile, Dennis carried on:

"Did I ever tell you about the murder that happened up here?"

"No," Thomas said flatly as he flicked sweat off his brow. The midday sun was beating down on us, and he was as frustrated as I was.

"Okay, then I'll tell you," Dennis said. "There was a famous murder up here back in the mid-1900s. A man named Rupert Byler shot and killed the sheriff."

"Rupert Byler?" I said, interrupting. "Is John Byler any kin to him?"

"Can't say…. Anyhow, one night the sheriff and his deputy went out to Rupert's house to arrest him, but before they had a chance to cuff him, Rupert shot the sheriff and fled with his wife. But Rupert might have thought that the sheriff was coming out to his house to kill him. It was rumored that the sheriff had been running a ring that stole cars and that Rupert was doing his dirty work, and the law was closing in on their car-stealing ring. So the sheriff had come out to make sure Rupert kept his mouth shut. It was the awfullest mess. They finally found Rupert and put him in jail."

Thomas and I, upon digesting Dennis's latest story, cut our eyes at one another.

"It's true that the sheriff got shot," Dennis said. "It is! It is!"

"Oh, I believe you," I said half-heartedly.

Later, I read an account of the Rupert Byler murder in a well-regarded history book titled *Arkansas*, by John Gould Fletcher, winner of the Pulitzer Prize for poetry in 1939. The book confirmed the essence of Dennis's story, though Dennis's version was definitely more colorfully told. Fletcher's account of the Byler murder and ensuing manhunt noted how the incident highlighted the provincialism of Ozarkers: how Rupert Byler, a man being hunted by virtually every branch of the law, had hid out for months in caves and barns during the winter of 1946, surviving on wild persimmons, and never even tried to leave Izard County, as if he lacked the will to reach out to a world beyond his own relatives and this rugged land that he knew so well.

With summertime came the unholy trinity of the Ozarks: chiggers, ticks, and snakes. The fierce, nearly invisible chiggers required constant vigilance: patting down with sulfur-laced powder before exposure, spraying with bleach-tinged water afterwards. Any lapse of discipline meant patches of awful bites. The vexing, hot-weather-loving ticks required close inspection of every cranny of the body, then painful removal by a sudden jerk of the tweezers.

Copperheads, however, were more than a mere nuisance. The Gillihans had warned us to watch out for snakes, though the aptly named king snakes were prized because their diet included other poisonous snakes. To me, this was pointless hair-splitting: I had no intention of getting close to any snake, bad or good.

But my intentions didn't matter. When out hiking, I feared being bitten. *What would I do?* I imagined putting a tourniquet on my swollen calf to keep the venom from spreading. How would I induce Bear, who ordinarily would not leave my side, to hurry back to our cabin and tell Susanne to come running with her snakebite kit? I was modestly encouraged by the phenomenon of dry strikes, though the mental terror of any dry strike would be the same as a strike filled with venom.

Despite my dark imaginings, I'd only seen one snake while hiking—actually, one-and-a-half, counting a baby snake.

But one day Dennis's eldest son, Jeff, was laying asphalt with a road crew along Highway 9, not far from our mailbox at Hogback Mountain. Not surprisingly, his crew killed a rattlesnake. Jeff loved snake meat, but before he skinned the viper, he took it down to his father's house and photographed it.

To make the rattler look even larger, Dennis, ever the prankster, draped the snake over a two-by-four and held it towards Jeff's camera. This trick of perspective made the rattler look as large as an anaconda. The photograph was texted to me and soon went viral among family and friends. "That thing could bring down a small fawn," someone commented.

We pledged to never venture into the woods around Hogback Mountain again, except maybe during wintertime when the snakes were dormant. This giant rattler was the third snake killed at our place so far this summer. The second, a copperhead, was under our porch, where we fired upon it with a pistol then summarily beheaded it with a garden hoe. We found yet another copperhead under the tractor-tire rim that served as our fire pit.

We were under siege, it seemed. And we weren't the only ones.

Down at their place, the Gillihans had taken matters into their own hands. One day, Dennis bragged, "We beat you-uns in snakes by two," and then explained that he and Carol had killed five snakes around their house, thereby besting us in the crucial competition of snake killing. Down at the Gillihans', even Bear had gotten involved in the action, signaling trouble by barking in what Dennis called a "funny voice."

To spook me even further, Dennis also told me about his friend who, when walking up his porch steps, was bitten by a copperhead so hard that the snake hung onto his bare leg. "And it's not the first time my friend was bitten," he added with remorse. "The guy just has a hard time with snakes."

I took some slight solace in the fact that because of the fearsome chiggers and ticks I never wore shorts in the first place when I was up at Hogback Mountain.

As it turned out, the best way to quell any concerns about snakes was to fixate on other threats. The famous razorbacks were said to be descendants of hogs brought to the Ozarks by the early Spanish explorers. In the forest, they found plenty of acorns to sustain them and bred prolifically.

Around our part of Izard County, speculation about wild hogs was routine. We heard that boars had been spotted over near Mount Olive, or that someone just two mountains over had killed a pair of baby pigs, or that the mysterious strip of rutted-up ground behind a neighbors' house was evidence of hogs.

One night over dinner on our back deck, David Blankenship bluntly informed me that one of his relatives over in Yell County was gored to death by a six-hundred-pound wild hog and then "had his guts eaten out." The next day, the man's kinfolk killed this huge and aggressive boar. But, obviously, the damage was done.

Despite all this chatter about boars, we never saw a wild hog, not even on the trail camera we'd placed at the back of our mountain. Nor did Bear, on any of our hikes in the woods, ever run upon any pigs (or none that he communicated to me anyway).

However, the lack of a verifiable presence of wild hogs at Hogback Mountain was no cause for us to relax, because tales of mountain lions also circulated. To fuel the general sense of alarm, the *Stone County Citizen* had published a front-page picture of a mountain lion taken on the edge of Mountain View. But this sighting was a secondhand account and therefore one I didn't take seriously.

But one day, when out hiking on Dr. Jackson's property, Ed Alexander told me that while driving on Highway 9 earlier that week, he'd seen a mountain lion stick his head out from the woods. Ed was a man of science (and music and photography and nature and other pursuits), a stick-to-the-facts empiricist hardly inclined to embellish.

"Are you sure it was a mountain lion?" I said.

"Yes. I saw its big head, and it was quite a bit lower to the ground than a deer's head. I know the difference."

"Where was the mountain lion when you saw it?"

He named a location that wasn't far away as the crow flew or, in this case, as the mountain lion walked.

20.

Local Characters of Different Sorts

The early pioneers of the Ozarks cut down too many trees and killed too many critters—deer, beaver, and bear, especially. By the end of World War II, the natural resources were approaching exhaustion. Around this time, the great Ozarks exodus began, with people leaving for better opportunities.

Now though, into the twenty-first century—when it came to the environment—trends were going the other way. The conservation movement, combined with the relatively sparse population in the Ozarks, as well as modern timber management techniques, had rejuvenated the land. The woods teemed with deer and other wild game, and trees were everywhere. Standing high on any ridge in our part of Izard County, I saw, in every direction, mostly pristine green hills.

This is not to say that the Ozarks were now an environmental paradise. The proclivities of the local populace set the ecological tone, and even triumphs like the designation of the Buffalo River as a National River in 1972 had its roots in a leave-us-alone attitude. The people who saved the Buffalo River, including Sam Walton of Walmart, saw how the White River had been tamed when the federal government built dams for hydroelectric power in the 1940s.

Up here in these hinterlands, property owners can pretty much do as they please. Want to burn some trash, including plastic? Go ahead and fire up a burn barrel. Want to cut down your timber and sell it off? Crank up your chainsaw. Want to clear a pasture or create an unobstructed mountaintop view? Start up your bulldozer. Want a new house? Go for it, because not much in the way of permitting is required. Want to build something totally out of character with your surroundings? Don't worry, because there are hardly any building codes.

The intrusive environmental oversight so stifling in places like California has blessedly not taken root here. Ozarkers are pretty much left alone, which is a good thing in general, though this can promote a certain nonchalance towards the environment, for sure.

Randy Sullivan was a vulpine, fidgety fellow who worked at Jack's Fishing Resort on the White River. Thomas and I had come down to the resort's boat dock seeking help: we'd poured bad gas from an old can in our barn into the tank of my father-in-law's fishing boat, and now it had to be flushed out before the motor would start. If it would start at all. Could Randy assist us? Pretty please? He was known to be the resident expert on boat motors.

As Randy darted around the dock helping his customers, he stopped long enough to say over his shoulder, "I'm kind of busy right now, youknowmean," this last run-on phrase seemingly his way of saying, "Do you know what I mean?" really fast.

It was late afternoon, and most of the rental boats had been returned to their slips. On the dock, fishermen gutted their trout—rainbow, cutthroat, brook, and brown—and packed them on ice. Thomas and I hung around and watched the river flow by. What else could we do? It took about five hours for water released from the upriver dams at Bull Shoals and Norfork to reach this far downriver. The water's rise comes imperceptibly and then recedes in a rhythm mostly determined by the demands for electrical power throughout the White River Valley, which peaks in summertime.

I tried to keep tabs on Randy as he scurried around. He was generally ignoring us, making it clear that he didn't have time for our problem, whatever it was. But as the luck of the Irish would have it, Randy's last name and my wife's maiden name were the same. Perhaps they were related, I loudly suggested as he hustled by us one more time. Somehow, for some reason, this most tenuous of familial connections softened him up.

"I have some cousins in the area, youknowmean," Randy said as he finally slowed down. "You never know, youknowmean?"

I eagerly nodded, then looked sideways at Thomas, who wouldn't make eye contact with me. Like me, he was trying to keep from busting out laughing at Randy's distracting verbal tic.

Soon, Randy led us up the riverbank to take a look at my father-in-law's boat. Indeed, the gas was bad, he readily confirmed after a few vigorous cranks of the motor.

"We've got to get rid of this, youknowmean," he said, pointing accusingly at the red, five-gallon gas tank in the floor of the boat. "But we can't do it around here, youknowmean."

The furtive decisiveness with which Randy had hatched his plan to get rid of our bad gas suggested that he had a holding barrel of some sort nearby—a suitable place to deal with the bad gas mistake that Thomas and I had made, which surely happened to other boaters and fishermen on a regular basis. There was a restaurant just up the cobblestone path. Perhaps the holding barrel for bad gas to which Randy was referring was somewhere up there.

He unhooked the fuel line, grabbed our red gas tank, and headed towards a utility vehicle parked nearby.

"Stay here with the boat," I said to Thomas. Because Randy had so firmly taken ownership of our bad-gas problem, I felt obliged to go with him to assist in any way possible, especially since I was no doubt going to need his help to get the boat's motor running after we refilled our gas tank with good gas.

As Randy and I drove along with the offending tank of bad gas in the back of the utility vehicle, he explained to me that gas of any type was not be dumped near the river. This sounded quite reasonable and even admirably conscientious. Who wanted to muck up the clear waters of what the French explorers called the Rivière Blanc? But this nattering statewide regulation, or boat dock policy, or mere noble sentiment in Randy's noble heart—whatever it was he'd just expressed—was not enough to deter him from what he now had in his mind to do.

We headed up a dirt path, back towards the tree line and not too far off the river.

"We're going to dump this gas back yonder, youknowmean," Randy said archly, as if we suddenly had a dead body on our hands.

We drove around a bend, past a stand of tall trees, gathering speed. The grass was almost waist high back here and if perchance we hit a hidden stump or a big rock, both of us would be thrown through the windshield of the utility vehicle—had there been a windshield at all.

Randy slowed to a stop, thank heavens, and then he took out the red tank full of foul gas. I looked behind us to make sure no fishermen floating by on the river saw what we were up to. Fortunately, the coast was clear. By the time I turned around, Randy was pouring the bad gasoline into the high grass. He gripped the red tank with both hands, turned it upside down, and shook it several times to make sure every last drop was emptied out.

As we sped back in our utility vehicle to my sickly boat, it occurred to me that in a stridently green state like California, what Randy and I had just done could probably have landed both of us in jail.

On a hot Saturday afternoon, Susanne and I ran into friends at Woods Old Time Soda Fountain in Mountain View. We were there for vanilla ice cream and fresh-squeezed limeades, while our friends, Margaret and Jay McEntire, a couple my parents' age, had just finished their BLT sandwiches. Jay was a businessman, oilman, geologist, and all-around renaissance fellow—I'd attended college with his son—and Margaret had recently sold her successful nationwide franchise. She was a striking blond and, though in her sunset years, full of energetic hospitality.

Soon, at their invitation, we were off to the McEntires' house down on the White River. They wanted to show it off, and with good reason: their sprawling manse sat on a highly desirable two-acre riverfront lot that probably cost more than the entire 123 acres of ridge land that we owned up at Hogback Mountain. Their place was in White River Estates, the closest thing Izard County had to any kind of upscale housing development.

"Solubria?" I said as I eyeballed the word carved into the house's massive front door.

"It means *healthy living* in Greek," Margaret explained as we went in.

Solubria was actually two houses, one with a long balcony that overlooked the river. It had a great room worthy of the name, plus numerous bedrooms for grandkids. Outside was a fireplace built into a wall of river stones: it was so well done that I took a picture of it. Margaret had combed the Ozarks for the finest in furniture and accents. Her taste was impeccable. The collection of rare arrowheads in handsome glass displays was a passion of Jay's. I coveted his high-windowed study that looked out onto their gently-sloping back lawn.

All in all, Solubria was a house that's built after one's dreams come true. This older couple was living a very enviable retirement life (recent trips to Cuba and, in their Mercedes Benz mobile home, to Marfa, Texas) and I was certainly in no hurry to leave their place. Homes down here along the White River had a different vibe—more stately and well-rounded than most of the cabins like ours up in the hills. Perhaps the McEntires would invite us to spend the afternoon trout fishing, followed by cocktails and a fine dinner on their deck overlooking the river with waters so cool that it was like nature's air conditioning.

To return the hospitality we'd so generously been shown, Susanne, at some point, said, "We'd love for you to come see our cabin sometime," and before I knew it, the four of us were headed, in our respective cars, up to Hogback Mountain.

On the drive up the dragon's tail of Highway 9, Susanne and I wondered what exactly we'd show our visitors when we got to our place. A tour of our small cabin would take five to ten minutes, at most. It was too hot, too snaky, too chiggery, too ticky to take the McEntires on a hike in the woods, and it was too early in the afternoon to offer them strong drink.

When we got to our cabin, I led our group straight around to the back deck to admire the view of Dark Hollow and the surrounding mountains. This was easily the best facet of our place. As we drank iced tea, I regaled the McEntires with the prospect of fun activities that lay just ahead.

"Come back in the fall and I will show you our waterfalls and our cave. They're just magnificent."

"Oh sure, we'd love to see all of it."

"Or maybe you could come up one night soon for a movie. Did I tell you about our cave cinema?"

"A cave cinema!" Margaret said, bright-faced. "Wow! We've never watched a movie in a cave."

"Well, we haven't either, yet," I said. "But we're going to do it before the summer's over, we promise. We'll be sure to call you when we do."

All of this conversation took place over the drone of our window-unit air conditioner as condensation from the upstairs unit dripped, dripped, dripped on the tin roof of our porch. It was so hot that Bear didn't even want to come out on the deck. He just looked at us through the sliding glass door like we were dupes for being outside.

"We're land rich and cabin poor," I said, summing up for Jay our obvious predicament at Hogback Mountain. This hardly needed to be said.

Finally, the heat forced us to retreat inside and, like a son showing his high-living parents around his first house, I gave the McEntires a quick tour of our cabin. When we got up to our second floor, I felt bad that they'd had to climb the stairs.

"You should've seen this place when we first bought it," I said in a lame attempt to justify their exertions. "You'd have fallen right through the staircase, and since the walls were only half-finished, wasps were everywhere."

"Oh, my!" Margaret said as if she had any reason to care.

"Yeah, it was a mess, you wouldn't believe it…" my voice trailed off.

After the McEntires rather hurriedly left to return to the comforts of Solubria, I poured myself another iced tea, sat down at our dining table, and said to Susanne, "Wasn't that an interesting way to spend a hot Saturday afternoon? I doubt we'll ever see those two up here again."

Susanne would hear none of it: "Oh, Margaret told me that our cabin has more character and charm than her big fine house."

"She did, huh? Then maybe she'll trade houses with us. I'll ask Jay about it the next time I run into him down at the soda fountain—I'm sure he'll jump on the idea of a swap. Maybe he'll throw in their Mercedes Benz motor home too?"

"Oh, what we have here is magic. Anybody can see that."

"I guess."

Susanne and I often differed on how to decorate our cabin, but thereafter, whenever we produced even a small triumph of interior design or architecture—even one as minor as hiring a workman to put in a rock-and-mortar stoop at the bottom of our front steps—I danced a little jig and, in mock defiance, said, "Eat my dust, Solubria!" In our never-ending efforts to better our decent little ole cabin up at Hogback Mountain, this became my rallying cry—though there weren't many occasions to invoke it, and even when I did, my wife just rolled her eyes at my petty harrumphing.

As we further refined our cabin (as much as possible), we asked Ben Harvey, our go-to furniture maker, to do some work for us. It was a minor miracle that he agreed, given his well-established reluctance to leave his property, only seven miles away.

On a Sunday morning, Ben drove up to Hogback Mountain and, predictably, the first thing he said to me was that he had to get back home by noon. I reckon he just never knew when someone traveling along Highway 9 would see his hand-painted wooden sign—INSIDE AND OUTSIDE FURNITURE SOLD HERE—and pull into his driveway to place a big order.

Ben came inside our cabin and took careful measurements for the shelves he was to build for our kitchen cabinets. For a sixty-year-old he was dressed rather youthfully in cargo shorts and a sleeveless T-shirt that showed off his tan, wrinkled biceps. His near-perfect teeth were so white they looked bleached.

Back out in our driveway, Ben set up his sawhorses and went to work, busily, efficiently. This job was to be quick if he had anything to do with it. Later, back at his shop, he'd build the doors for our cabinets, as well as a new credenza for our bedroom. While he fashioned our kitchen shelves from planks of wood stacked in the back of his Chevy truck, I sat on the porch in a rocking chair and tried to carry on a conversation.

"I hate to travel," Ben said as he sawed, head down, peering through his thick-lensed eyeglasses.

"It's not for everybody, for sure."

"I just wasn't made to travel."

So how did this Yankee homebody from Illinois wind up in Izard County? Well, years earlier, he'd visited his sister-in-law in nearby Calico Rock and eventually bought some land near Melbourne from the same realtor from whom I'd earlier bought the thirty-six-acre parcel that adjoined the Gillihans to our east.

Not surprisingly, these days Ben wasn't too fond of visiting his sister-in-law up at Calico Rock. "At her place the dogs and cats just come and go as they please," he complained.

"Hmm," I said, feeling a bit embarrassed. Bear had been coming in and out of our cabin, scratching at the front door when it suited him, following me around like, well, a puppy dog. "Nice weather, huh?" I said.

"My wife was chilly last night," Ben replied. "She's cold natured."

I considered this to be quite persuasive. Although it was mid-July, the temperature had dropped to a near-record low of sixty-one degrees. I'd found this heavenly. Such weather was about as good as it gets during the summertime in Arkansas.

"After we moved here to the Ozarks, my wife suggested that maybe we didn't move far enough south," he said. "But I told her that if we moved further south, we had to account for the hurricanes."

"That's true."

"I never go back to Illinois unless somebody dies."

This I was hardly surprised to hear.

While Ben worked away on our cabinet shelves, I took the opportunity to suggest a more ambitious project. Granted, he'd pooh-poohed my earlier idea to build a human nest, but a week or so ago I'd watched a television show about how to build tree houses, so I explained to Ben what I had in mind, which was a really cool tree house. More like a house up in a tree. Finally, I stopped my gushing—I sounded like an infatuated Cub Scout.

"Do you think you could build something like that up here at my place?" I said hopefully.

Ben stopped his sawing, his eyes still on where he'd been cutting with his saw. I took this as a positive sign. But as his pause lingered, I realized that he was struggling not so much with practicalities of executing my idea for a house in the trees—this was relatively easy for a skilled craftsman like him. Rather he was wrestling with the notion of having to be away from his property for any length of time.

"Could you just make prefab sections at your shop?" I offered. "That's how they built the tree house that I saw on the TV show. They just trucked the sections in. It looked pretty easy to assemble it on site."

"I don't think I could do that," Ben said, finally looking up at me. "My shop's not big enough."

Disappointed, I stared off in the direction of Brandenburg Mountain and rubbed Bear's head. A few minutes later, I asked Ben if perhaps he could make a wooden door for us to replace the cheap-looking metal one that presently graced our entryway. "Wouldn't a wooden door look nice here?" I mused aloud.

"I've never made a door," Ben said.

I was curious. Was it was just me who had a hard time relating to Ben? Perhaps he just didn't cotton to an over-educated flatlander with goofy ideas like human nests and houses built up in trees. So I said, "Have you got many friends around here? You met many people?"

"I just meet people who drop by my shop. I don't get out much."

"How much time do you spend on your woodworking?"

"I just work awhile in my shop and then go up to the house and have some coffee or tea with my wife."

One of Ben's daughters resided in the next county over, and another daughter lived on his property. His son lived out near Death Valley, California, and apparently this offspring of Ben's had inherited his mother's sensitivity to ambient temperature. "My son came here once," Ben noted. "And he complained when it got below eighty-five degrees, and then he complained when it got above ninety-five degrees. He tells me that since I'm retired I should come out there to see him."

Somehow, the strong bonds of parentage notwithstanding, I could not imagine that a trip out to Death Valley was in Ben's future.

I continued to rub Bear's head. He always napped in a state of vigilance, his head typically resting on his buckshotty-colored paws and ever alert to any movements, especially mine. There was not much left for Ben and me to discuss—not that I could think of, anyway—so I turned on some music and called out from the porch, "Do you like Frank Sinatra?"

"I just listen to country," Ben replied without looking up from his sawing. "But it don't matter."

Over these last months, Susanne and I had done so much business with Ben Harvey—numerous Adirondack chairs, our deluxe chicken coop, pole bean towers for her garden, kitchen cabinets, a credenza—that whenever we passed by his place, we joked that he was up there in his house atop his hill, drinking coffee with his wife, living high on our money.

Each weekend, to reach Hogback Mountain, we drove west from the flatlands, tracing the paths of the early pioneers, who'd followed trails the Indians left behind. This two-lane highway was crooked and mostly empty. We traveled for miles without seeing another vehicle and, as we sped along, Susanne said, "These have been the best days of my life."

Despite my obvious awkwardness up in Ozarklandia, I felt the same way. We had finished the hard but rewarding work of making Hogback Mountain reasonably comfortable, and in doing so we'd learned a lot about ourselves and each other: the joy of discovery is not to be underestimated. We'd had a lot of fun so far too, and it only promised to get better as time went on. This weekend, we had big plans, beginning with dinner that night with friends out on our deck. We were antsy to get there.

However, somewhere on this highway into the Ozarks, in the no-man's land between Flat Creek and the Strawberry River, we noticed our SUV was running on empty. *How can this happen?*

We stopped at a red brick house that somewhat resembled a small-town fire station. But no one answered our insistent knocks at the front door. There was a can of gas out in the garage—maybe enough fuel to get us to the nearest gas station, some twenty miles ahead in Cave City. But the gas in the can was diesel. *What now?*

The idea of hitchhiking to Cave City—and back—in this searing heat was discouraging. Moreover, beyond Cave City, it was another fifty or so hard miles to Hogback Mountain. In just a few hours, our neighbors were coming over to drink rosé wine and eat barbecue chicken wings, as well as the homegrown tomatoes and watermelons we planned to buy at a produce stand when we passed through Cave City.

Desperate, just up the highway we stopped at another house where an older man answered the door. He said his name was Darryl, and he wore only gray gym shorts and white terry-cloth slippers, each adorned with a little red Razorback logo.

I introduced myself, then, to set him at ease, I looked him squarely in the eye and said, "You know, I'm a Razorback fan too."

This, it seemed, was all Darryl needed to hear. In a welcome show of modesty, he put on a shirt; he was fairly fit for a sixty-five-year-old living in the middle of nowhere. In his garage, he found a five-gallon plastic jug that was half-full of unleaded gas. Under his watchful supervision, I poured the fuel into our vehicle.

"It fills faster if you undo the top latch of the jug," he said over my shoulder. "It lets it breathe."

Darryl had likely inferred from my khaki slacks, fancy loafers, and button-down shirt that I was not from around here, though by now my mind had drifted to how exactly I was going to get our SUV out of his driveway. We had a trailer hitched to our vehicle, and I wasn't comfortable backing it up. In fact, backing up a trailer was among my worst nightmares. I'd jackknifed ours a few weeks ago while turning around our SUV; it seems I'd somehow forgotten that I was pulling a trailer at all. At this particular moment, I sensed the following was about to happen: I was going to try to back out of Darryl's driveway and then, frustrated with my ineptitude, Susanne would order me out of the driver's seat of our SUV and back out the trailer herself.

I got into our SUV, turned to look behind me, and then from the kindness of his Razorback-loving heart Darryl said through the open window of my vehicle, "You can drive around this way." He helpfully motioned with his hands, as if directing traffic. "Just drive straight ahead across my front yard if you have to," he added. "It's mostly just rock anyway."

I barely managed to miss the chain-link fence stretched across Darryl's front lawn. I had no idea who—or what—he was trying to keep out with this fence. There was hardly anybody living anywhere along this stretch of highway through the eastern edge of the Ozarks.

Before we left, I wanted to pay Darryl something for his gasoline and for his hospitality, and he accepted my twenty-dollar bill with such eagerness that for an instant I felt I should hand him another one.

After we got back on the highway, Susanne looked over at me and again said, "How in the world did we manage to run out of gas?"

"Well, I guess we got so excited talking about our weekend plans. Believe me, it won't happen again back here on this desolate road, of all places."

"What was that man's last name? He was a nice man."

"I never even thought to ask him," I said. "All I know is that Darryl is a great American."

Seldom had we beheld a sight as welcome as the gas station fifteen miles up the road in Cave City.

After filling up, we headed to a roadside produce stand. It was on the front lawn of a run-down house with a dusty old pale-green Impala parked in the garage. I assumed a little old lady lived in the house—it looked like such a place—even though the produce stand was always unattended and we'd never seen anyone in the garden behind the house.

The tomatoes here were always fleshy and full of flavor—real Arkansas tomatoes, as we called them. But the true prize was the watermelons stacked two-high like rounded sandbags, each bearing a trademarked Cave City certification, like a bottle of French wine that bears a note of its appellation, the specific *terroir* from which it originates.

Cave City watermelons are famous throughout Arkansas. I had heard about them for years, though until recently I had only a vague idea of where Cave City was. It is basically a forlorn little town on the highway between Batesville and Hardy, not exactly a compelling destination from either direction. Cave City watermelons are easily the best I've ever tasted, never mealy and full of sweet flavor, which the locals attribute to the rocky soil.

Susanne and I paid for our watermelon and tomatoes and, for encouragement, left a little extra cash in the honor box. We were all stocked up for our dinner party in the hills, if only we could get there in time. We got into our SUV and stepped on the gas pedal. And why not? We had a tank full of gas, and this area of the Ozarks was so remote that there were never any cops back here anyway—they'd have to be lost to wind up back here.

At Hogback Mountain, our back deck overlooking Dark Hollow had become a gathering place for our friends in Lower Izard County. Susanne and I had unwittingly become local matchmakers, mixing friends like the down-to-earth Gillihans with retired professionals like the Alexanders with multi-talented longtime Ozarkers like the Blankenships, our fellow catastrophists who owned a picturesque farm over at Mount Olive.

In the twilight, we all gathered around our communal table while I served drinks in my new white plastic cups with the Hogback Mountain logo emblazoned on them, my latest attempt to brand our retreat, to make the name stick. The heat broke around sunset, and when our dinner of chicken wings, potato salad, tomatoes, and watermelon was finished, we poured more rosé wine as David Blankenship and his daughters pulled out their guitars.

Jennifer Blankenship, the mother, was a descendent of the Jeffery family, among the first settlers to the area, and the entire Blankenship family, while quintessentially Ozarkian in many respects, also served as an impressive counterpoint to every long-standing stereotype of Ozark backwardness and provinciality imaginable: Jennifer, a pharmacist, had just returned from another of her medical missions to Peru; Megan, their daughter, had recently visited London, Bath, and Wales, and was presently dating a Brit whose father was a lifelong Maoist, if such a thing were still possible. Annie, their other daughter with her fiancé in tow, studied anthropology and aspired to be a folk singer. The family was joyously religious, yet they drank wine and beer. They were conservative yet didn't watch Fox News or any television at all for that matter—David, the father, who'd lived in Panama while in the army, had grown up without TV at his father's insistence.

Under the glow of the tiki torches ringing our deck, the Blankenship daughters sang ballads by Gillian Welch, Hank Williams, and the Avett Brothers. Annie, wearing her hippyish headband, crooned and swayed, while Megan, a poet, strummed her guitar. The two of them looked like Joan Baez, with nearly the talent to match. David played backup guitar and sang too. Our guests were rapt. Encores were called for.

It was another glorious evening at Hogback Mountain and certainly worth the various obstacles Susanne and I had overcome in order to get there.

21.

Meetup of a Mountain Clan

At the front door of the Twin Creek Church of Christ, my wife and I signed the logbook for the annual Twin Creek reunion. We were the last to arrive, fashionably late amongst a group who considered tardiness a sign of bad character. We'd come at the invitation of Dennis Gillihan. Susanne and I were otherwise faux Twin Creekers, our only connection to the little hamlet—other than our burgeoning love and affection for Dennis and his wife Carol—was that we lived on a mountaintop between the two creeks (East Twin and West Twin).

Attendance this year was dampened by the hot August weather. Still, the conversation inside the narrow, low-ceilinged room was loud. "It's good to come to these reunions because you find out what's really going on," Dennis said with the relish of a gossip-loving housewife.

Certainly, it was easier to be in the know if you were somehow related to the Gillihans. Dennis introduced us to a woman named Jimmalene, who with pride noted that of the seventy-four people in attendance, she was somehow kin to all but eight of them. Her count, I presumed, included my wife and me. For the first time I met Dennis's mother, who shook my hand, caressed it, then, like I was her long lost son just home from a war, raised my hand to her lips and kissed it.

"Come see me," she said softly. "I live in Melbourne, near Roger, my eldest son. Have you met him?"

"Oh, yes ma'am, I know Roger." I waved at Roger.

Dennis and Roger grew up in nearby Melbourne, but as soon as Dennis could afford it, he bought land at Twin Creek, where their father was born, and where the three Gillihan brothers, the original settlers, had stopped on their migration from Tennessee back in the 1840s. The brothers' affection for this remote part of Izard County had been passed down to their descendants, now sprinkled like pixie dust over the surrounding hills and hollows. Dennis's eldest son, Jeff, lived over at Mount Pleasant—some thirty miles away—but, in anticipation of his eventual move back home someday, he'd named his metalworking business Twin Creek Ironworks.

Dennis ushered me over to a well-dressed, older gentleman from Springfield, Missouri, who, he declared, once owned ten manufacturing companies and employed more than a thousand people. Dennis showed off his prosperous kin as if the man was Warren Buffett himself.

My eye was drawn to an older lady who wore an Arkansas Razorbacks blouse. We chitchatted about the upcoming football season: she was surprisingly knowledgeable, and of course, her last name was Gillihan. Another lady—Elizabeth Gillihan, Dennis's sister-in-law—told my wife and me that her father was once asked if he was a Gillihan and he'd answered, "No, but I wish I was."

All of us laughed knowingly.

Finally, Dennis introduced me to someone who wasn't related to him: an older, red-nosed, barrel-chested man. "Here's Samuel Durm, the fella that invented the machine that exchanges dollar bills into coins." He spoke as if the man had outdone Thomas Edison himself.

I felt obliged to shake the old man's hand. "You mean you invented those coin machines like the ones they have in laundromats and arcades?"

"My, that coin machine was a long time ago," Samuel Durm noted, less than impressed with his invention than Dennis was. The man's cap bore a Texas A&M logo, so I asked if he went to school there, but he told me he'd studied at the University of Arkansas.

Such sideways answers are typical up in the Ozarks, where appearances often deceive. Things aren't always what they seem; people not only don't put on airs, they typically downplay any worldly success they have achieved. There is no such thing as a flashy, braggart hillsman. Not long ago, I'd told Dennis about a poor old woman I'd seen stranded alongside Highway 9, and after I described what her old broken-down car looked like, Dennis shook his head at my presumption of pity and told me that the lady was one of the largest landowners along Greasy Bottom, a beautiful stretch that bordered the White River.

I was getting hungry. The big room smelled of all kinds of food. There was a buffet of chicken casserole, macaroni, green beans, potatoes, pot roast, pulled pork, hot dogs, meatballs, fried okra, fruit salad, and three kinds of slaw, bread, banana peppers, tomatoes, and broccoli: the buffet was seemingly endless. Desserts included pound cakes in flavors of orange and vanilla, lemon icebox pie, and a chocolate tunnel cake. All of this was the typical hearty, straightforward fare that mountain people preferred, and most of the dishes confirmed the reputation of Ozark women as average-at-best cooks. Indeed, among innovative chefs and trend-seeking food lovers across America, there is no such thing as an Ozarks cuisine per se, an anomaly many attribute to the distrust of outsiders and the poverty so prevalent in these hills.

As we sat at one of the communal tables, I overheard Dennis tell someone about how he'd learned to fly an airplane and about his dicey landings on crude, grass airstrips. His talk of his ad-hoc piloting evoked the scene in the movie *Out of Africa* when Karen Blixen climbs into Denys Finch Hatton's two-seater biplane and asks him when he'd learned to fly, and he says, "Yesterday."

Dennis quit talking long enough to pass me the salt, and then he looked down and studied his plate: there was a yellow jacket in his potato salad. "He's just trying to make a living," he said of the mayonnaise-coated bee as he gently moved it aside with his fork. When a stocky man walked by, Dennis leaned over and said, "That fella just moved back to Twin Creek. He's an engineer of some sort. He doesn't do any kind of physical labor."

I winced. Dennis had hit upon a crucial distinction that hill folk make between those who do physical work and those, like me, who do knowledge or managerial work. The former is virtuous and highly valued, while the latter is seen as a sign of over-education and softness.

Someone took up a microphone and awarded plaques to the couple who'd been married the longest (fifty-six years); to the oldest person in attendance (almost eighty-four); to the youngest person (an eight month-old infant). To close the reunion, a raffle was held, and as a fellow named Jim Hainey walked to the front to accept his prize, Dennis informed me that Jim had the same double vision in one eye that he sometimes suffered due to his diabetes—the difference being that Jim's ongoing eye trouble was because a bull had once kicked him in the head.

As the afternoon progressed, Dennis held forth at our table about his memories of his family and of this little hamlet he so treasured—a place hardly anyone beyond those gathered at this reunion gave two hoots about: "My granddad lived in a house just down the road here at Twin Creek," Dennis recalled fondly. "At his kitchen table, I ate many a helping of speckled gravy. That's an old-timer's gravy. I just loved it!"

After we left the reunion, Susanne and I once again spoke of how fortunate we were to have bought a cabin next to the Gillihans, proverbial good people in every sense of the word. Thanks to our good luck, we felt as if we'd become honorary members of a truly unique mountain clan.

22.

Drama at the Cave Cinema

It was another hot, muggy August night—perfect weather for our second movie down at Sandy Wallow Cave, where deep inside it got down to fifty-eight degrees. The weekend before, we'd christened our cave cinema with a movie called *Take Shelter* in which the main character has premonitions of a coming cataclysmic storm but doesn't know if he's prescient or delusional. He frets his plight is inherited—his mother was a paranoid schizophrenic. Here, in the land of preppers, such a fraught, apocalyptic story line seemed somehow fitting.

Now, after our soft opening with only a few people in attendance, we were ready for our well-attended grand opening.

Our invitations to our neighbors went like this:
 Would you like to come over Saturday night and
 watch a movie down in our cave?
 Say what?!
 We're going to watch a movie down in our cave.
 A movie down in a cave?
 That's right, and we're having a picnic dinner down
 there too. Come on, it'll be fun.
 I'll be there! Now, what time?

For Susanne and me, it wasn't so easy to arrange for dinner and a movie in a cave. My job was to set up the movie projector, speakers, our gas-powered generator connected to several long extension cords, and a six-foot wide inflatable movie screen. Susanne prepared grilled chicken, cole slaw, pasta salad, even popcorn. We iced down wine and beer and soft drinks. It took most of the afternoon to make all the preparations, and then, just before show time, lug all the food and drink and equipment down to the cave.

Our guests arrived well before dark, parking along the highway. There was an easily navigable footpath that dropped down into a crease between big limestone rocks. Into the gentle slope that began at the mouth of the cave, I had arranged fifteen Adirondack chairs in a kind of stadium-style seating. Susanne placed the food on a red-checkered tablecloth covering one of the many earthen mounds. The only thing Sandy Wallow Cave Cinema lacked was ushers. I'd even rigged up several spotlights to shine into the low-arched recess at the back of the cave: it was like Jonah peering into the throat of a whale.

Our guests were appreciative. David Blankenship, our fellow prepper from Mount Olive, walked towards the spotlights in the rear of the cave and in wonderment, said, "Wow, brother, now this is great!"

Another guest, a twelve-year-old boy, found my shovel and dug deeper into one of the pothole bunkers.

"What's down here?" he said, full of insistent curiosity.

"Who knows?" I said. "There might be a prehistoric animal underneath us."

The boy dug further into the brown sand, but all he found was a few rocks. "If I keep on digging, what will I find?"

I had no good answer for him.

An hour before dark, we started the evening's movie, *Legends of the Fall*. I was tickled with the atmosphere, at what we'd created inside our cave. The cinema had come off even better than I'd imagined months earlier when we'd first bought the cave. The overall effect was very close to magical.

Fifteen minutes into the film, one of our moviegoers leaned over towards me and said, "I can't believe I'm in a cave," as he looked around in amazement. "I get caught up in the movie and then I have to remind myself of where I am."

I looked back: Dennis was not in his seat. He was standing outside the mouth of the cave, just beyond the flames of the tiki torches, whispering to his wife. I went to see him, picking my way through the crowd.

"Are you enjoying the movie?"

"I heard something." He motioned upward with a flick of his head. "Some noise, like a thud. I'm going up on the highway to look around."

I returned to my front-row seat and tried to focus on the movie. Ten minutes later, I looked back and again saw Dennis standing outside the mouth of the cave, talking to his wife. I was reluctant to get up from my seat again—I was distracting the others—but I got up anyway.

"You and your guests might want to come up to the highway," Dennis said quietly yet firmly. "There's been a wreck up there. It's right above us."

I returned to the cave, turned down the volume on the movie, and announced the news to the other guests. We all began to make our way up the steep trail.

It was not a pretty sight out on Highway 9. One of the Harley-Davidson riders—amongst a group of four—had wiped out in the curve. Near his wrecked bike, he lay on the ground and moaned, while his fellow riders tried to figure out what to do. On the pavement was a trail of skid marks and spots of blood. From what I soon gathered, the wreck had been caused when two of the bike riders somehow bumped into one another.

Susanne, a nurse practitioner, took over, attempting to comfort the fallen biker. His name was Pete, and he was skinned up pretty badly and had a head wound. His breathing was labored, halting. Susanne tried to talk to him and stabilize him.

The rest of us moviegoers diverted any oncoming traffic and stood around helplessly. An ambulance had been called, of course. While we waited in the twilight, I watched as one of the Harley drivers rode his bike a little further down the road, where he dispensed with several beer cans that he'd stashed away in his saddlebags.

As we all gathered around Pete, the fallen biker, Susanne looked up. "This is serious," she said to us. "You breathe like this when you're about to die."

The police arrived first—they'd traveled from Mountain Home, fifty miles away. Ten minutes later, the ambulance showed up. Clearly, the emergency services in Izard County weren't very prompt. This was one of the worst places to have an accident of any consequence.

It took four of us to lift Pete into the ambulance. He weighed almost three hundred pounds. I worried that the stretcher was about to break.

"You can't take pictures of my patients!" the driver barked at Dennis just before she shut the back door to the ambulance. "That's illegal! I won't have it!"

Chastened, Dennis retreated. He'd only brought along his small camera—the one he'd not so long ago bought at the so-called Potato Chip Auction—to take photographs of the grand opening of our cave cinema. As Dennis backed away, I came over and put my hand on his shoulder to console him, whereupon he smiled mischievously and with a knowing nod, said, "I'd have made a good newspaper reporter."

Though I confessed this to no one, I had a sinking feeling that somehow—with my zany idea to show a movie down in our cave—I'd played a part in Pete's wreck. There was little doubt in my mind that the pack of motorcyclists, as they rounded the switchback turn, had been surprised to see eight cars parked alongside the otherwise remote and deserted roadside. When rounding a curve on a motorcycle, even an instant of distraction can be fatal. Poor Pete. Think of it: that cave—Sandy Wallow Cave—had been there for millions of years, and he'd chanced to drive by it on a motorcycle on the one night that a large group of people had driven their cars over to the cave to watch a movie, of all things. Of course Pete had certainly not helped himself by riding too close to his fellow motorcyclists, not wearing a helmet, and, probably, having drank a few beers. But still...

For days, we followed the news about Pete in the local newspaper and on the ten o'clock news. I was hopeful he'd pull through and perhaps one day even be well enough to come to our cave to watch a movie, if he was so inclined—to be our guest of honor. But about a week after his accident, we learned he had died.

Even with this tragedy on the night of our grand opening, our Sandy Wallow Cave Cinema went on. It was our hot weather sanctuary, with a movie season that ran from mid-July until the end of August, when the college football season started—a stretch when it was otherwise difficult to escape the summer heat in northern Arkansas.

23.

Among the Arts and Crafts Gentry

After wandering along several gravel roads in the darkness for half an hour, we finally found Freda Cruse Phillips's house down on the White River. Freda was spry for her autumnal age, and with her blond hair and lively blue eyes she exuded a free-spirited, bohemian air. Among her past adventures, Freda had left Mountain View at seventeen to attend college in San Diego, where she eventually worked for Richard Avedon, the famous fashion photographer.

It's been said that the Ozarks area does not have a historian, but don't tell Freda, who self-published a series of books called *The Vanishing Ozarks*. I admired Freda's moxie—she'd circumvented any and all academic and commercial gatekeepers and gone straight to her readers. Her books—mostly chronicles and interviews of local people—were sold at places like Anglers White River Resort, where we sometimes bought gas and bags of ice.

Freda led us to her well-stocked kitchen table, where we nibbled on cheese dip and fresh veggies and honey-baked ham. Her guests this night were mostly members of the local arts and crafts community, folks whose work Susanne and I admired even though we didn't know them well. Even so, they served as an inspiration to us. Our life at Hogback

Mountain had assumed enough genteel trappings for us to ponder taking up a craft. Thus far, however, all we'd done that could be considered remotely creative was to decorate our cabin, conjure up names for hiking trails, and spray paint some wrought-iron furniture. By contrast, the folks here at Freda's house were dedicated craftspeople: potters, nature photographers, oil painters, candle makers, woodworkers, and welders of metal art.

Up in the Ozarks, class distinctions don't hold much sway. There's just not much class to distinguish. Not many folks have serious money—much less old money—and those who are wealthy, like the Walton family of Walmart, aren't begrudged because they somehow retain their common touch and don't put on airs. Nevertheless, among Ozarkers, one not-so-subtle distinction—at least over here in Stone County—was between those who belonged to the arts and crafts gentry and those who do not. Craftspeople were considered bulwarks against the flattening homogeneity of modern culture, and the crafters up here worked hard to perfect and promote their trades. Locally, the epicenter of this effort was the Arkansas Crafts Guild in Mountain View, and its undisputed leader was Becki Dahlstedt.

Right away, I detected this intense, silver-haired woman wasn't a native of the Ozarks, though I was surprised to learn that she hailed from Berkeley, California. It was as if Dennis Gillihan had just informed me that in his youth, he'd hung out on the streets of Haight Ashbury.

Becki, like our host Freda, was a sparked character: long interested in pottery making, after a stint as a Berkeley city planner, she'd moved to the Ozarks and married David Dahlstedt, already well-established as a regional potter. Their pottery was sold at such high-minded places as the Historic Arkansas Museum down in Little Rock.

I asked Becki what her proudest accomplishment as a city planner had been, and without hesitation she said it was providing handicap access throughout Berkeley. One suspects the town's merchants didn't have much choice but to go along with what Becki thought was best for them. Nowadays, she was the driving force behind the Off the

Beaten Path Tour, a popular, self-guided fall event featuring open houses at the homes of craftspeople around the Mountain View area.

Out on Freda's screened-in porch, some of the menfolk had congregated. This was a gathering of the local chapter of the National Public Radio-listening crowd, with the progressive politics to match. What these liberals lacked in numbers up here in the arch-conservative Ozarks, they made up for with their fervor. There were enough conversational digs at things Republican to warm the heart of any Upper West Side Manhattanite. I could drive hundreds of miles in any direction from Freda's back porch and not encounter leftist politics such as this.

I watched Bo Phillips, Freda's new husband, slip out of the room, so I took the opportunity to follow him. Bo was dark-headed and, in his cowboy boots, stood a shade over five and a half feet tall. He too was a flatlander, a native of Memphis, where he brokered airplanes.

"This is Freda's crowd," he said conspiratorially. "You and I are the only conservatives here."

"How do you two newlyweds manage to get along?"

"We just stay away from politics."

I tried not to let my skepticism show.

Afterwards, Susanne and I drove back up the Dragon's Tail of Highway 9, grateful that Freda had included us in her party. Granted, we weren't craftspeople, but we'd been reasonably well received at the gathering. We looked forward to more evenings in their company. For the most part, this group of crafters was an antidote to the hard-right preppers with whom we regularly met. Yet another dimension had been added to our new lives up in these hills. We congratulated ourselves on how well rounded we were.

"Maybe one day I could take up pottery making," Susanne offered as we neared Hogback Mountain. Like me, she'd realized that up in the Ozarks, among a certain subset of educated people, pursuing a craft of some sort was pretty much obligatory. "We could set up a studio for me out in the barn."

"Well, you'd probably be good at pottery making. You have a sharp eye, and you're definitely good with your hands. But we'll have to clear some stuff out of the barn, including the monkey cage."

"Oh, I forgot about that monkey cage. But of course we can clear out the barn—we need to do that anyway." Susanne thought for a moment, then frowned as if something perplexing had suddenly set in on her. "But what about you?" she said. "What can you do for a craft?"

"Well, that's a tough question," I answered as I drove on. "I'll have to give that some serious thought."

Soon, I was surprised to discover that even Dennis Gillihan aspired to join the arts and crafts gentry. One Saturday night, as we sat the deck of our cabin at Hogback Mountain, he said he was not happy with the way his day had gone. He'd driven over to the flatlands—more than three hours' round-trip—to attend a regional art show, but as he saw it, his whole day had been a waste of time.

"Did you know they wouldn't let me show my picture frames there at that art show?" he said, his indignation rising. "I'm telling you, framing pictures is an art. There's a lot to it! What does a photographer do but push a button?"

"How many artists were at the show?" I said in a diversionary reply to Dennis's attempt to elevate his trade into an art.

"Lots of them! Lots! They come from Arkansas and several other states around us. But none of them were framers, as far as I could tell. If they'd let me exhibit, I'd have been the only framer at the show. I could've done a lot of business!"

"So, you really asked them if you could participate?" I said, impressed by Dennis's chutzpah. Then again, he was such an instinctive and able trader that I should not have been surprised.

"Of course I did. I showed them my frames. But those people don't know nothin' about art!" Dennis threw up his hands. Then, his ire settling, and perhaps realizing he'd overreached, he added, "Now, that's just my opinion."

24.

The World Underground

As fall progressed, Bear and I hiked more and more around Hogback Mountain and, to my delight, still occasionally made new discoveries. When out on the western side, I practically fell into a house-sized sinkhole. How exciting! A big sinkhole is often a telltale sign of a cave. My first thought was to have Dennis bring up his old bulldozer to move around some dirt and unearth the magnificent cavern that surely lurked somewhere just below the surface.

Perhaps underneath my feet, in limestone rock honeycombed like Swiss cheese, was another Blanchard Springs Caverns with its vast underground wilderness. Remarkably, some have speculated that there's as much so-called land underground in the Ozarks as there is above ground.

I hiked on, exploring further back on our mountain, and soon I heard the out-of-place sound of dripping water. *What the heck?* I tracked this noise and came upon a reasonably large cave with a wide mouth that narrowed gradually into a low, wide passageway in the rear.

I could scarcely believe my eyes. Who knew what was back in this recess: Indian arrowheads? The carcass of a saber tooth cat? Perhaps the remains of early settlers? Dennis had spoken of a married woman whose body was long ago found in a cave somewhere in Izard County:

her corpse lay alongside that of the traveling salesman with whom she'd allegedly had an affair. Per Dennis, it was never found out how the two star-crossed lovers got there, or who'd done them harm. Their fate was an eternal local mystery.

To explore the passageway at the rear of this newly discovered cave, I got down on my hands and knees and crawled along. It got darker as I went deeper. I heard a strange noise and froze. Did Bear just make that sound? I hoped so. In any case, I heard *something*.

Many caves up the Ozarks were discovered by the early white homesteaders while on bear hunts, and as I crawled along it occurred to me that perhaps going further back into this cave wasn't such a good idea after all. Too, if the roof of this low passageway somehow caved in, my corpse, unlike those of the long ago star-crossed lovers, would never be found, for I was pretty sure that no other living human being even knew this cave existed.

Back at our cabin, I described my findings to Susanne and asked her to come explore the cave with me.

"Get Ed Alexander to go with you," she said. "You guys take some big flashlights and a gun, and take Bear with you too."

A week later, on an overcast afternoon, I set out with Ed and Bear to return to the cave. But we soon ran into a problem: I couldn't remember where exactly it was.

"It's around here somewhere," I called out as we tromped through the woods. "It has to be." How embarrassing, I thought—I'd already lost the cave that I'd only found a week ago. I listened for the sound of the dripping water that was near the mouth of the cave, but heard nothing. It hadn't rained in a while, I realized. Was my mind playing tricks on me?

We came upon a thin rock outcropping that was compressed into a curtain of rock: most unusual. Ed took out his ever-present camera, and while he was occupied I finally found the cave. It was over a hundred yards down the mountain from where I thought it was.

Ed and I stood at the cave's high entrance. "You know," he said, "it's a tradition in the Ozarks that if you find a cave, you get to name it."

"Then I reckon I'll name it after myself."

"And so it is."

With the cave officially named, Ed took my flashlight and crawled back into the tunnel-like recess of the cave. Better him than me, I thought. With Ed leading the way, I was now at ease as we crept further inside into a low-ceilinged room. My imagination took flight. This hard-to-find cave was perfect for a wine cellar. It had it all: a cozy space, a constant cool temperature, filtered light. My wine cellar would be magnificent! Deep in this remote cave, we'd soak up a sense of ancient mystery and listen to the echo of our voices.

Later that week, back in the flatlands, I bought a wine rack—a metal one that wouldn't rot in a cave. I further resolved to put only my finest wines in my newfound cave, vintages worthy of the effort required to crawl on all fours through the low passageway at the back of the cave to get to get to the wine. To facilitate this crawl, I even bought leather work gloves and carpenters' kneepads, as well as cushions for my guests to sit on. I also procured a fancy corkscrew and several noteworthy California wines, plus matches, candles, flashlights. Like my cave cinema over in Sandy Wallow Cave, my wine cellar in my new eponymous cave was going to be another of my grand innovations.

The next weekend we had another dinner party on our back deck, our communal canteen, and as our guests mingled and chatted, I started in with my enticements: "So, before we eat dinner, how about we go to my new cave for a wine tasting? We've got plenty of daylight left. You've just got to see it."

Several guests ignored my invitation, but, to the ones still paying attention, I added that I'd even cleared a path through the woods that led down to the cave. All we had to do was to pile into my utility vehicle and follow Hogback Road to the back of our property. "Let's do it!" I said, rising from my chair. "It'll be an adventure!"

Still firmly seated, Ed Alexander, the master outdoorsman who'd explored the cave with me, said, "Uh, I don't think so."

"It's getting dark," someone else chimed in. Another guest objected to the idea of a crawl. Several others were skeptical this newly found cave of mine was as magnificent as Sandy Wallow Cave—and it wasn't, I admitted.

"You won't have to crawl very far to get to the wine," I pleaded. "And I've got pads for your knees and gloves for your hands and even seat cushions for you to sit on while we drink the wine… *No, I'm not kidding!*… Just imagine the candlelight lapping against the walls of the cave. And I've got some great wines back there too. For crying out loud, all we have to do is get to them!"

My audience dispersed.

"Y'all are no fun," I said after them. "None at all."

A week later, I went to the cave to retrieve my wine rack, fancy corkscrew, kneepads, gloves, wines—all the stuff I'd so enthusiastically bought for my soon-to-be-aborted wine cellar.

I tried to coax Bear into following me into the deepest part of the recess. But he was too smart for that. Crawling on, I saw that varmints had chewed the straps off several of my seat cushions. They'd also completely scratched the labels off my best bottles of pinot noir and cabernet. I wouldn't be able to tell what wine was in each bottle until I opened it and read the name of the winery on the cork.

It took me several trips up and down the steep hillside to haul all of my wine-cave paraphernalia back to my utility vehicle up on Hogback Road.

That night, at our kitchen table, I drank a glass of one of the red wines I'd bought for drinking in my cave. By this point I was so tired and frustrated that I didn't particularly care whether it was the bottle of hoity-toity pinot noir or the posh cabernet.

25.

The Fall Churn

It was September—harvest time—and with James Bell's permission Susanne and I raided his fifty-year-old pear tree, so laden with fruit that its lower limbs touched the ground. Thomas, already taller than me, swung a long two-by-four to knock the fruit off the higher limbs. These Kieffer pears were the size of baseballs—and almost as hard—and tasted sour when eaten right off the tree. We filled up three large buckets—more than enough for us to share with friends and have plenty left over to cook on our wood stove throughout the upcoming winter.

As recompense for his magnificent pears, I told James he could have some of the firewood that John Byler had cut up for me. It was stacked just inside my front gate. All James had to do was go get it. But of course, with fall coming on, this meant I'd need more firewood. So to build up my log pile, I, in turn, asked James if I could borrow his prized thirty-ton log splitter. As he stood in the shade of his porch, a tall shadowy grayed figure, he readily agreed.

Susanne and Thomas and I took our buckets of pears and left, more than happy with our swap: pears and the use of James's log splitter for some of our firewood.

The following weekend, Thomas and I ran James's log splitter for about an hour, but when we went to start it again the next day it was completely locked up. Defeated again by machinery, my nemesis, I hitched the log splitter to our utility vehicle and hauled it back to James's trailer home at the base of Brandenburg Mountain.

I offered to buy James a new one if I'd broken it. *Had I broken it?* All I knew was that the darned thing would not crank at all. I was at the mercy of his skills at small engine repair, not to mention his goodwill towards me. James, cradling his little Pekingese dog, Trouble, in his lank arms, said he'd work on the log splitter and let me know if it could be fixed.

Meantime, back in the flatlands, I bought my own log splitter, thinking that I'd give it to James if indeed I had torn up his. If not, then I'd keep it. It was silly that I hadn't already bought one since firewood was the only source of heat at our cabin. Moreover, when it came to splitting logs with a maul, I wasn't exactly an Ozarks version of Paul Bunyan.

The next weekend, when I drove back over to Brandenburg Mountain to see James, he told me that his log splitter—the one I feared I'd broken—was running just fine. He'd fixed it. But James's other news wasn't so good.

"I'm moving back to Mississippi," he said in his raspy voice from the steps of his porch. "Peggy has asked me to leave, and I don't have anywhere else to go."

"Wow, I'm really sorry to hear that.... We'll certainly miss you." While saddened by James's news, it was not unexpected given his longstanding surly attitude towards Peggy-the-Polish-Lady, his ex-wife and current landlord. His eventual departure seemed inevitable.

"I'm trying to sell off some of my stuff around here," James said after a sip from his ever-present water bottle. "You wanna buy my log splitter? I won't be needing it anymore."

"Well heck, I just bought a new one last week. I felt really bad about tearing up yours, so I got one of my own."

James gave a downtrodden shrug, then, with reasonable cheer, given his circumstances, said, "Dennis has offered to buy my four-wheeler and maybe my lawn mower."

"Good! Glad to hear it! That Dennis is a great neighbor."

"Yeah, I know. I'll miss him. Do you have any use for a lawn mower?"

"Not really," I said. "It would just be something else I'd tear up and not be able to fix." I turned up my hands as if they were worthless, but James just looked off as if confirming in his mind what he'd surely long ago deduced: I was an unreliable part-time neighbor from the flatlands with no skills he could depend on, whereas Dennis Gillihan was precisely the opposite. As a neighbor, I had pretty much failed James Bell.

"What will you do with Trouble?" I said as James's Pekingese dog went on squirming in his long arms.

"Agh, Trouble goes wherever I go," he said with nary a hint of self-mockery.

It takes a while to make all the subtle refinements necessary to fully enjoy a cabin in the woods. More can always be done. Granted, in our living room we had a big-screen television, but into our second fall in the Ozarks, this wasn't enough: I wanted to sit out on our deck, admire the view of the autumn-kissed hills, and watch college football games. So I finally bought another TV and called the satellite cable company, which gave me a four-hour window of time as to when the installer, Jody, would show up to run a second cable line out to our deck.

To get this outdoor TV installed, I was on a tight schedule. It was Saturday morning; the Arkansas Razorbacks played at noon. It promised to be a sun-drenched fall day, with temperatures around seventy and a gentle north breeze: perfect football weather. I was ready to rumble.

At 9:00 A.M., Jody, the cable installer, sent me a text message: he'd be there between 10:30 and 11:00. When 11:00 came, there was no sign of him. At 11:30, I got another text message from Jody that read, *Call me.*

Oh, boy.

By now, I had given up on watching the kickoff outside in the sun-dappled shade. I only hoped that the work Jody was to perform to hook up my second television out on my deck would not require him to disable my first television in my living room, leaving me with no TV at all on which to watch the game. *This just could not happen!* While I had Jody on the phone, I asked him about this critical technicality.

"Never mind," I said when I sensed his puzzlement over my rather convoluted question. "Just hurry on out here to my cabin and we'll figure it out."

I gave Jody directions from Melbourne. He sounded confident that he could find Hogback Mountain, noting he was only ten miles or so away.

Forty-five minutes later, Jody finally showed up.

"No, I won't have to turn off your main television when I hook up your second television," he said, as if he'd been thinking on this during his drive up and down Highway 9, the last leg of his meandering journey from Newport, which had taken him practically all morning.

"Good," I said. "Because the Hogs' game has already started."

It took Jody an hour to drill a hole in the wall through which to run the cable line and then to run the cable line under the deck to my desired viewing location—a shady spot under the hickory tree. To keep Jody happy and helpful, I fed him a chicken sandwich and some real Arkansas tomatoes that I'd bought at the little old lady's roadside stand in Cave City.

"How about some barbecue potato chips?" I asked.

"No, thanks," he said. But before I could dart back into my living room to catch the score of the football game on my big-screen TV, Jody added, "I saw several tarantulas on the road from Melbourne. Big suckers."

"They come out this time of year. It's mating season, I guess."

"I read that some one hundred of them once migrated across a road up in Missouri. Wouldn't that have been a sight to see?"

Indeed, it was the season when tarantulas were out looking for love—and granted, all this spider-talk was passably interesting—but my world pretty much stopped when the Arkansas Razorbacks were playing football. To me, it would not have mattered if Jody had said that on his drive that morning up to Hogback Mountain, he'd bagged Sasquatch and had the behemoth in a cage in the back of his van.

Thanks to Jody's handiwork, I was indeed able to watch the second half of the Razorbacks' game out on my deck. I propped the TV on a cedar post; it looked like it belonged there and the glow of it warmed my heart.

"See! Look!" I said to Susanne, who'd been skeptical of my plans for a television out our deck—she wasn't much of a football fan. "Isn't this nice? I've basically got myself an outdoor sports bar. What a deal!"

"Okay," she said. "You were right. This is pretty neat."

After the Hogs' game, I watched another late-afternoon college football game, followed by several night games. I drank more wine and ate more cheese and olives and cooked trout on my charcoal grill. When the evening chill set in, the fire in our chiminea kept me warm.

All told, before bedtime, I watched eleven hours of college football and, in the process, thoroughly enjoyed nature's abundance, especially the view out over the fall-hued mountains. It was a glorious day, beginning to end—a true breakthrough in Ozarks living as far as I was concerned.

Peggy-the-Polish-Lady dropped by to our cabin at Hogback Mountain to borrow some sugar. Though it was high noon—the light sharp and clear—I didn't immediately recognize her with her graying hair cut short like a man's except for the long, thinly-braided rattail that fell down her back.

Peggy lived in Horn Lake, Mississippi, near Memphis, and occasionally came up to Izard County to stay at her trailer home at the foot of Brandenburg Mountain. We rarely saw her. But lately, with her ex-husband James Bell back in Mississippi, she was spending more weekends up here. I was always glad to see Peggy because of course I still secretly coveted her eighty acres of mountaintop land. *I don't want to own all the land; I just want to own all the land that touches mine.*

"Have you heard from ole James lately?" I said. "We miss having him around."

"He just found out he has lung cancer," Peggy replied without any inflection. "It's the third place on his body he's had cancer. I told him he was so mean and ornery that nothing was going to kill him."

I smiled wanly at Peggy's droll joke and expected her to at least half-heartedly smile back, but her expression was stone cold. "I invited James to visit me up here," she went on. "But he told me he didn't want to come up to the hills because it would just make him miss the place too much."

Soon enough, Peggy took her sugar and left.

At Hogback Mountain, one refinement to our cabin led to another. The more we had, the more we wanted. The hedonic treadmill spun at high speed even up here in the wilds of the Ozarks. Soon, after we'd considered buying a telescope to watch the stars out on our back deck, we instead bought a pizza oven. This was an expensive purchase yet one we rationalized as eminently practical because otherwise we had no real oven. Susanne had cooked many meals on a portable cook-top grill we'd received as a wedding gift. Often, her fare was remarkable: trout almandine with potatoes, corn salad, and garden-grown peas.

Our new pizza oven had a shiny green patina and was wide enough for large pizzas. Its appearance on our back deck put me in a worldly, expansive frame of mind. Like a Sicilian chef, I walked around, saying, "Fresh pizza, hot pizza," in a mock Italian accent. Included with our oven were instructions for cooking a pizza. I considered this condescending. Come on, how hard could this be? I dropped the instructions into the trashcan.

Soon, we had friends over for pizza. The ladies all gathered in the kitchen to prepare our first pie. Cloves of garlic were sautéed in olive oil, along with chopped onion, oregano, basil, rosemary, and parsley. A store-bought tomato sauce was stirred in, then mozzarella cheese, jalapeños, sausage, and pepperonis piled on top.

Meanwhile, out on the back deck, us menfolk prepared the fire, using scraps of wood left over from the unique cedar pinstriping that graced the cabin. Soon enough, embers glowed in the corner of the new oven. So atmospheric! I was set to revel in my mastery of pizza cooking, just as I'd mastered cooking steaks, hamburgers, and barbecue chicken wings. Up in these hills, I'd developed a reputation as a man who knew how to grill meats.

With considerable fanfare, the ladies brought out the heaping, uncooked pizza. I used a long wire brush to push the coals further to one side of the oven. In went the pizza. But as time went on, we noticed the top of it cooked faster than the bottom—at my suggestion, we'd used a stone platter instead of a metal one. But it was too late now. I also belatedly learned that if the pizza wasn't turned frequently, the searing heat from the fire burned the edges of the crust.

It took forty-five minutes for me to cook our first pizza, and when it came out, with its charred top and edges, yet gummy inner crust, it was like something a teenage trainee at the Pizza Inn in Mountain View would've been embarrassed to serve. But our guests oohed and aahed over it anyway—by this stage of the evening almost anything would've tasted good—and we washed down the doughy pizza with beer and mourvèdre wine from Provence.

Our appetite was only whetted by my first ill-cooked pizza, so the ladies went back to the kitchen to prepare another—an all-veggie pie on a metal platter with mushrooms, tomatoes, green and black olives, plus more ingredients from Susanne's garden including red and green bell pepper, green onions, jalapeños.

Before the ladies brought out this second pizza, Susanne pulled me aside. "I'm cooking this one," she said sternly.

"No, I'll do it. I just have to make a few tweaks. We're in a learning mode here."

"That last pizza was operator error."

"Operator error?" I patted my chest as if flabbergasted. *"You mean me?"*

"All I need you to do is build a big fire right in the center of the oven. Don't build the fire off to one side like you did the first time. Just get me some hot coals. Get a big fire going this time *right in the middle of the oven!*"

I did as instructed. It took only fifteen minutes for Susanne to cook her pizza—a third of the time required to cook my first one—yet her crust was done to slightly-crisp perfection and the vegetables were cooked just right too. It was all in her technique: she used a metal pan, plus she burned the wood down to hot coals, then pushed these hot coals from the center of the oven and immediately placed her pizza onto the hot surface. I reckoned these details were in the instructions that came along with the pizza oven—the instructions I'd heedlessly tossed away.

"Good, isn't it?" Susanne said as our guests chowed down.

"Maybe the best pizza I've ever had," I said between bites.

"I told you it was operator error."

"Pass the wine, please."

26.

Bear Mountain Flirtation

The news echoed like a thunderclap along Highway 9, and even beyond: Dr. Howard Jackson's property was in foreclosure, all twelve hundred acres, plus his four-thousand-square-foot cabin, in toto. Predictably, in a shameless effort to exploit the situation, a number of folks went into overdrive, including of course Susanne and me.

After several phone calls, including one to the good doctor himself, we learned that his house and property—every acre of it—was to be auctioned off by the bank in one week on the steps of the courthouse down in Little Rock. This did not faze us. Who in their right mind would buy all that acreage? Jackson's land was nothing but a series of hills and hollows, virtually all of it thickly wooded and much of it so steep that it was impassable, even if anyone ever had any earthly reason to try to get through it, or over it. Though admittedly, the terraced waterfall on his property—the one I especially loved—was indeed spectacular.

Three days later, Susanne and I stood in the great room of Dr. Howard Jackson's sprawling cabin. His caretaker, Denys Clardy, had left the door open for us. We had the run of his place for the weekend.

The view from this house was a grand sweeping vista over the heart of the White River Valley. We could see forever, it seemed—or at least to Marshall, two counties to the west. Mountain Home, fifty miles north, was also visible. It was, as the saying goes, a million-dollar view—no, it was a two-million-dollar view, especially with the layers upon layers of hills burnished with their fall colors.

The house itself shamed our decent little ole cabin over at Hogback Mountain. It had a big kitchen and a formal dining room (the perfect size for a billiard table) and two fireplaces, including one in the gentleman's study. The master bedroom had beamed ceilings and built-in closets. There was a sizable pantry and a two-car garage with a subterranean space for a wine cellar. The upstairs, with its views of the surrounding woods and the vast valley to the west, felt like a plush tree house with five bedrooms, huge walk-in closets, and two bathrooms. All in all, the Jackson house was a bona fide, ready-made mountain retreat and hunting lodge.

Susanne and I surveyed every foot of the house and all therein. Dr. Jackson and his wife had their belongings packed in boxes, and it appeared that they too were quite the preppers with stashes of molasses and honey. We also saw plenty of camping gear and emergency equipment and medical supplies, as well as cans of gas and diesel down in the garage.

The Jackson house had other endearing features: it was close to the Alexanders, our friends. We even spotted an abandoned red chicken coop. We could only imagine what wonders Ben Harvey could work with it.

For us, the only question that remained—discounting the slim chance that the Jackson property sold at auction with its reserve price of $1.5 million—was how much of his land we should purchase to go with his house. We didn't need, and couldn't afford, all twelve hundred acres; we wanted, say, only one hundred or two hundred. And, oh yes, we'd have to sell Hogback Mountain—our cabin and all our acreage. Well, on second thought, we'd sell the original twenty-seven acres, plus the additional thirty-six acres that joined the Gillihans to the east, excepting of course the prized sixty-acre parcel to the west with the three waterfalls and Sandy Wallow Cave. We'd keep that land. We were giddy with excitement. Our plan was perfect.

"What will we call our new place?" Susanne said.

"We can't call it Wildcat Mountain," I noted. "The Alexanders already call their mountain by that name, and it's even on the topographic map, which makes it official. But I didn't see any name for this mountain on the topographic map."

"What about calling it Bear Mountain?"

"We can't call everything Bear this and Bear that. We need something more original."

"Who do you know has a place named Bear Mountain?"

"How about Beargrease Mountain?" I said.

"Seriously."

"What about Quanah?"

"*Quanah?*"

"It was the name of a Comanche chief: Quanah Parker."

"Were there ever any Comanches in the Ozarks?"

"Maybe not. There were Osage, Shawnee, and Cherokees, but those words are overused around here. Quanah just rolls off the tongue. It's a really cool name."

"We're not naming anything Quanah."

"Quanah," I repeated. "The Lodge at Quanah. Would you like to come for the weekend to Quanah Mountain Retreat? Or we can call our place just plain ole Quanah."

Susanne winced. "I like Bear Mountain better."

One hour after the auction ended, I called the judge down in Little Rock, and he told me what I expected to hear: the so-called winner of the auction was the bank that owned Jackson's property in the first place. As Susanne and I had figured, they'd found no immediate buyer for the entire Jackson property. Now, all we had to do was to work out our purchase with the bank, which would surely be eager to get rid of at least some of the twelve hundred acres of land and of course the four thousand square foot house.

When I called the banker several hours later, he told me his other bidder—offering $1.7 million for the entire property—had backed out. *Sure, right*, I thought, figuring the banker was working me over. He also said his boss had just undergone emergency gall bladder surgery and, as a result, his bank wouldn't know of its final plans for the property for at least another week or so.

Meantime, we put up a FOR SALE BY OWNER sign down at the front gate of Hogback Mountain. Susanne was especially intent on this, and it was presumptive, no doubt. We still weren't certain what the bank planned to do with Jackson's property. But, hey, why not put up a sign at our place and see what happened? If by some miracle we were able to quickly sell our land and cabin, then it would only embolden us to go all out for Bear Mountain (or whatever we decided to call our new place).

But the only immediate response to our For Sale sign at Hogback Mountain was that it upset our neighbors, unaware as they were of our flirtation with Bear Mountain, which was nearby. As far as they knew, Susanne and I were packing up and heading back to the flatlands. The outpour of concern made us realize how much they cared for us.

Even the prospect of our moving only a short distance away alarmed the Gillihans, our dearest neighbors. In his own gentle way, Dennis noted several problems with Jackson's property: the well wasn't very reliable (he'd heard that the owner before Jackson had driven to town once a week to fetch water); the roads that led up to the house were steep and ragged (we could get stranded in icy weather); the big, many-windowed house would cost a fortune to heat during the winter. Despite Dennis's waving of red flags, I figured that if, or when, the time came for us to move over to Bear Mountain, he'd be the first to offer to help us.

Soon enough though, our homemade For Sale sign at the front gate of Hogback Mountain did attract at least one interested buyer.

One overcast afternoon a dingy car came chuffing up our driveway, and a man in denim overalls stepped out of the driver's seat. He was gaunt and snaggle-toothed with a gray-brown beard that fluttered in the early October breeze. He looked like a character straight out of *Lum and Abner*.

The gaunt man said that he and his wife—who still sat lumpen in their car with the doors and windows closed—were just out driving around, looking for some property. They lived in a trailer home just outside Melbourne, and he went on about all the deer he saw on his two acres of land and how beautiful it was.

When I told him our asking price for the cabin and surrounding sixty-three acres, I felt as if I might as well have given him the price of an upper-floor penthouse in Trump Towers. But the gaunt man didn't seem outwardly fazed by the number. I asked if he wanted to come inside our cabin and look things over, even though I didn't especially relish the thought of him poking around. After a few seconds of consideration, he turned me down, thankfully.

He then got back into his car and spoke briefly to his wife, who thereupon, as if unhinged by what he'd said, removed her eyeglasses and covered her face with her hands.

As their car headed down our driveway, past our For Sale sign, I cut my eyes at Susanne as if to say, *Well, what do you think of that?*

27.

Close Encounters with Fellow Dreamers

The next day, Bear and I hiked over to Dr. Jackson's former house. As I made my way up the mountain, I realized I'd forgotten to wear my bright orange vest. I was exposed to any deer hunters who might be lurking nearby with their deadly accurate compound bows. Their steel-tipped arrows could pierce armor. I thought of the movie *Deliverance*, specifically the scene when the hillbilly rapist gets speared through the chest by the character played by Burt Reynolds and slowly dies in agony with his glazed eyes wide open.

I walked briskly on, calling out, "Man and dog, man and dog, woo-hoo, woo-hoo," in hopes I wouldn't be mistaken for a trophy buck. I was startled when Bear flushed a flock of turkeys out of the brush and then, just ahead on the trail, I saw a man get out of a white pickup truck.

Like me, Denys Clardy had long enjoyed the absentee ownership of Howard Jackson. Though Denys was ostensibly the caretaker of Jackson's property, in the good doctor's absence from Izard County he'd pretty much had unlimited access to his land over on this side of West Twin Creek.

I reminded Denys of my name—we'd met only glancingly a few weeks ago—and right away, he pointed at his neck. "I had throat cancer," he said, "so it sometimes makes it difficult for me to talk. You'll hear my voice falter." He reached into his truck to get his deer hunting gear, of which he had plenty. "Never smoked and never chewed," he added in a why-me tone. "The doctor told me that sometimes lightning just strikes. The chemotherapy damned near killed me. I'm still weak and can't much hike these ridges around here."

As I stood alongside Denys, I realized that Bear and I had just hiked across the zone where he'd planned to hunt. This ridge, with its gorgeous views, was the choicest land of all that Dr. Jackson once owned, and of course—after hiking it twice over the past few weeks—I now wanted to buy this parcel of land to go along with Jackson's former house. (Before the Great Recession, Marvin Rash, the major domo local realtor, planned to develop the ridge into White River View Acres, yet another abandoned Ozark dream.) This ridge also linked into the tract of land where my three waterfalls and Sandy Wallow Cave were situated.

"Here's how we signal one another," Denys said after he cleared his throat. He had thick gray hair and a curious scar on his bulbous nose. "When my truck is parked here, it means I'm hunting back there, and when I'm hunting in the other clearing I park back towards the road."

"Okay, next time, I'll pay more attention," I said. "And I'll wear something bright orange too, so you won't shoot me by mistake."

Denys told me about the hunting club he ran—so far, they'd downed two bucks and three does. He kept charts that showed two of the does had not been lactating, which meant there were too many of them. Denys was obviously a meticulous, by-the-book hunter. Formerly an engineer for the U.S. government, he'd long been stationed in Cairo, Egypt. "There's a lot of good there," he said of Egypt. "And there's a lot of bad. It depends on your focus." He showed me pictures of deer taken with his trail camera. His philosophy was to let the smaller bucks grow up and shoot them later. "I'm after that big boy," he said of a fourteen-point buck.

Eventually, we spoke of Dr. Jackson's predicament, about the auction and how the bank now owned all of this property. "I want to buy this forty acres of ridge land," Denys said. "I love to hunt it. Been hunting it for years. But I'm only going to offer the bank seventy-five percent of market value."

I was dumbstruck upon hearing this. Heretofore, I'd thought I was the only person scheming to carve up Jackson's land. With my best poker face, I said, "So, you've already talked to the bank about buying this acreage?"

"I sure have. But I'm not going to buy it unless I can get a good deal."

My poker face cracked. "Well, just to be upfront, I'm thinking about buying Jackson's house, and if I did, I'd like to own this land too." I did not mention to Denys that I was willing to slightly outbid him, whatever it took.

Bear barked and barked, a welcome diversion since it seemed Denys and I were at loggerheads. After Bear let up, to steer the conversation in a more amiable direction, I asked Denys about his family.

He laughed knowingly, as if I'd just stepped into a trap, and said, "I picked my wife up on the roadside." One summer afternoon Denys had driven by a house in Little Rock and noticed a pretty lady in the yard. There was a basketball goal in the driveway but only one car. From this, he inferred that the woman was a single mother. So he stopped and pretended to be lost. "I've told my wife that inviting me into her house was a big, big mistake," Denys added.

He was having trouble speaking around his partially amputated tongue, but he managed to talk on: "Usually, when I check on this place for Dr. Jackson, I just fly over it."

"Now that you mention it, I've probably seen you a few times, or at least heard your plane."

"Yeah, it's an easy way to see if anybody is up here. I had a tough choice this afternoon deciding whether to fly one of my airplanes or hunt for deer."

Still seeking some sort of compromise, I said, "How about if I get this land, I'll let you continue to hunt up here? It's the kind of land that needs to be hunted."

Denys raised an eyebrow. "By law, if I bought the land, I'd have to give you egress and the right of passage," he helpfully offered.

"Well, if you get this land perhaps you'll agree that I can buy it from your wife when you're gone." I cringed because I'd just implied that Denys himself might not be around too much longer. But he took no offense at my off-the-cuff proposal and nodded in agreement.

A few days later, I called the banker in Little Rock to see if his boss was back at work, but, incredibly, the banker was off at Disney World on vacation. Later, when he finally got back, he told me that though the auction had not produced an immediate buyer, there were still two parties interested in purchasing the entire Jackson property: one from south Arkansas and one from Texas. For now, the bank wasn't interested in selling off the land and the house in piecemeal fashion.

For Susanne and me, this was not good news. Yet we still figured the bank would have a hard time finding anybody to buy all that Jackson owned. The odds were against it.

It was during this period of ongoing limbo about Bear Mountain that I saw a newspaper headline: "In Fracking, Sand Is the New Gold." Energy companies were blasting billions of pounds of sand down oil and gas wells to fracture rocks and let the trapped gases flow—and the demand was increasing.

I had the sinking feeling that the banker down in Little Rock—when he wasn't off at Disney World—was trying to sell Jackson's property to one of the big sand mining companies mentioned in the article. In fact, if I were him, that's what I'd try to do. It only made sense.

I called Denys Clardy, but before we discussed the latest news about Jackson's former property, I asked if he'd been flying any of his airplanes.

He replied that he'd gone up recently to scatter the ashes of a woman over the hills of the Ozarks. "I do flyovers like that sometimes," he noted. "But with the woman's husband in the plane with me, it was kind of a hard thing to endure."

"I'll bet it was."

"The fellow cried like a baby. It was terrible."

Denys had heard nothing new vis-a-vis Jackson's property, and I hadn't either. My call was merely an excuse to feel him out. All Denys and I could do was console one another. For sure, it was most unlikely that someone would come out of the woodwork and buy up all of Jackson's property, including the ridge that both of us sought to buy when, or if, the bank sold off the land piecemeal. Denys speculated that any such bulk buyer would have to be someone interested in running a deer hunting operation—the highest and best use of this land, according to him. Any other productive use for it, by his lights, was pretty much inconceivable.

Even though the two of us both desperately wanted at least some portion of Jackson's former land, still we found a way to talk the property down, like competing bidders trying to give each other a convincing head fake.

"There are easier places to deer hunt in Arkansas," I said. "Walking up and down those damned hills isn't easy."

"That's right!" Denys said. "Not only is the land flat in south Arkansas, but there are bigger deer down there too. Really big deer."

We ended our phone conversation, each privately convinced that our respective Ozark real estate dreams were on the verge of coming true.

Lately, my mind stirred by the availability of Dr. Jackson's vast property, I had begun to think more about the stewardship of land—mine as well as any of Jackson's acreage I might purchase and even, indeed, this entire unique area. My time horizon had expanded well beyond just the next five or ten years—out to fifty years, even to one hundred years. At some deep and growing level, I wanted to leave a hundred-year legacy for John and Emily, my stepchildren, for Thomas, and for others in my original family as well as the new family created when Susanne and I had married. Perhaps I would even leave a legacy for the populace at large in the form of a nature preserve or some such. Maybe, amidst all these day-to-day machinations involving Jackson's former land and his proposed sand mine, something permanent and lasting and suitably worthwhile would come out of it.

This had become my hope, my dream—grandiose though it might be—even though as recently as just over a year ago, before I'd first ventured up to the bed-and-breakfast at Bear Gap, the very idea of something like this bubbling up in my mind would have been totally unimaginable.

Soon, I again hiked over towards Bear Mountain. Susanne and I were still obsessing over the prospect of buying Jackson's former cabin and some of his acreage. It dominated our conversations. Accordingly, I wanted to walk the land as often as possible to get more familiar with it.

Sure enough, along the winding driveway that led up to the house, I stumbled upon one of the spots where Helios Mining LLC, Dr. Jackson's company, had taken a core sample. The perfectly round hole was as big as a softball and went ten feet or so deep. What had this sample revealed? Was the sand here like the white sand up in Wisconsin, which, owing to its big round granules, was preferred by the fracking companies? I wished I knew. The suspense was killing me.

I started up a steep hill: I wanted to catch a faraway glimpse of Jackson's house again—the house that, if everything fell just right, we were soon to buy from the bank in Little Rock at a great price. After I reached the crest, I paused to catch my breath in the brisk, cool breeze. I looked down the tree line, away from the house, towards the front gate of Bear Mountain and watched in astonishment as a white pickup truck revved its engine and then drove *around* the gate, bouncing and clanking off a rocky ledge.

I figured this was Denys Clardy, the caretaker. But then I thought, why in the world would Denys practically tear out the undercarriage of his truck to drive around the front gate, when surely he had a key to it in the first place? This truck wasn't Denys's—it belonged to someone else.

I hid in the tree line and waited. After the truck circled around the long driveway that led up to the house, I followed, emboldened because Bear was with me and also because, for once, I also had my five-shooter pistol, even though there was one empty chamber in the cylinder. (Like Rooster Cogburn in *True Grit*, I never carried a fully loaded gun for fear of accidentally shooting myself.)

Phil Laubach had the firm, aggressive handshake of a businessman who typically got his way. He wore a white short-sleeved shirt—the chill wind on the mountaintop didn't faze him a bit—and in no time at all he told me that he and his wife were considering buying Jackson's former house and all twelve hundred acres from the bank. The way Phil made it sound, their purchase was pretty much a done deal.

I didn't tell the Laubachs of my interest in Jackson's property. Instead, I introduced them to Bear—he and I were big hikers, I said—and pointed in the general direction of Hogback Mountain: we were just passing through. Soon, Bear and I left.

Well, that was that, I thought. *End of story*. Our hope of owning the big, fine home at Bear Mountain—and my nascent dream of acquiring hundreds, if not thousands, of the surrounding acres and then passing it all on to my family and to posterity as a hundred-year legacy—was over.

28.

Genuine Ozark Wedding

This was a genuine Ozark wedding, if ever there was one. Annie Blankenship, in her flowing white dress, waited on the front steps of the Mount Olive Cumberland Presbyterian Church. Near the door was a plaque honoring her forefathers:

> The first elder to represent the church at the Presbytery was Jehoida Jeffery in 1827.
> The current building was erected by E. W. Jeffery & Sons.
> The land was donated by Ambrose Jeffery.
> The materials were donated by Miles Jeffery.

Annie's mother, Jennifer, was a descendent of the Jefferys, the first family of Mount Olive, where, as Annie's father, David, was fond of repeating, they were all blessed to live.

The little church was decorated with cedar wreaths and white roses and stands of ferns. As the door swung open, the crowd of one hundred people stood in unison from the rough-hewn pews as Annie walked down the aisle. At the altar, the bride and the groom exchanged simple vows while a wasp hovered above Pastor Steve's head.

Soon, we all headed to the wedding reception at the Blankenships' farm, which sat on an alluvial plain, easily the best land in the area—and it should have been. As one of the first settlers to this region back in 1815, Jehoida Jeffery got first dibs. This spot was remarkably flat, close to the White River, and ringed by mountains. It was a property that, as David sometimes said, had never been bought or sold. The Blankenships' house was a two-story craftsman with a wide front porch. Their yard was filled with buffets of food and casual groupings of mismatched chairs and an old wagon loaded with pumpkins and baskets of red apples. The setting had a shabby-chic-in-the-mountains vibe, and to top it off, the fall air quivered and the trees shimmered with peak colors of gold and red. All of it was like a postcard.

This reception was a high-low affair, with country folks mixed with city folks (the groom hailed from North Little Rock). I mingled out in the yard, where the groom's father expressed his disappointment that he hadn't brought his fly fishing rod. That morning he'd wasted three hours sitting on the porch of their rented cabin watching the river flow by. The groom's mother said her two five-year-old grandsons had been in four weddings over the past year, and when it came to that sort of thing, the boys were "going pro."

Annie's sister, Megan, a poet and graduate student in creative writing at the University of Arkansas, called everyone to the porch where she read her poem "Epithelium," just a fancy word for "wedding song," she noted. It was a tribute to her deceased grandfather, Steve Blankenship. Everyone was charmed.

Soon enough, the menfolk congregated at the back bar where, after boasting of his intention, one middle-aged guest from Little Rock went to the ground, rolled onto his back, raised his butt into the air and grunted as he lit his fart. He rose up red-faced from exertion and declared, "My gas is so wicked that it's better to light it than to smell it." Clearly, this otherwise solid urban citizen—a family man at least forty years old—considered the Ozarks to be a place where he could really let loose.

I sought out Marvin Rash, the local real estate major domo, who, prompted by my questions, told me more about Phil Laubach, the man

I'd run into at Jackson's former house over on Bear Mountain: Phil was a manager for a mining company near Mount Pleasant, and he owned quite a bit of property in the northern part of the state. A few weeks ago, Marvin had escorted Phil to the auction of Jackson's property down in Little Rock.

"I'm interested in buying Jackson's place too," I said. "I've looked at it."

At this, Marvin Rash's eyes brightened. *"You have?"*

"Well, buying some of the property anyway—the house and maybe a hundred acres or so."

"I don't think Laubach's going to buy it. He still has to convince his wife, plus he has to sell off some of his other properties too. It's complicated."

"Tell me about it." I tried not to show the glee I felt over what I'd just learned about Laubach. This deal over Jackson's land had more moving parts than a Ferris wheel.

Marvin stared off into the sunset, then turned back. "I could talk to the bank about you trading some of your land at Hogback Mountain for some of Jackson's land."

I hesitated, unsure why I couldn't strike such a deal with the bank myself. Why did Marvin Rash need to be involved?

"And I also know of some land for sale down by the White River," he went on.

"Well, I'm looking for mountaintop land, not riverfront land. I like the mountains." Truth was, I coveted riverfront land too, but it was just far too expensive.

"I know of a fantastic house and some mountaintop land for sale down a road called Dogwood Hollow. Do you know where that is?"

"Yes. Sort of."

Marvin handed over his business card and said he was going home. But a few minutes later he reappeared to talk more about the Dogwood Hollow property.

"Does the house have south-facing views?" I said to be polite.

"You know about south-facing views?" he replied in a tone intended to flatter me for my gift of insight into the proper orientation of a house on a hilltop.

Finally, Marvin Rash left again—the two of us had thoroughly milked one another for information. As the sun hovered just over the tallest westward mountain, I wandered out towards the fire pit, where a crowd was gathered.

Jeanine Jeffery was sitting back from the fire, alone. A tall, dignified older woman, she wore a tan jacket with a green felt vest and slacks: she looked quite natty.

"How are you today?" I said.

"If I can keep off the floor, I'm doing good," Jeanine replied. For her, this was a proud day—her granddaughter had just gotten married—but Jeanine did not seem exactly overjoyed. In fact, with her drawn face and stoic expression, she seemed perpetually worn out from seven decades of living up here in these remote mountains.

"Do you want to move closer to the fire?"

"No."

"It's warmer by the fire."

"I'm fine here," she said as she tightened the collar of her tan jacket.

Earlier, I'd learned from Jeanine's brother that one of her nephews was my roommate at the University of Arkansas: more proof of the influence of the Jeffery family across northern Arkansas. I told Jeanine, as if she didn't know this already, that my college roommate and her daughter were cousins.

"Yes, first cousins," she elaborated, as if she carefully tracked such things as first cousins, second cousins, third cousins, and so on.

"Well, your family has quite a history in this area," I noted. "At least by American standards you have a long history, not so much by European standards."

As if this was old news to her, Jeanine replied, "It's believed that during bad times in England, when they didn't have enough money or food, my ancestors set out for the new land."

In the 1750s, James Jeffery migrated from England and had three sons, one of whom somehow made his way to Mount Olive, Arkansas. Nowadays, the descendants of James Jeffery numbered 3,826, not including their spouses, so documented in a spiral-bound book titled *The Jeffery Family of Izard County, Arkansas*, a kind of *Burke's Peerage* for this quintessentially Ozarkian family.

The sun finally slipped behind the mountain, and as dark came on, more guests gathered around the big stone fire pit. Alongside his daughters, including the lovely bride, David Blankenship played guitar as they sang songs like "Shoeshine Man," a Tom T. Hall tune.

Amidst the firelight, the forty-year-old fellow from Little Rock, the torcher of his own farts, pulled out a pair of rotted, irregular false teeth: hillbilly teeth. He'd been waiting for just such a moment to unveil them. "What a scene, what a scene," he said buck-toothed, as the others around the fire ignored him and blithely carried on with their song and drink.

I couldn't find Susanne—I hadn't seen her in almost an hour—so I went inside the Blankenships' house, where she sat at the kitchen table, talking with Cindy and Bill Dawson. As I walked past, the three of them cut their eyes in my direction and lowered their voices as if I was not to hear what they were discussing, which I assumed was prepping. What else?

With the sale of the Jackson property still pending, there was blood in the water—ours especially—and the real estate men circled. A few days later, I got a phone call from Marvin Rash, the broker in Melbourne. This was not surprising, for Marvin saw his mission broadly: his company also provided consulting services for large-parcel estates, hunting leases, and timber management. When it came to real estate dealings in Izard County, he was both the knower and the man to know.

"Don't buy Jackson's place until you see this other house up on Dogwood Hollow," Marvin said.

"How much land does this seller have?"

"We can put together a couple hundred acres. I can get you all the way to the White River," he added, as if this were heaven-on-earth itself.

My oh my, what forces had we unleashed with our dalliance with Bear Mountain, not to mention the innocent little For Sale sign that we'd posted near the front gate to Hogback Mountain?

Seeking a second, closer look at Jackson's house, Susanne and I went over to Bear Mountain soon after the Jacksons had completely moved out. Amazingly, the bank, which now owned the house, had not even bothered to lock the doors.

On this visit, the empty house seemed cavernous, drafty, unloved. The weather was cloudy, and in the flat light every blemish stood out: places where the paint was nicked, nails left in the walls, worn-out patches on the pine floors. The great room was, upon further review, not so great. The only air vent in the master bedroom was underneath the spot where the bed should go. The upstairs bedrooms were full of hundreds of dead wasps. Squirrels had gnawed away at the wooden rafters on both porches. The deck off the kitchen was sloppily built of untreated, warped lumber. The condition of the well and the availability of water were still unknowns.

Susanne and I looked out through the living room windows at the magnificent, multi-million-dollar view over the White River Valley. My, what a sight! Then we looked at each other: perhaps we'd gotten ahead of ourselves. If we bought Bear Mountain, we'd own far more house and land at our second home in the Ozarks than we did at our main residence back in the flatlands. Then again, were we even flatlanders anymore? My mother claimed we now practically lived in Izard County anyway.

We had a host of other questions related to Bear Mountain, many related to my long-standing thirst for property and my newly-concocted desire to leave a hundred-year legacy of some sort up here in Izard County.

We drove back to Hogback Mountain, where I studied the topographical map on our bathroom wall once again to see just how much of the twelve hundred acres of land we could afford to buy—or even really wanted.

The next day, over on Bear Mountain, I ran into Denys Clardy. He was driving around in his white truck with his wife, showing her the forty acres along the ridge that he still hoped to purchase at a sweet discount from the bank. She had the what-am-I-doing-here look of a wife only humoring her husband by riding around with him.

"I'm just out hiking with my dog," I said in answer to Denys's unsaid question as to what I was doing over on what had been his domain when Jackson had owned the property. "Bear's around here somewhere. I'm not sure where he went. He must be off chasing a squirrel or a deer."

"Your dog's back at Jackson's house looking for you," Denys said through the window of his truck. "We just saw him sitting on the porch when we drove by."

It seemed that even Bear had picked up the lingering scent of my interest in Dr. Jackson's former house: indeed, he was a sharp dog. I told Denys about my earlier conversation with Phil Laubach, the man with the firm handshake from Mount Pleasant, and also what I'd learned from Marvin Rash, the real estate agent from Melbourne. It was hard to say how all this ultimately affected Denys's ambition to buy part of Jackson's land. Heck, I was confused too, so with a shrug, I added, "And now you know everything I know," and then slightly smiled at Denys's wife.

"I know where the deer are up here," Denys said as if to justify his ongoing obsession. He put his hand to his throat as his voice faltered. "I know where the turkey like to feed. I know everything about this ridge."

"But you could learn to hunt some other land."

"I've hunted this land for years," Denys went on, undeterred.

Our ongoing flirtation with the purchase of the house and land over at Bear Mountain had only whetted our appetite. Our interest in local real estate grew ever keener, and Susanne and I became more inquisitive about everything going on around us.

A place I called The House That's Never Finished sat perilously close to Highway 9—so close that an inattentive motorist could easily miss the curve and run into it. It was a two-story home with a back deck perched over a deep hollow. But the place was not entirely completed, with only sheetrock covering its wooden frame. In all our trips up and down the highway, we never saw any cars there, or even any signs of life.

Until one sunny day we did.

I figured that anyone who truly valued their privacy wouldn't build a house only thirty feet off the roadside, so I stopped and parked our car in the abbreviated driveway, making sure our rear bumper did not hang off into the road. My wife thought it best that I make this house call alone, so while she and Bear waited in our SUV, I went to the front door. A thin, sallow-faced man answered my knock, and as I introduced myself, I instantly knew from the way his dark eyes narrowed that he was not at all pleased that I was there.

"I was just driving by," I said, trying to sound casual. "I have a cabin just up the road, and I've always wondered who lived here."

"Nobody lives here," the sallow-faced man grumped. "It's not finished." He looked back, as if to make sure I wasn't seeing anything inside the house that he didn't want me to see.

"Well…" My voice trailed off as I eased back down the front steps. "Thanks for your time. I guess I'll just be moving along."

Susanne and I drove on to Hogback Mountain knowing that for the foreseeable future, and perhaps for time immemorial, The House That's Never Finished would sit half-built on the edge of a hillside just barely off Highway 9.

29.

The Glories of Bean Fest

Was the Bean Fest and Championship Outhouse Races, held annually in late October in Mountain View, just another second-rate event so typical of the Ozarks? Were the town's progressives, few though they may be, right to ask, "Why advertise that we're backward?"

It was another golden fall afternoon, and cars crept ahead on the main road. We parked on the edge of town, then meandered through a gauntlet of vendors peddling scented candles, leather belts, sunglasses, and garish paintings of Ringo Starr, James Gandolfini, Al Pacino in *Scarface*. Nearer town, among the many booths, I saw a sign for a bread company—no wait, I'd misread the sign—that was the Independence Beard Company, which sold *Fear the Beard* T-shirts.

In the center of Mountain View, quite a crowd was on hand—some twelve thousand people or so attended Bean Fest each year. A young man stood amidst them on the busiest street corner and shouted about the wages of sin and about Jesus, as if this white-bread, mostly Protestant crowd needed reminding of who their Lord and Savior was.

The big lawn surrounding the Stone County Courthouse was full of people watching a variety show, a kind of boondocks version of *American Idol*. Up on the stage, a young woman sang "Falling In and

Out of Love (With You)," a fairly racy, modernish song for this older-trending audience. I couldn't help but cringe.

On the west side of the courthouse was a cluster of big cast-iron pots like the settlers would've used for boiling hogs. These black pots had been spray-painted with orange numbers—earlier that morning, the Bean Fest contestants had used them to cook up their beans. Then, after the winner was declared, festival attendees had eaten all those beans, which was why just one street from the courthouse some unusual races were underway.

The Championship Outhouse Races—hundred-yard sprints, really—were cheeky in a British kind of way. The victors won a toilet seat trophy. I appreciated how these Ozarkers made light of themselves and their festival of beans. Their outhouse-themed buggies were human-powered and sponsored by local merchants: Jack's Fishing Resort, JoJo's Catfish Wharf, Sonic Drive-In, Bank of the Ozarks. Another buggy, not surprisingly, was emblazoned *Rural Special Rebels*.

At one of the food stands north of town square, we bought a corn dog to share with Bear and then walked over to where the local artisans were clustered. A young man in one of the booths detected my interest in his wares. Broom making was a family business, he said, though he admitted he was new to his trade. His business card read, LAFFING HORSE DESIGNS—BROOMS AND MORE, a local enterprise, I noticed. But it was the young man's first name that truly stood out:

"*Arjuna?*" I said.

"It's part of my Indian heritage."

I shot him a look, for his last name was Larson and he was a tall, big-boned Caucasian; his name and appearance suggested a northern European heritage.

He shrugged. "I tell people that the name Arjuna, when translated, means My *parents were hippies*."

I smiled to let Arjuna know that I appreciated his self-deprecating joke and then mentioned that, hey, my first name was just as unusual as his was, even though this was debatable.

"This is all made out of broom corn," he said as he ran his meaty hand through the bristles. "So, what it is is a variety of sorghum, but not like they use for molasses—it's actually grown for that long seed tassel." Appropriately, Arjuna then explained why his brooms lasted much longer than those found at Walmart. Such a point of differentiation was essential to the survival of almost any merchant in the Ozarks, even Laffing Horse Designs.

Doc Tatum, husband of the recently deceased naturalist Billy Joe Tatum, and our neighbor up on Highway 9, had set up a booth to peddle his wares—various wood pieces he'd carved, little baubles to put on a bookshelf or table. But Doc Tatum, aged eighty-two, was nowhere to be found. His children were selling his wares because, they said, he'd never tried to do so. Doc's carvings were made of zebrawood and catalpa collected from his travels to California and even Ireland, where a retired woodworker had given over the last of his stash. I bought a wine stopper—I wanted to own something made by Doc Tatum, especially since I'd missed the chance to meet his legendary wife.

Ed Alexander, our outdoorsy neighbor from Wildcat Mountain, had a booth too, though he noted he was *showing* but not necessarily *selling* his photography, which in their artful depictions of nature were maybe a tad bit too refined for Bean Fest. Ed was perhaps the most talented nature photographer in the Ozarks. His pictures of our waterfalls—High Twin, Maidenhair, and Switchback—had recently been framed by Dennis Gillihan and hung in our living room.

Next to Ed's booth, a man named Darwin Fontentot peddled his violins and fiddles, which cost thousands of dollars. He was a kind-faced, balding fellow in his early sixties who'd retired early from Hewlett Packard. Nestled down in a felt-lined case was a gorgeous viola he'd wrought from red maple.

"Did he make that for you?" I asked a man who caressed another of Darwin Fontentot's violins. This man had been strumming "Ashokan Farewell," the song from Ken Burns's Civil War documentary. "I wish he'd made this violin for me," he said longingly, "but Darwin made it for himself."

Overhearing us, Darwin rhetorically said, "How do you make one?" as several onlookers took an interest in what he was about to say. "You just follow a whole bunch of little steps and use the right materials, and if you follow all of these little steps you wind up with a violin. It takes several hundred hours."

Like many expert craftsmen, Darwin Fontenot—while clearly no showman—made what he did sound relatively easy. Just hanging around his booth made me want to learn to play the violin (summoning a fleeting image of myself brandishing a bow and strumming a Mozart concerto). It was surprises like coming upon a luthier from Pelsor, Arkansas, who built handcrafted instruments from Stradivari models that made Bean Fest worth attending.

By 3:30 in the afternoon, the exhibitors were already taking down their booths. I passed by the tent for the Izard County Antique Tractor Club, which was about to hold a drawing for their giveaway prize. Susanne and I were startled when, just behind us, a lady galloped by on a white horse. Before we reached our car on the edge of town we passed a few last booths, including one where a couple from Vilonia was selling hand-knitted caps. They told us they had moved to Arkansas ten years earlier from Michigan.

"Was it worth your time coming to Bean Fest?" I said. "Have you sold much?"

"It was worth it," the man replied. "We sold a lot of the Razorback hats."

"Well, they're cute," I said, walking away even though I was a die-hard Razorback fan.

"Thanks for stopping by," the woman said in her Yankee accent.

On the way out of town, Susanne and I passed the local hardware store where a pony ride was set up for the kids. Three Shetlands walked in a tight circle just in front of a big white sign that read, AMMUNITION SOLD HERE, as if anyone driving along the road wasn't aware they were in the very heart of gun country.

A side attraction during Bean Fest weekend—the undercard, as it were—was the aptly named Junk Fest. This giant yard sale was held out in an open field ringed by an old barn and several outbuildings. In the bright sunshine, dozens of vendors were set up side by side, their bric-a-brac spread out over several acres in a sprawling tableau that included, though certainly was not limited to, a collection of old Coke bottles, boxes labeled *Taters* and *Onions*, decrepit gasoline cans, rusted gardening tools, fake flowers, dusty jars, and a rickety sled rendered less valuable by the fact that Bear had just peed on it. There was even a beat-up pontoon boat for sale.

All in all, Junk Fest put to severe test the old adage that one man's trash is another man's treasure. It was a wonder these vendors made enough money selling their junk to even pay for the cost to haul it in.

While Susanne scouted around, I sat at a picnic table and drank lemonade and listened to a band play "Amazing Grace" and "Glory to God." When I asked the sound technician the name of the band, he said he didn't think they even had one. This unnamed band consisted of a young man and a young woman, backed up by another woman who looked like their mother and an older man who probably was their grandfather.

When the band finished, I told the young man I'd enjoyed their music. "Praise the Lord," he replied, handing me a flyer that advertised a tent revival at the nearby Arbanna Baptist Church.

I found Susanne, her caramel-blond hair glinting in the sun. She'd been diligently sifting through the junk—a task worthy of Hercules if ever there was one. She pointed to a chest of drawers that, she said, was just perfect for our bedroom. But after much discussion we passed on buying it. The policy at Junk Fest was cash-and-carry, and at that moment we had no way to haul the chest back up to Hogback Mountain.

In the following days, this unbought chest of drawers, with each of Susanne's retellings, became like the whopper trout that wriggled off our hook. It was as if this Junk Fest chest of drawers—the proverbial one-that-got-away—had been made of pure gold.

A few weeks later, I went into Melbourne to get groceries. Melbourne wasn't exactly a bustling commercial center; it lacked any of even the modest tourist appeal of Mountain View. But the town did have two grocery stores, though a friend of ours always complained about the poor quality of the merchandise at both places. She was convinced that they regularly rounded up all of the bad food in Izard County and brought it to Melbourne to sell at both stores. I think she was onto something.

As I walked down the produce aisle at one of these two decidedly ho-hum grocery stores, I ran into Mary and Morgan. Haggard and disheveled, Morgan was on furlough from his latest stint as a cook at one of the fishing resorts down on the White River, now closed for the season. When he first moved to the Ozarks, he'd looked like a hip, long-haired Generation Y refugee from any big city. Now, with his blunt haircut and long woolly beard, Morgan more resembled a worn-out settler from 150 years ago.

When I asked what he'd been up to, he said he'd just been sitting around eating pork. Remembering some of the lean times this young couple had endured up here these hills, I replied, "So you have a hog now?" and then, like a Hindu who believes in the cycle of life, Morgan said, "We did have a hog. But he's with the Lord now."

"We've been preparing for winter," Mary added more cheerily. She gave me their good news—they were getting married in June, when the weather was warmer. Too, it seemed Mary and Morgan had hit another milestone in their young lives: without water for over a year now, they'd had a well dug and only had to go down 145 feet to hit water.

With undisguised envy, I said, "Only one-hundred forty-five feet? Wow!"

Mary nodded. "The well digger had a shocked look on his face when he told us."

"I'll bet." I did a quick calculation in my head—Mary and Morgan's well only cost them only a fraction of what our 1,040 foot-deep well cost us at Hogback Mountain.

"I had butterflies in my stomach yesterday," Mary said. "I had my first hot shower at our trailer."

I, of course, could relate to Mary's hot-shower euphoria. I glanced at Morgan, who seemed unimpressed by the shallowness of their new well. I suspected that, as he saw things, every modern convenience he acquired—even hot running water—was just one more way he'd given in to The Man.

"Let's bounce," Morgan said to his bride-to-be, and off they went to the checkout line.

Second Winter

30.

Deer Season, Full On

By early December, the days grew colder and deer season kicked into high gear. The sounds of gunfire echoed across the hills and brought a frisson of excitement. Sometimes this sound seemed close, sometimes far away: always, it was hard to place. Regardless, the sharp guttural sound like a small canon was unmistakable, and whenever heard it was easy to imagine that somewhere in these mountains a deer was felled.

I was no avid deer hunter, though John, my stepson, and his friends certainly were. Our cabin and porch were cluttered with their hunting gear: guns and gun cases, boxes of bullets, camouflage clothes of impressive cunning and variety. Inevitably, our young deer hunters got word of a husband and wife who'd driven down from Calico Rock to hunt on Brandenburg Mountain, directly across from us, and promptly shot a fourteen-point buck. Oh my!

Talking about deer hunting, preparing to deer hunt, and deer hunting itself can occupy quite a chunk of mountain life. Many hours had been spent locating deer stands, setting up feeders and keeping them filled, strategically placing trail cameras to photograph the deer, and then poring over the footage from the trail cameras. It was a lot of work, yet John, just home from college on the East Coast, was more than happy to take it all on. His enthusiasm, announced by his scraggly seasonal beard, was infectious (though I resisted infection).

Weeks before, back when archery season opened in late September, one of our young hunters had shot a buck with an arrow. The wounded deer fled deep into the woods, and to track him, we searched in vain for some sign of blood on the ground. Darkness came on. Finally, Bear let out a yelp and I ran after the white tip of the dog's tail as he darted through the forest. We came to a thicket of downed trees. There was a puddle of blood and then—nothing. The blood trail disappeared. Bear soon lost interest, leaving us to mutter amongst ourselves. To serve as a natural check on over-hunting, our rule at Hogback Mountain was that any deer shot had to be cleaned and processed—the meat was not to be wasted. But first, we had to find the dadgum deer.

Now, though, it was gun season. Show time. So on a cold Saturday morning, our crew of young hunters rose before dawn. The night before, I'd kindly requested that before they left our cabin they put a few logs on the fire to keep me warm in my bed. If they shot a deer and needed help tracking it, I was available. Otherwise, do not disturb.

Later that morning, when the group returned to our cabin, they said their hunt had not been good.

"I got winded," John explained.

I looked at him, blank-faced. Had he literally run after a deer and gotten short of breath? Or perhaps he'd passed a little gas in the direction of his prey? This couldn't have been a good thing for any living creature. But John was speaking of a far more subtle olfactory effect.

"The deer smelled me," he explained with a sad wag of his head. "I didn't take a shower this morning. The deer just snorted twice and took off."

I was surprised to hear this, given that our cabin was littered with pump-spray bottles of Scent-A-Way in a flavor called Fresh Earth. Too, all weekend the rails on our front porch had served as a clothesline for the hunters' clothes, which flapped in the wind and got wet in the rain. Our young deer hunters wouldn't bring their camouflage gear inside our cabin because it would be exposed to the smell of humans.

Later, after Susanne's breakfast of scrambled eggs (from our very own chickens), John showed me a picture of a so-called scent control device. This little black box, which cost hundreds of dollars, was small enough to fit in a backpack. He should buy one of these gizmos for the group's next hunt, he said, countering my skepticism that it would really work as advertised with assurances that the device came with a money-back guarantee.

Our young hunters' obsession with scent sounded like an excuse (though of course I didn't dare say this). Moreover, the suppression of scent was offered as the reason they drove their loud four-wheelers into the woods at six o'clock in the morning. To me, it made more sense to walk stealthily back into the forest. But what did I know? Among cagey deer hunters, any such exertion was verboten. Walking involved movement, and movement caused sweating, and sweating caused odor, which of course any deer worth killing could readily smell.

This no-scent policy set up a kind of hunter's nirvana. In the early mornings or late afternoons, all the fierce young deer hunter had to do was walk about thirty feet from our cabin to his four-wheeler, drive back into the woods, walk another sixty feet or so from his four-wheeler to the deer stand, climb up and wait for the deer to come to him, and then pull the trigger of his high-powered rifle. Easy breezy.

Despite all the folderol involved in killing (and finding) a deer, it wasn't long before we had a gut-shot buck hanging from a sturdy tree limb at the front of our property, only twenty-five yards or so from Highway 9. The young hunter's rifle had left a baseball-sized exit wound in the rib cage. A rope was tied around the buck's feet: he'd been hoisted out of the dense brush with the aid of a four-wheeler. What unadulterated fun!

With long serrated knives, our young hunters cut up the deer and packed the strips of still-warm meat in an ice chest. Bear was up on his hind feet, licking at what remained of the poor animal's flanks.

Through the cold night, the carcass of the deer hung from the tree and, with morning's light, greeted passersby out on the highway.

Any motorist riding along would glimpse the bloody remains that dangled from a limb. Gutting a deer so close to the highway was not good etiquette, even by the laissez-faire standards of the Ozarks. But on Hogback Mountain, this was our first deer killed and actually tracked down. For our next deer, we'd find another tree further back in the woods.

Winter was the best time to hike in the Ozarks, but our young deer hunters had declared many of the trails around Hogback Mountain off limits. They didn't want any disruption of their prey. But this was my property, so I hiked anyway.

Of course, I'd been repeatedly warned to never hike during hunting season without wearing the appropriate attire. Near our front door hung my bright orange-colored vests, sweaters, and caps. Yet I often forgot to wear any of this loud garb, so eager was I to go out hiking with Bear. This was a bit reckless. What if some poacher was on my land, ready to shoot his rifle at anything that moved?

One afternoon, when I was out hiking down by Sandy Wallow Cave, I stopped dead in my tracks when, through the naked trees, I spotted a makeshift deer blind—basically, it was a camouflaged tent with slits at eye level. Fearful of being fired upon, I dropped to the ground behind a tree and called for Bear, another likely target for any trigger-happy hunter. I quietly backtracked, staying in a low crouch as I headed down West Twin Creek. My heart raced, and for an instant I considered crawling on my belly like a soldier in combat.

In due time, I made my way up the hillside to Highway 9 and then hurriedly walked back towards my cabin. I was in no position to confront any poachers: for one thing, I didn't have my five-shooter pistol with me—recently my old leather holster had fallen apart. Too, when I'd earlier gone to the ground in fright, the walkie-talkie that I sometimes carried had fallen out of my coat pocket. I needed backup in order to confront any poachers. I considered calling Dennis, but down in this hollow the signal on my cell phone was too weak. *I had nothing.*

As I rounded the sharp curve that led towards Hogback Mountain, I saw the tracks of a pickup truck on the highway's shoulder, evidence of where the hunters had earlier pulled off and parked. Like a cagey detective, I was piecing together the clues, and I deduced that the hunters had heard me and then made their getaway.

With the poachers gone, I decided to approach the makeshift deer blind from the opposite direction. So I left the highway and walked to the bottom of Switchback Waterfall, then headed down West Twin Creek, walking in a stealthy crouch with Bear behind me. As a precaution, just in case one of the stubborn hunters still lurked in their tent-blind, I shouted, "Man and dog, man and dog, yoo-hoo, yoo-hoo," and listened for any sound in return.

As I waded deeper into the desolate woods, it slowly dawned on me, step-by-step, that what I had earlier thought was a deer hunter's makeshift blind was really just a large triangular-shaped rock. Granted, this particular rock was only visible when the trees had dropped most of their leaves, but still…

I chuckled at the paranoid trick I'd played on myself. Thankfully, I had not summoned Dennis and his son Ernie, a policeman over in Batesville, to come and confront the phantom poachers on my land.

Back in the flatlands I received, via text, a photograph of a bear taken up at Hogback Mountain. The giant bruin stood on its back legs and looked right into our trail camera mounted on a tree at the back of our property.

"That's a big bear!" Susanne said.

I was determined to handle this calmly. "You know, black bears are only violent if you come between a mother and her cubs," I replied, invoking the standard caveat used to allay any overblown fear of bears.

"Do you even carry a gun with you when you go hiking?"

"Sometimes. But not lately."

"Well, you need to."

"Even when I do, it's just my five-shooter pistol, which I'm told will only aggravate a bear as big as that one."

"Then you need to carry a bigger gun."

Chastened, I more closely inspected the photo in the text message on my phone. "Is this even real?" I said skeptically. The original picture was allegedly taken from my stepson John's trail camera. I had not seen this photo firsthand. It looked too perfect, too posed, as if the bear was performing for our camera. I suspected I was being pranked, even though I'd recently seen what I thought could have been bear tracks at the crest of Hogback Mountain, not too far from our cabin.

A few weeks later though, I saw firsthand—right off John's trail camera—more photos of the mama bear and her cubs. In one photo, the mama bear walked towards our camera. In another, one of her cubs was climbing a pine tree. These photos were date- and time-stamped. I pieced together the timeline—I'd been hiking back in the woods about two hours before these photos were taken.

It was not unheard of to run into bears up in the Ozarks. Bear hunting season ran for about two months, and each year a couple hundred were killed across Arkansas, once known as "The Bear State." Throughout most of the Ozarks, it was even legal to bait bears on private land. But I had no interest in killing a bruin—they seemed like docile beasts in general, sometimes to their detriment. Dennis had once told me about a camper who, while in his sleeping bag, saw some animal press his nose against his tent and run it all the way around; the next morning the camper got up and killed the bear.

Later, when I hiked to the back of our property, I saw for myself that the mama bear in our photographs had demolished our deer stand. Apparently, she'd climbed up in the pine tree and yanked down the metal scaffolding and then, for good measure, ripped open the seat cushion—its foam innards were strewn across the ground. It was if the mama bear had wandered by and, knowing the deer stand was a place for a hunter to sit, decided she didn't want it there anymore.

The next weekend, David Blankenship invited us over for a sing-along around his fire pit. Over at Mount Olive, a small group of Ozarkers gathered in a corner of his yard that overlooked his remarkably flat and picturesque farm, the place he said where his family was blessed to live and had never been bought or sold. We drank beer while David and his musician friends sang tunes like "Pancho and Lefty," the only Merle Haggard song I knew.

During a break from his music, David—whose standard reply whenever asked how he was doing was, "Hard work and never-ending worry"—told a story about shotgunning a poor whippoorwill. It seems he'd wanted to carve out some private time each day to read the Bible, so he'd prayed to God to help him rise at 4:30 every morning. Two days later, a whippoorwill showed up outside his bedroom window. But after a week, this constant, heaven-sent bird was driving him and his wife, Jennifer, crazy. They became uncharacteristically bloodthirsty, David noted.

After we all laughed, David spotted a few buzzards circling overhead. "Pallbearers of the sky," he said. "That's what my dad called them." But before he played another tune, he turned to me. "Did you hear about the mountain lion?"

"What mountain lion?"

"My neighbor said he saw one crossing the highway right there at the second overlook."

I stared wide-eyed into the roaring fire: the so-called second overlook on Highway 9 was just around the corner from our driveway. Dozens of times, Bear and I had hiked through the glade of cedar trees just below it. Too, the second outlook was on the opposite side of our property from where Ed Alexander had previously told me he'd seen the shadowed profile of a mountain lion.

David went on, "I heard this mountain lion was so long that it stretched from one side of the highway to the other."

I grimaced. "Oh, don't tell me that."

David strummed his guitar to find the tune. "The thing about a mountain lion is that you never see the beast coming," he said before he started singing. "They sneak up on you from behind and then pounce."

It seemed that potentially dangerous beasts—bears and mountain lions, especially—were closing in. Dennis had recently even mentioned rumors of wild goats in the area, the first of this I'd ever heard.

31.

Prepper Fatigue

Our prepper meetings continued—vigilance was required to be truly prepared—and on a cold winter night our group met again at our cabin on Hogback Mountain. For this gathering, a bit of extra effort had gone into the food: homemade oatmeal cookies, cream cheese and pepper jelly, spinach dip, and venison jerky. Jennifer Blankenship, an excellent cook, also brought homemade jalapeño bread.

"You-uns are eating good up here," Dennis said as he chowed down. Though not officially in our group—Dennis wasn't listed in the Red Book—he'd come at Susanne's invitation. He wanted to see what, if anything, he'd been missing out on.

This evening's program featured a short film titled *Variety Buckets, Sensible Food Storage*, produced by the Mennonites who owned a grocery store in Mountain View. We learned how to pack and seal a five-gallon grab-and-go bucket filled with everything a person needed to survive for two weeks in the event of cataclysm.

This emergency bucket was a nifty feat of spatial engineering, with a bottom layer filled with split peas, great northern beans, chia seeds, and Colombian coffee. Wedged in was a hygiene kit that included a bar of soap, burn ointment, razors, toothbrushes, Band-Aids, and a single antacid tablet. The top layer was dry butter, white sorghum, lentils, rice, vinegar, iodized salt, baking soda, ground mustard, cinnamon, toilet paper, red pepper, black pepper, dark-chocolate chips. All of these essentials were packed in separate polypropylene bags, and any gaps in the bucket were filled in with five pounds of loose red wheat.

The full bucket, as heavy as compressed sand, was a miracle of economy, not to mention highly useful in the proper situation. When the-end-of-the-world-as-we-know-it came, and it was time to bug out, all we preppers had to do was grab our bucket and go. Where? Well, *somewhere*.

After the video, Bill Dawson, our wizened leader, informed us that twenty-eight nations were now capable of detonating an electromagnetic pulse bomb over the United States that would cripple our power grid. "Some people are just now becoming aware of some of this stuff that *could* happen," he said as he stood somberly before us. "Whether it happens or not, we don't know… Now, how many countries can hit the United States with an electromagnetic pulse bomb?"

Belatedly, someone seated on a nearby couch answered, "Twenty-eight."

"That's right! Twenty-eight!" Bill echoed, pleased we were paying attention. "So the possibility is there, and that's just one thing that could happen. Or it could be a meteorite or an earthquake or whatever."

I glanced at Dennis—he was too sensibly skeptical, his worldview too naturally sunny to be much affected by all this—and yet I detected a look of consternation on his round, ruddy face.

Thereupon ensued a rambling group discussion about the perils of Obamacare, which segued into talk of the gold standard and newfangled virtual currencies and even the privately issued currencies used in the Ozarks back during Civil War times. The dollar was doomed, all agreed.

Somebody asked who was building the big structure on Highway 9 near Melbourne, and Dennis proudly declared it was Mary Gillihan, kin to him of course. Her barn-like house was barely framed up, yet in the center of it was a giant safe room built of cinder blocks. Everyone in our group had admired this safe room from the highway. No doubt Mary was a wise, forward-thinking woman.

Bill Dawson passed around an article from Mother Earth News, lamenting the magazine's typically leftist viewpoint. The article spoke of herbal medicines and the overuse of antibiotics in American-style medicine, more evidence of how foolhardy modern life really is.

My wife led a brief discussion of a menacing comet that was beginning its trek towards earth. We were reminded that a comet was in the sky when the New Madrid earthquake occurred in 1811, according to written eyewitness accounts. None of these were recorded by anyone in the Ozarks, however, for back then there were only a few Indians in these mountains.

It was almost nine o'clock, a late hour for any gathering in the Ozarks, and by this point we'd all pretty much scared ourselves to death. Prepping can be an act of faith like awaiting the second coming of Christ, and as our meeting wound down David Blankenship mused about his "prepper fatigue" and how he was tired of preparing for, and spending money on, an eventuality that never seemed to happen.

No one particularly disagreed.

As we milled around our kitchen, eating the last of Jennifer Blankenship's jalapeño bread, I sidled up to Cody Dawson, who had been featured some months earlier in American Frontiersman, a magazine for resourceful tamers of the frontier. I was ever curious about Cody's involvement with the group that went on organized campouts, during which they attempted to live like fur trappers back in the early 1800s. Such deliberate, willful anachronism intrigued me.

"Tell me more about the Early Arkansas Reenactment Association," I said, struggling to enunciate the group's name.

"Yeah, try saying that five times real fast," Cody said through his thick beard. "It's a good group of people. Ministers, doctors, construction workers—people ranging from kids to men in their eighties." With a nod towards his wife, Rebecca, his dark eyes came alive. "I got her into it about five years ago at a Rendezvous down in Greenbrier. She fell in love with it and started making her own clothes for the reenactments."

"Skirts and shirts and dresses and blouses," Rebecca elaborated. "I started knitting too, and I make our blankets and ponchos and towels and even dishrags for the reenactments. My new serging machine makes it easier to do ruffles."

All her talk of frilly things confused me. I'd somehow imagined that AERA members really roughed it, like back in the days of Lewis and Clark's expedition circa 1804. "When you camp out, just how rugged is it, really?" I asked.

"We have a canvas tent, and of course inside our tent I have my heater," Rebecca said.

"And we have a stove and our own stovepipe," Cody noted.

I frowned. "But I thought the purpose of the campouts was to live like they did in the early 1800s?"

"Everything on the outside of the tent is pre-1840s," Rebecca assured.

Cody clarified: "A lot of our reenactments are in state parks, so you can't really do exactly like they did back in the 1830s. We have an ice chest to keep our food cold, but we just keep it out of sight, and also things like a plastic water jug. We just cover that up so nobody sees it."

"I see…. Now, why 1840? Why is that the cutoff for the era of the Rendezvous?"

"Well, that marked the end of the fur trade," Cody replied. "The last Rendezvous they had was in 1840."

"March of 1841," Rebecca corrected. "Up in the Rocky Mountains."

"They used beaver pelts for top hats in England," Cody said. "It was just a fashion quirk, and by the time 1840 rolled around, they were making the hats out of silk."

"The end of an era," I confirmed.

"You wouldn't think something that lasted only twenty years would have such a big impact on our history," Cody intoned. "Our son,

Cody Don, loves going to the reenactments too. Last spring, he made sixty-five dollars just putting up tents."

"Uh, yeah, he's told me about that," I said, recalling my conversation with young Cody Don last summer at the Ruthie Mountain Volunteer Fire Department Bake Sale.

Before he left, Esker Brown slipped me a bottle of his wine—a merlot he'd made with grapes imported from Germany. The dark green bottle bore a hand-written label that read *Vinifera Merlot Wine* and included a born-on date that established Esker's merlot as being just over a month old.

Later, I tasted his wine. After any prepper meeting, a nip of some sort was in order. The merlot was passably dry, reasonably smooth, and not too high in alcohol (I guessed). I'm sure Esker—yet another of these hardy, multi-talented Ozarkers—considered me a spendthrift for all the money I'd spent purchasing, at marked-up retail prices, bottles of wine from California and France. And it was a fair point to make.

32.

A Dreaded Campout

Like many ridiculous ideas, the notion for a wintertime campout was one man's tipsy brainstorm. It sounded like an exciting adventure when David Blankenship suggested it over dinner with our wood stove roaring and the wine flowing. Wouldn't it be fun to camp out in Devil's Backbone Natural Area?

But as the campout approached, a sense of dread came over those of us who'd committed to go. The week before, when Dennis Gillihan had run into David at his wholesale spice company in Melbourne, David said, *"What the heck was I thinking?!"* No doubt the unrelenting cold weather weighed on his mind. "Be there or be square," Dennis had replied, echoing the group's gut-it-out attitude.

There would be four of us campers, plus possibly a friend of mine from Little Rock. The weather the day before our campout was milder, but my Little Rock friend was still concerned, with evening lows forecast to be twenty-five degrees along with high winds. When pressed, I admitted that we planned to camp on the top of a mountain.

"To get up in the wind, right?" he said.

"We'll find a way to shield ourselves, don't worry."

"Well, I'm worried."

"Look, if it gets too cold we'll just come back to my cabin and sleep in our warm beds beside our wives."

I was hardly a seasoned camper. In fact, the last time I had camped out was in college when I went on a float trip on the Mulberry River in western Arkansas with a bunch of sorority girls. I was counting on my neighbor, Ed Alexander, the consummate outdoorsman, who, thankfully, had plenty of extra gear.

At three o'clock on the appointed day, Dennis picked me up at Hogback Mountain. He told me to put my gear in the bed of his pickup truck. This proximity of his parked truck to our front door was quite handy, so I kept bringing out my stuff: my Posturepedic pillow, a few books, two bottles of cabernet, extra blankets, my Russian Cossack hat, gloves and coats of various fabrics and thicknesses and—tah dah!—five Porterhouse steaks, including one for Bear. (My friend from Little Rock had backed out at the last minute.)

On the drive over to Devil's Backbone, as we passed the lookout high above the Gillihans' ranch, Dennis said, "The last time I camped out was about forty years ago."

"*You're kidding me?*" I'd assumed that Dennis, as the complete hillsman, was an experienced camper. Then again, he always seemed to surprise me.

"It was up at Lake Norfork and I slept on one of those concrete boat ramps that has ridges in it, and when I woke up the next morning I had deep ridges in my back. I thought for a while that I'd seriously injured myself."

I laughed at this. I had a vivid image of the ridged boat ramp that Dennis had just described, having spent numerous summer days of my youth water skiing on Lake Norfork.

He continued, "I'd been out on the lake all day and then decided to fish for catfish after dark. But I got so hungry that I built a fire and cooked all the chicken livers I'd been using for bait."

I did not mention to Dennis that, whenever I was at Lake Norfork, I'd dined and slept in the lap of luxury at my grandparents' house just above Tracy Ferry Marina.

At the Devil's Backbone access point we met Ed Alexander, who, surprisingly, was shocked that Dennis and I had showed up at all. He said that until the very moment he'd left his house over at Wildcat Mountain, his wife was convinced he wouldn't go on the campout and that the rest of us would back out too. Ed was, as usual, well prepared with all his gear tucked away in a reasonably sized backpack. He'd also brought along a tidy backpack for me, complete with a tent, sleeping bag, and a pad to sleep on.

Soon David Blankenship arrived. He too carried a tidy backpack on his sturdy shoulders. Both David and Ed looked prepared to ascend the Himalayas.

The four of us started up the steep trail, but Dennis and I soon lagged behind as we hauled up our unruly assortment of gear, armload-by-armload like two poorly organized hobos. Dennis, like me, had brought along an odd assortment: plastic grocery sacks full of crackers and cheese, bags of potato chips, sodas, enamelware plates, and silverware forks. He and I staged our stuff in a pile at our probable campsite—a bluff that faced the stiff northwesterly wind. Ed and David had ambitions of going deeper into the woods, even over to the next mountain, to find a better campsite. But they realized that Dennis and I, with all our gear to carry, couldn't possibly go any farther.

We started a fire and began to set up our tents on the grassy hillside. It didn't take Dennis long to put up his tent, for it was just a plastic tarp draped over a pine sapling he'd bent to the ground to form an arc. Regardless, he was quite pleased because his makeshift tent was further from the campfire than any of ours. "One thing about it," Dennis noted. "If the grass catches on fire, I'll hear you-uns scream first before it gets to me."

I tried to put up the one-man tent Ed had brought for me. I was determined to do this, to prove that I was an educable camper. I futzed with it for about fifteen minutes and then, from the distance, I faintly heard Ed say, "Need help?" and loudly answered, "Yes!" Left to my own devices, I'd have never have gotten my tent up.

The four of us huddled around the campfire as the wind whipped in a swirling fury. "Can we go into town and get a motel room and not tell anybody about it?" Dennis suggested. "I think I'll enjoy this more tomorrow when I'm at home talking about it."

As darkness fell, the only light on the horizon was the surreal glow from the bright security lights at the state prison near Calico Rock. It was as if a giant spaceship had landed just over the farthest ridge of mountains. David Blankenship had predicted that the wind would die when it got dark, but the williwaw still blew out of the north. Even Bear was cold. He laid down on one of my spare coats with his back to the fire while I cooked the steaks.

"I'll guarantee nobody has ever eaten T-bone steaks up here on this mountain," Dennis said.

"They're Porterhouse steaks," I noted and then launched into a wholly irrelevant explanation about the difference between various cuts of beef. By now, we were all so hungry that we would have devoured dried pemmican. We enjoyed the steaks with the baked potatoes that Ed's wife had sent and my two bottles of red.

Despite the blustery cold, I was having a great time with these men, all friends I'd made over the past year, people I'd never have met had I not ventured up to the Ozarks. They were as different as could be: David, the former school counselor-cum-businessman who, in his spare time, also ran his farm down at Mount Olive; Ed, the retired music professor, naturalist, and photographer, who'd also built his own retirement home; and Dennis, the kind, deep-souled Ozarker extraordinaire.

After dinner, we put more logs on the fire and Dennis launched into a tale about buying, from a lady in Memphis, a plot of land he'd always coveted along the creek bed between his property and mine:

"This is true, so help me God, this is a true story," he said, limbering up. "It was getting dusky dark, not real dark but dusky dark, and I pulled up on my four-wheeler... There was a fence with strands of barbed wire, and when I cut the first strand I heard something about the size of a bowling ball fall into the creek. I looked around. I didn't know what to think!... When I cut the second strand of the barbed wire, a giant tree fell. *Eeerk!* The tree made a huge crash. Do you know how loud a tree sounds when it falls in the woods? And when I cut the third strand of barbed wire, I heard the sound of tapping on a tree. *Tap, tap, tap.* This went on for several minutes. That's a long time!"

"What happened when you cut the fourth strand of barbed wire?" Ed said.

"I'm not sure there was a fourth strand," Dennis answered. "All I know is that I got the heck out of there." He chuckled and said, "I swear it's all true. I swear!"

As the wind blew, Ed regaled us with tales of his solitary campouts in the Buffalo National River Wilderness Area, where he'd carry in a forty-pound pack and a water filter and stay for days on his photo safaris. He had it down to a science. "If I came back with even one piece of leftover food I was mad." Ed's wife had quit worrying about him while he was on his camping trips; she figured that if he died while he was out in the woods, then he'd die happy.

David Blankenship told us about his first job out of college with the Conservation Corps instructing local farmers on how to properly handle their chicken litter. From his very first day at work, he'd heard stories about a legendary family who lived out in the sticks near Mount Pleasant.

"The Pringles were the most backwoods, inbred people you've ever seen. They had so many kids, all of them red-headed and all in special education." David made a squinted, compressed face. "Before I went to go see them, I told the lady I worked with what I was up to and she said, 'Oh, I'll go with you.' And thank God she did, or else the Pringles would've killed me, or worse yet bred me with one of their daughters. When I introduced myself, the first thing the Pringles said was, 'Aha, you're with the chicken police!'"

As the fire burned down, Dennis got his second wind and spoke of a man he'd known named Edris Fox, who had a curious habit of finding money in odd places. "Edris's dog treed a squirrel up inside a tree—sometimes that happens—and he got a long switch and went to probing up in the tree and soon silver dollars fell out. Edris was lucky like that.... Years later, after he told me what happened to him, I found a billfold in an old fireplace near the creek."

Expecting a happy, profitable ending to Dennis's story, I said, "Was there anything in it?"

"No. Not a durned thing."

We doused the fire amidst talk of rising early to hike over to the next mountain. Up the hill, I unzipped the flap to my tiny one-man tent and Bear went inside ahead of me. I didn't even try to get him out. He'd keep me warm through the night. It was thirty degrees and the wind roared, but not loud enough to drown out the howl of coyotes or Dennis's snoring. In the middle of the night, I got up to pee. I wasn't getting much sleep anyway. The wind had at last died down. I stared up into the pitch-black sky pondering the twinkling heavens and gasped when, out of the corner of my eye, I saw a shooting star.

After sunrise, from inside my tent, I heard the sound of far-off gunfire, the heavy chug of a train along the not-too-distant White River and, eventually, the crackle of the campfire. I rousted Bear. Down at the campfire, Dennis moved around stiffly. He'd just returned from the east side of the mountain to watch the sunrise, which he described as a "religious experience." After a yawn, he said, "You know, I've learned a lot on this camping trip, and one of the most important is that I should've bought the fifteen-dollar sleeping pad instead of the seven-dollar sleeping pad."

David Blankenship brewed some coffee and, after he bragged that it was Starbucks, Dennis said, "I've never tried it," confirming that he was perhaps the only adult in the Western Hemisphere never to have drunk Starbucks coffee. (Blessedly, there wasn't a single Starbucks up here in Izard County.) David had brought cinnamon rolls too, but somehow we burned them over the open fire.

Soon it was time to do something I'd dreaded, which was carrying all my gear back down to Dennis's truck. As Bear followed my every step up and down the mountain, I said to him at one point, "I know you'd help if only you had hands and arms." He was indeed the kind of dog who liked to have a job to do, something to keep him occupied.

Eventually, the four of us gathered at the access point to say our goodbyes, and as Dennis and Bear and I drove off in Dennis's truck, he reminded me that, on the other side of the road, lead was once mined.

"You can see where they dug into the mountain," Dennis said, pointing in that direction. "There was a man who lived up here during the Civil War who made lead bullets, and the Union Army captured him and took him to Mount Olive, but they couldn't convict him. So they brought him back out here and hung him anyway."

We sped along, admiring the clear blue sky, when Dennis offered up one last tidbit of his vast and mostly reliable local knowledge: "Bushwhackers lived over there," he said, with a nod towards the nearest hill. "They'd rob people along this road and hide out here. Finally, the townspeople got tired of it and sent a posse out here and hanged 'em." He cut his eyes at me to gauge my reaction and then added, "Now, I believe that's a true story. I really do."

33.

Deep Wintertime

When back in the flatlands, I closely watched the weather forecast, anticipating cold, clear days up in Izard County. But rain was no disappointment either, because it stoked our three waterfalls. Basically, no matter the weather, my attitude was akin to that of the naturalist John Muir, who said, "The mountains are calling and I must go."

It was deep wintertime, and the barren hills were iron dark. The smell of wood smoke hovered over our cabin, and even on the coldest and windiest days I could hike down to West Twin Creek where the air was calm and warm myself in the sun. Bear and I often went to Little Grand Canyon where the ice along the thirty-foot high limestone walls was like a white mustache. Sometimes I'd spot a deer across the canyon and hear the sound of ice falling off the ledges.

As happy as I was during winter, Bear was even happier. The cold energized him, and any snow that fell only amplified his joy. He wallowed in it on his back like a kid making an angel in the snow. Whenever I picked up my hiking pole, the dog went into near fits. We'd go out hiking for hours, come back to the cabin and rest for a while, then he'd start barking, ready to go out again. Physically, emotionally, spiritually, I was as fit as I'd ever been. The dog, by pushing me out further and further into nature, had bettered my life. Because of our long hikes, my mind was sharper at work, my patience wore longer in all matters, and my mood was usually better.

To extend our weekends in the Ozarks, Susanne and I had taken to staying over on Sunday nights. Our minds were increasingly occupied by the possibility that our weekend life in the Ozarks was a gateway to something more permanent.

What had begun as an experiment, a lark, really—our buying a run-down cabin on a curvy highway along the southern rim of Izard County—had evolved into something unexpected: the place, and the people, had gotten into our souls. Of course, over the past year or so, there had been the joy of discovery that comes with any new experience, but there had been other compensations as well—developing new skills, making lifelong friends, exploring nature, adapting to and expanding upon the ways of Ozark life. All of this had created a kind of cumulative bliss—a joy of experience that we craved and treasured. Day by day, weekend by weekend, we knew we were making memories with our family and friends that would last a lifetime.

Not long ago, Dennis had spoken of a local character by the Dickensian name of Coon Dog Moser who'd brought him some homemade moonshine (though Dennis rarely drank). That name—Coon Dog—stuck in my head, of course, but his last name resonated too. There were a number of Mosers up here in Izard County, including Shane Moser, the digger of our well. Curiously, my mother's side of my family was full of Mosers, originally from Bavaria. Just how or when they came to America I wasn't sure. Perhaps they'd read Friedrich Gerstäcker's dispatches from Arkansas back in the 1840s—the tales his mother had published back in Germany—and feeling cramped in western Europe, some of the Mosers had up and moved to Tennessee. Then, maybe some offshoot of the Mosers of my heritage had migrated to the flatlands of Arkansas and then, somehow, wound up in the Ozarks. Who knew? It was something I'd have to check out. In any case, perhaps my newly evolved affinity for these hills owed more to heredity than to culture, or proximity, or mere chance. Certainly Susanne's affection for this region of the Ozarks was inherited from her father and now she'd passed it on to our son, John.

Deeper into wintertime, we got snowed in again. This storm began with sleet and then, overnight, gracefully transitioned to a few inches of snow. By morning, the sky was sunny, everything was white, the temperature near a record low.

I bundled up and went outside to see how the road looked. Apparently, it wasn't too bad, for I saw an orange Camaro come barreling along Highway 9, kicking up a plume of snow as it streaked past our driveway. I was shocked at how fast the car was going given that the highway had yet to be cleared by a grader. Perhaps later that afternoon, Susanne and I could drive back to the flatlands. After all, it was Monday and work beckoned.

As the Camaro disappeared around a bend, I trained my eyes towards the lookout along the highway where it would soon pass after it circled around the hollow, out of my line of sight. I watched and watched and watched. But the orange car never came around.

I walked along the snow-covered highway in that direction and eventually saw the idling Camaro, nose down in a ditch. A dark-haired lady heard my beseeching voice and climbed out of the driver's door.

"I'm okay," she said as she reached back to turn down the loud classic rock music on the radio in her car. "I just slid off the road. I was only going about fifteen miles an hour. I had to go to Mountain View this morning to file my marriage license."

The Camaro had left a trail in the snow. Luckily, the driver had barely missed hitting a road sign and a stout oak tree. "I've called Skeeter Beene," she said, referring to the local wrecker service in Melbourne.

"My wife and I live just up the hill. You can come up and wait with us if you want to."

"Oh, I'm just fine. I'll wait here. There are only a few scratches on my car."

Later that day, I went back down the highway to check on the lady, but her Camaro was gone—Skeeter Beene had already been there with his tow truck—but I saw that the rocks underneath where the lady's car had been were all scarred up with orange paint.

It was snowing almost every week now, with such delightful regularity that I went into our barn and got out a pair of skis—in his haste to bolt off to Texas last year, Barry Helton had left them behind. What a deal! Boy, I was going to have some fun with these.

My goal was to start my ski run atop the hill above Dennis Gillihan's ranch—a wide-open space that I could easily traverse—and make it all the way down to his house. All I had to do was follow Dennis's crude dirt road that led down the mountain, much like I'd followed old logging roads, typically the so-called green trails, when I'd snow skied out in Colorado as a kid. On my inaugural run in the Ozarks, I'd use my two best hiking poles as ski poles. I imagined myself schussing through Dennis's lower pasture in an aerodynamic tuck like Jean-Claude Killy, my long red scarf fluttering in the wind.

But before I rode my four-wheeler over to Dennis's mountain to begin my triumphant run, I decided to try out my new gear by skiing down our driveway, a bunny slope of sorts. I had no ski boots, though; unfortunately Barry had not left a pair of those behind. So, as best as I could, I fastened my rubber-soled work boots into the skis' binders. This took some doings, but my skis-and-boots pairing seemed fairly functional, if not exactly stylish enough for a chichi resort like Aspen or Vail.

By now, it was snowing hard atop Hogback Mountain. I had no goggles to help me see, though my dashing red scarf was indeed tied loosely around my neck. I started down the hill but quickly discovered that with my makeshift rubber-soled ski boots I had no control of the edges of my skis: I couldn't turn. As I went down the driveway, I gathered so much speed that to keep from crashing into the barbed wire fence near our front gate, I deliberately fell to the ground. Behind me, strewn all over the hillside, were my skis, poles, and red scarf.

From the top of the driveway, Susanne shouted, "You're going to hurt yourself!"

"Whatever!" I shouted back as I lay on my back, making sure I was all right.

"No, really!"

"I know! I know!"

Before the next wintertime storm arrived, I needed to buy some proper ski boots. Or, better yet, just use my sled.

34.

Chimney Sweep Triumph

Before wintertime ended, Susanne and I faced one more crisis at Hogback Mountain: our chimney would not draw, which meant we couldn't burn a fire in our stove and consequently no heat in our cabin. Nighttime loomed, and the day's temperate weather would not last. Already, it was turning colder. I'd have called John Byler to assist me in sweeping our chimney, but he was otherwise occupied with his skate rink, which was open every Sunday afternoon. And Dennis, with his stiff right leg, not to mention all his work down at his ranch, was off limits.

From our neighbors the Dawsons, we'd just borrowed a chimney sweeper—basically a metal brush with long, attachable rods. As Susanne and I gazed up at our chimney to assess the situation, she informed me that she wasn't going up on the sharply angled, metal roof. That was my job. The man's job.

Fortunately, behind our cabin was a rickety wooden scaffold over our thousand-gallon backup TEOTWAWKI water tank: the scaffold was the perfect aid for climbing up on the roof. Susanne double-tied a rope around my waist—my makeshift safety harness—and I climbed up. Down on the ground, Bear barked angrily, as if he knew I had no business at all up there.

With the loose end of my safety harness, I lassoed the short chimney, then eased out onto the roof and grabbed the chimney with both hands so I wouldn't slide off.

So far, so good.

Then, predictably, I discovered that the metal cap on the top of the chimney would not come off: a clamp had to be loosened. While Susanne fetched pliers, I clung to the chimney and leaned into the slope of the slick metal roof to get out of the brisk wind.

Finally, pliers in hand, I loosened the clamp and, with a tug, pulled off the chimney cap. A major accomplishment! I cleaned black soot from my eyes then put my ear to the clogged flue: I could barely hear the basketball game on the television down in our living room. When I peered down the flue, I saw nothing but pitch black. Of course, I had not thought to bring a flashlight with me. Pressing on, I took up the wire brush and prepared to force it down the flue.

So many times thus far in our Ozarks adventure, I found myself thwarted in performing almost any chore I faced. I felt like Sisyphus always pushing the heavy rock up the steep hill, consigned to an eternity of unending frustration. Consider, for example, a simple task like operating my new chainsaw. It inevitably would not start when I wanted it to—I had not choked the engine properly, or I'd flooded the engine, or I'd not put in the right mix of fuel in the engine, or *something*. Then, when at last I got the chainsaw started, I would discover the chain was too dull, or there was too much slack in the chain, or the chain needed to be lubricated, or the chain had broken, or, when sawing, the chain would get pinched and stuck between the two lengths of wood. Buying a new chain was no solution, for I'd inevitably discover that I'd bought the wrong length of chain, the wrong brand of chain, and so on. In short, for me, no chore was simple and easy, and all this was further complicated by the fact that we lived out in the sticks. Whenever I tried to break out of my epic unhandiness by doing something like sweeping our chimney, there seemed, as now, to be a silent conspiracy against me.

Down the flue, I inserted the wire brush. The brush was brutally stiff and about six inches in diameter, and I fully expected this borrowed brush to be too big, or too little, or too round, or just plain wrong-sized for our flue. But it fit perfectly.

Emboldened, I forced the brush down the chimney, attaching four-foot lengths of rod, end-on-end, as I pushed it deeper. At this point, I counted on one of the rods to snap thereby permanently lodging the brush inside our flue, thus necessitating either the chimney equivalent of a Roto-Rooter or a completely new flue, whichever was the most expensive and/or the biggest hassle. Eventually, I felt the wire brush hit bottom: a good sign. Then, I slowly pulled the brush up the flue, waiting for—nay, expecting—the long connecting rods to pull apart at their hinges. But the brush came out of the flue exactly like it was supposed to. Astonished with my success, I cleaned the nasty soot out of my eyes and put my ear to the flue: I could hear the basketball game on the television down in our living room much more loudly than before.

As a confirmation of my fine work, Susanne went to light a fire in our stove. Soon, puffs of white smoke came out of the chimney, which I regarded with the expectant satisfaction of a Roman gathered in St. Peter's Square to watch for the white smoke from the Vatican when a new pope is selected.

Susanne came back outside, her face buoyant as she looked up at me.

"I fixed the chimney!" I shouted down from the rooftop. "I absolutely fixed it!"

"Yay!" she said, waving her hands like a cheerleader.

"We'll have some heat tonight, thanks to me! We're not going to freeze, by golly!"

As I climbed down, one of the rotted boards on the rickety scaffold came loose and I nearly fell off. I hung by my arms like I was on schoolyard monkey bars. When I finally let go, I hit the ground clumsily and slightly sprained my ankle. After I walked it off, I said, "Did you ever think you'd be married to a first-rate chimney sweeper?"

Susanne's admiring smile was all I needed. I had gained what urbanites call street cred, or the hillbilly equivalent thereof. How true Ozarkers managed to be so self-reliant in matters far more complicated than sweeping a chimney—in all matters, really—was completely beyond me.

Epilogue

Back in the flatlands, I received an email from our neighbor Ed Alexander:

> The house and all of Jackson's land sold to Perry Orr of Heber Springs (this from a friend of his who came up to hunt). I asked if Perry might be interested in selling part of it and he said he might, but there was a deal to sell it to another party. (Now it gets bizarre.) That other party is … Dr. Howard Jackson.

Ed and I usually communicated by text or email, but this news warranted a phone call.

"I'm confused," I said.

"Me too. Just when I thought the sand mine had died."

"Agh, Jackson will never get the money to buy back all that land. He's just trying to hold onto his dream. You can't blame him for that."

"I guess not."

I hung up and called Denys Clardy, longtime caretaker of Jackson's property.

"What do you know about this fellow who just bought Dr. Jackson's house and land?"

"I'm told he bought it all as an investment."

"Anything else?"

"A friend of his made it clear to me that I wasn't welcome to hunt on the land anymore."

"I'm sorry, Denys."

"Me too."

Regardless of the disposition of Bear Mountain, or Quanah as I still sometimes called it—or whatever the new buyer named his new place—our flirtation with buying it had passed.

Perhaps Dennis Gillihan was right all along when, from our first meeting, he'd advised me, *"Just enjoy your land, just enjoy it."* Maybe his contented approach was better than mine, which was to own my land while also coveting everyone else's property too. (Then again, Dennis owned almost twice as much land as I did, didn't he?) There's much to be said for having the ability to keep wanting what you have, to heed the saying in the fortune cookie, *"Be satisfied with what you already own."* I had to control myself, lest I wind up like so many other overextended Ozark dreamers. Susanne and I would be content with our 123 acres at Hogback Mountain and our decent little ole cabin, with its endearing limitations and checkered history. It was where we belonged. For the time being, anyway.

Our first year up at Hogback Mountain seemed to have passed in slow motion, but the longer we were in the Ozarks, the faster the seasons seemed to slip by. Since settling in, our life was easier though still pleasurably rough in certain aspects, which provided a stimulating contrast to our more mainstream life back in the flatlands.

Come early summertime, Mary and Morgan's wedding approached. A shower for the bride-to-be was held down at the little white church in Mount Olive. Eight women were gathered, including Susanne. Bear, as was his custom, pushed his way through the door of the anteroom to say hi to everyone, so I followed him inside. The ladies were sitting in a circle drinking punch and eating cake. Mary wore a sleeveless dress that complemented the subtly colored flower tattoo that ran up her arm and the knob of her shoulder.

The bridal gift basket from Susanne and me included a bottle of champagne, two wine glasses, and a vial of balsamic vinegar. Though Mary and Morgan were avid readers, my suggestion to include a copy of *Pissing in the Snow* by Ozark folklorist Vance Randolph was deemed too randy. I signed our card, *"To our fellow Ozarkers…"* though none of us—neither Mary nor Morgan, nor Susanne and I—were real Ozarkers.

I felt a kinship with these two young adventurous Yankees. Like us, they'd gone without electricity and running water, though they'd lived their misery full time and even, unimaginably, through a hot summer, whereas Susanne and I had endured it only one winter and a portion of the spring.

"Look at you!" I said to Mary. "You've got electricity, running water, and now you're getting married."

"We're in a house now too, and out of our trailer."

I smiled. "You got some really nice gifts today."

"Our kitchen just got a huge upgrade," she said, adding they'd also gotten a second dog, this one named Cujo.

"As in the writer Stephen King's rabid dog named Cujo?"

"Morgan insisted," Mary answered with a rueful shake of her head.

I winked at Susanne, then slipped outside to let the ladies talk. After all, Bear and I were not officially invited to the wedding shower.

It was a sunny hot afternoon with temperatures near a record high for the month of May, and Pastor Steve was spraying weed killer around the edges of the church's parking lot. "I guess I'm the custodian as well as the preacher," he said as I passed by. "That's why they pay me the big bucks."

Bear raced excitedly ahead. Near the White River I saw a road called Manor Drive, a name bestowed by someone with a sense of irony, for sure. I crossed the railway—the original Missouri & North Arkansas Railroad. This particular crossing, like many along the river, had no flashing light or boom arm to warn of a coming train. Apparently, it was thought to be so quiet and peaceful back here that anyone in a car, or on foot, was expected to hear an approaching train.

All along the track, spaced at fifty-yard intervals, lay bunches of new railroad ties, each cut to the same length and width. The ties smelled strongly of creosote and evoked the tie-hackers who, back in the pioneer era, cut ties from the forest and hauled them to the river, where they were corralled into rafts and floated down to Batesville and from there transported all over the United States for railroad building. With his typical heartfelt reverence for the past, Dennis Gillihan once told me that one of his forebears had worked for a year as a tie-hacker for twenty-five cents an hour, until he found another job that paid him thirty-five cents per hour, a trade-up career move that Dennis no doubt admired.

The White River had swollen during the rains earlier that week and the boat ramp was muddy from the rise. I headed down the shoreline, below the secondary bank, atop which was the Old Mount Olive Cemetery with its thirty-seven age-blackened headstones, almost half bearing the early settler name of Jeffery, plus eight headstones for infants, a stark reminder of why hill folks often had to have numerous offspring just to make sure a few survived.

Down on the river, I sat on a rock and petted Bear, his black fur almost hot to my touch. Just upriver, Pelham Creek spilled in and below the White River rippled across a pebbled shoal: it was like a symphony of running water. Overhead, a bald eagle hovered in the cloudless sky and the southerly breeze hit my face. This was about the coolest spot on the river and—on a hot day such as this—perhaps cooler than any other place in the Ozarks. The river's clear green current rolled on with its swirling eddies and occasional swarms of tiny bugs that moved across the water's surface like dust. Pieces of flotsam floated by—sticks, tree limbs, even a cigarette butt—and when I trained my eye on one thing I could tell just how swiftly the current moved.

I waded out onto the flat rocks that protruded like underwater stairs into the cold water. I looked for trout but couldn't keep my feet in the frigid river for too long. Eventually, Bear slipped off the rocks and panicked when his head went under. But at least he was cooled off now.

Further out in the current, a boat floated by with painted letters on its side that read *Jack's Fishing Resort*, the place where Susanne spent the summers of her youth trolling with her father and her sisters. The silhouette of the boat was familiar, with a man seated in the front and another man in the back, next to the motor. As they cast their lines, their rods caught the sharp sunlight. I heard the sound of a small plane headed in the direction of Hogback Mountain. Perhaps it was Denys Clardy, spreading someone's ashes over the beloved Ozark hills.

This particular bend along the White River was a good place to fly fish, but I'd yet to even assemble the fancy rod I'd bought months ago. I just hadn't found the time, nor had I gone to see Blanchard Springs Caverns, or Hemmed-In Hollow up on the Buffalo River, or Raimondo Winery up in Baxter County, or the trout hatchery up at Norfork, or the nearby Syllamo Mountain Bike Trail. There was so much more out here in what was considered an American hinterland—mere flyover country, according to coastal elites—with nothing going on and nothing to do. Just a bunch of hillbillies in those mountains, they said.

Thinking of John and Emily, my stepchildren, as well as my nephew Thomas, I snapped a picture and group-texted it to them—in Myrtle Beach, South Carolina; Fayetteville; and Little Rock respectively. *Wish you were here... Love ya much!* At this little spot along the river, I felt at peace, even curiously at home. In the years to come, could I really ever retire up here in Izard County, this land of innocent and rewarding pleasures? I was not sure I'd ever formally retire. Nevertheless, this was a possibility that, as recently as two years ago, I would not, in my wildest flights of fancy, have seriously entertained. Perhaps our weekend life up in the Ozarks was a phase Susanne and I were going through. Certainly, there were other weekend lives—or even full-time retirement lives—out there to be lived. I'd always loved Santa Fe, New Mexico, as well as of course several big cities, and

Epilogue

Susanne loved the beaches of Florida. Then again, no place in the world was quite like this, like the people we'd encountered out here in this little lost corner of the Ozarks. No place, at all.

www.ingramcontent.com/pod-product-compliance
Lightning Source LLC
Chambersburg PA
CBHW020610300426
44113CB00007B/579